Caring for Children in Family Child Care

Volume II

by

Derry G. Koralek

Laura J. Colker   Diane Trister Dodge

Design and Layout by
Elisabeth Hudgins

Graphics and Cover by
Jennifer Barrett

P.O. Box 42243
Washington, DC 20015

Published by
Teaching Strategies, Inc.
P.O. Box 42243
Washington, DC 20015

Distributed by
Gryphon House, Inc.
P.O. Box 275
Mt. Rainier, MD 20712

ISBN: 1-879537-10-9 (Volume II)
ISBN: 1-879537-08-7 (Two-Volume Set)
Library of Congress Catalog Card Number: 93-61317

ACKNOWLEDGMENTS

Caring for Children in Family Child Care is based on a set of training materials originally developed for the U.S. Army Child Development Services, under contract #MDA-903-90-C-0180. It draws much of its content from three previous publications by the authors and others: *Caring for Infants and Toddlers, Caring for Preschool Children,* and *The Creative Curriculum® for Family Child Care.* All of these materials address the profession's standards for quality: the competencies of staff as outlined by the Council for Early Childhood Professional Recognition, and the "Guidelines for Appropriate Curriculum Content and Assessment in Programs Serving Children Ages 3 through 8" as defined by the National Association for the Education of Young Children.

Many individuals supported the development of these comprehensive training materials. First, we would like to acknowledge M.-A. Lucas, Chief of the Army Child Development Services, who recognized the importance of family child care as a quality child care option, and contracted with Teaching Strategies to develop these materials for the military. Next, we want to convey our deepest gratitude to Patricia Kasold, Family Child Care Program Manager for Army Child Development Services, who thoughtfully guided us through the development of this training program and provided meaningful comments and feedback. We also wish to thank Sandra Nation, Child Development Services Program Manager for U. S. Army Pacific Command, who contributed to the training design and reviewed all of the modules. And finally, we would like to recognize the role of Carolee Callen, Head of the Child Development Services Branch for the U.S. Navy who introduced the idea of a self-instructional training program and contracted with Creative Associates International, Inc. to develop the original modules for staff working with infants, toddlers, and preschoolers.

Several modules were reviewed and tested at Army installations. We offer our sincere thanks to the family child care providers and education program specialists at these sites for the time they spent trying out the modules and reporting on their experiences. Their feedback was invaluable. Additionally, all branches of the Services reviewed the modules and we thank them for their suggestions and comments. We are very much indebted to Professor Charles Flatter, University of Maryland, who provided extensive comments on the content and format of the training modules, ensuring that they reflect appropriate practice.

The production of a document of this size required the specialized expertise of several dedicated individuals; Martha Cooley, who edited the manuscript; Elisabeth G. Hudgins, who designed the layout; Jennifer Barrett, who designed the cover; Frank Harvey, for word processing; Kerry Harris, who revised several sections to reflect national family child care standards; Debra Foulks, who served as production coordinator and assisted with final editing; and John Fay for final production and printing coordination.

It is our sincere hope that as family child care providers undertake this training program they will gain new knowledge and acquire new skills that will allow them to offer children the highest quality of care. We also hope that family child care will continue to grow and be valued by parents as a desirable child care option.

Volume II

Module 7:
CREATIVE

Promoting children's creativity involves:

- arranging the environment and providing materials to encourage exploration and experimentation;

- offering a variety of activities and experiences to promote creativity; and

- interacting with children in ways that encourage and respect creative expression.

Everyone has creative abilities.

Creativity is a way of experiencing the world. Creative people are innovative and resourceful. They can take an idea, a plan, or an object and adapt it to make something new. Although some people are more creative than others, everyone has creative abilities that they use on the job and at home. Artists, musicians, architects, and writers are all creative people—but so are cooks, secretaries, lawyers, plumbers, and family child care providers. You don't have to be able to paint a picture or write a book to be creative. Thinking of new ways to help children learn self-help skills, making up a song to sing when you are changing an infant, or rearranging your home to create a cozy reading area are all examples of creativity. Being creative is really an attitude, a state of mind.

Exploration is the beginning of creativity.

Children are eager learners, naturally imaginative and creative. They learn by doing as they interact with people and things in their environment. Children are curious about how things work and why things happen as they do. They naturally see more than one possibility for how a toy can be explored or an art material used. In a supportive environment they feel good about their efforts and accomplishments.

Infants learn about the world primarily through their senses. Everything is new to them, and they want to explore everything around them. Martha (5 months) reaches for a mobile because she sees it hanging over her crib. Her exploration leads her to discover that when she hits the mobile, it moves. This exploration is the beginning of creativity.

As toddlers develop their motor and language skills, they can play with a wider variety of materials than they could when they were infants. They begin learning how to play with each other, and they make use of materials in many inventive ways. Toddlers need many opportunities to develop their senses and their creativity: playing with water or sand; finger painting; squooshing a plastic bag filled with a mixture of corn meal and food coloring; or being asked open-ended questions.

3

As preschool children develop their motor and language skills, their play with one another is more inventive. They can make plans and carry them through. Their ideas may not always work and their answers may not always be "right," but when children feel that their ideas and plans are appreciated and valued, they feel good about themselves and their abilities.

School-age children can use all of their skills—cognitive, language, physical, socio-emotional—in creative pursuits. In fact, almost everything they do involves using these skills in imaginative ways. They make up jokes, enjoy open-ended craft projects, plan and then carry out their ideas in drawings and paintings, conduct experiments, and invent new ways to play traditional games. They have the capacity to be excellent problem solvers and often can resolve their own disagreements. In addition, children in this age group have special talents and interests that they want to explore in creative ways.

Feelings of trust and security support creativity.

The relationships between children and providers set the stage for creativity. When children develop a sense of trust and feel secure with their providers, they feel free to express themselves and to explore. Providers can support children's creativity as they plan the day and set up the environment. A schedule that allows children plenty of time to explore and play at their own pace, and an environment that includes interesting materials and activities, are both effective means of supporting children's creativity.

Listed below are examples of how providers demonstrate their competence in promoting children's creativity.

Arranging the Environment and Providing Materials to Encourage Exploration and Experimentation

Set up the environment so children can easily select, replace, and care for materials and equipment. "Sonia, I put some fabric scraps on the school-age shelf. You and Cassie might like to use them in one of your projects."

Provide time in the daily schedule for children to make plans and carry them out. "Hayley and Jamal have spent every afternoon this week working on the clubhouse they are building in the backyard."

Arrange the indoor and/or outdoor environment so children can move freely and work alone or in small groups. "Marybeth and Tyesha, would you and your babies like to eat your picnic in the backyard? You could spread your blanket under the oak tree."

Hang interesting and beautiful pictures and objects at a child's height on the wall. Invite children, beginning in infancy, to explore and enjoy the world around them. "Lamont, I put a new picture of a cow on the wall. Would you like to come over and see it?"

Provide and rotate according to children's changing interests a variety of materials, props, and real things, including some from the children's own cultures. "Perla, your mom brought us some beautiful fabric and hats from the Philippines, where she was born. You and the other children can use them for dress-up."

Provide space for school-age children to store their ongoing projects and special supplies. "We can put your puppet theater in the storeroom and your puppet-making supplies on top of the kitchen cabinets. Before you arrive tomorrow afternoon, I'll get them out."

Display or help children hang their own creative work attractively and respectfully. "Carlos, where would you like me to hang your potato print?"

Offering a Variety of Activities and Experiences to Promote Creativity

Extend children's dramatic play. "Thank you, grocery shoppers, for bringing me an apple. You must have known I was getting hungry."

Use descriptive language as you talk with children, even a very young infant. "Close your eyes. I'm going to pull your green fluffy sweater over your head now."

Provide for "messy" open-ended activities that are enjoyed in different ways by children of different ages. "Today is a perfect day for chasing bubbles. Let's look in the supply closet for things we could use to make bubbles. I know there are some berry baskets in there and some wire coat hangers."

Call attention to sensory experiences. "How does it feel when the soapsuds squish between your fingers while you wash your hands?"

Avoid using coloring books or craft kits. Instead, provide a variety of materials and tools. "Alison, you'll find lots of crayons, markers, paste, paper, scissors, and craft supplies right here where you can reach them any time you want to use them."

Include a variety of music, movement, and dance activities in the daily schedule. Teach children songs, chants, and rhythms from a variety of cultural groups, including those represented by the children in your care. "Let's wave the streamers in little circles. Now let's make the circles as big as possible."

Encourage children's use of imagination by telling stories, playing make-believe, and singing songs. "The dragon ate 3 tons of mashed potatoes, 2 boxes of hot dogs with chili, and a big pumpkin. What do you think he had for dessert?"

Provide materials with which children can do many different things, such as blocks, finger paint, dough, clay, or water. "Jacci is using all her fingers to roll her playdough, and Anna is using her fists. What different shapes you're making!"

Interacting with Children in Ways That Encourage and Respect Creative Expression

Encourage an infant's exploration of sounds. "I hear that gurgling you're making in your throat, Stephanie. It makes me think of a little bird song."

Respect the creative process as well as the creative product. "Lenny, you've cut out some interesting pictures. How do you plan to use them in your collage?"

Share your interest in and appreciation of children's explorations. "Ana, it sounds like you're playing a drum when you slap the floor like that." "Leslie, the way you're playing with your cereal makes me think you're ready to finger paint."

Accept and value each child's creative expression. "Maya, would you like to tape yourself singing the song you made up so you can share it with your whole family?"

Hold an infant, sing a song, smile, and make eye contact, encouraging the infant to join in with her sounds. "Fa, la, la, la, la...Cheryl, some day you may be singing in the choir!"

Give children positive feedback about their creative thinking. "Al, you made a great hat out of that basket. Decorating it with feathers made it look very exotic."

Ask open-ended questions that encourage creative thinking. "Raoul, what can you do to get the other children to play your game with you?"

Share your enjoyment of language. Introduce children to fun and interesting words. "Betty, can you make up a word that rhymes with chrysanthemum?"

Model creative thinking. "I'm thinking about reorganizing our storage closet. Do you have any ideas about where things should go, Manny?"

Respect each child's creative expression. "Jeremy painted a picture of the farmer. Mary wrote a poem to send to the farmer's family. They both have a special way to thank the farmer for our field trip."

Show your respect for children's creativity by not interrupting them. "Henry and Dion are busy crawling back and forth through the tunnel. I'll wait until they are finished before serving lunch."

Promoting Children's Creativity

In the following situations, FCC providers are promoting children's creativity. As you read each one, think about what the providers are doing and why. Then answer the questions that follow.

Arranging the Environment and Providing Materials to Encourage Exploration and Experimentation

Before the children arrive, Ms. Rizzi checks the "junk" building supplies that were so actively used yesterday. She adds shoe boxes, oatmeal boxes, and wrapping-paper tubes. She checks the supply of glue, paper fasteners, pipe cleaners, and twist ties on the shelf. She adds more Popsicle sticks, strips of fabric, and the dryer lint she has been saving. She covers the kitchen table with butcher paper and leaves it empty.

During free play Kira (4-1/2 years) works on the house she started building the day before. Ms. Rizzi stops by the table to watch for a minute. Then she asks, "How's your construction coming along today, Kira?" Kira smiles and tells Ms. Rizzi about the boxes she has glued together. "This is the kitchen and this is my room and this is the porch." Ms. Rizzi nods and asks, "What do you do on your porch?" Kira responds, "That's where my new puppy sleeps. I didn't make him yet." Ms. Rizzi asks, "Do you have everything you need to make your puppy?" Kira responds, "I need some very soft stuff." Ms. Rizzi shows Kira the cotton balls, dryer lint, and yarn, and says, "Yes, puppies are very soft."

1. **How did Ms. Rizzi arrange the environment to promote children's creativity?**

_____

_____

_____

2. **How do unstructured (or open-ended) materials promote children's creativity?**

_____

_____

_____

Offering a Variety of Activities and Experiences to Promote Creativity

Ms. Vaughn and the children are making banana bread. Emily (24 months) picks up some flour and rubs it on her hands. "How does that flour feel?" Ms. Vaughn asks. "Soft," she says as she smiles proudly. She lifts up the measuring cup and pours the flour in the bowl. Maggie (6 years) mashes the bananas. "This is hard work," she says, "but I can do it." Tomas (30 months) cracks an egg against the side of a cup and gently pours it out of the shell. He looks concerned. "Don't worry," says Ms. Vaughn. "You are doing a great job!" As Maggie and Emily stir the ingredients together, Ms.

Vaughn asks the children, "What else can we put in this banana bread?" "Pineapple," says Maggie. "I want raisins," says Tomas. "Yeah, raisins," says Emily. "You all have some good ideas about what to put in the banana bread," says Ms. Vaughn. "Can we do raisins this time and next time try another suggestion?" All the children agree on raisins this time. Maggie gets the jar of raisins from the cupboard.

1. **Why are cooking activities such as making banana bread good opportunities to promote creativity?**

_____

_____

_____

2. **How did Ms. Vaughn support creative thinking?**

_____

_____

_____

Interacting with Children in Ways That Encourage and Respect Creative Expression

Ms. Sanchez hears the front doorbell. "It must be Mariah and Bryanna," she thinks to herself. She opens the door for two very excited children. "Hi, Ms. Sanchez," says Mariah. "We're in a hurry to work on our song and dance," says Bryanna. "I've been playing music in my head all day long. I could hardly keep my feet still in school." The two girls dash into the house and quickly put their coats and backpacks away. Then they go into the bedroom and pop a tape into the cassette player. Through the closed door Ms. Sanchez hears a familiar tune (she's been hearing it every day for the last two weeks): "Tomorrow, tomorrow, I'll love you tomorrow…" Half an hour later, two hungry girls emerge and go into the kitchen to get their snack. Ms. Sanchez comes in to talk to them. "When you are ready, the other children and I would really like to see your performance." "That would be great," says Bryanna. "The little kids can be the other orphans. They can wear their pajamas!" "We'll be ready tomorrow," says Mariah. Ms. Sanchez smiles and says, "Okay. We'll be ready too. I'll ask the parents to send the children's pajamas in their bags tomorrow. We can move the furniture back against the wall so there will be plenty of room for your performance."

1. **How did Ms. Sanchez encourage the girls' creativity?**

_____

_____

_____

2. **How did the way Ms. Sanchez responded to Bryanna's idea create an atmosphere that supports creativity?**

_____

_____

_____

Compare your answers with those on the answer sheet at the end of this module. If your answers are different, discuss them with your trainer. There can be more than one answer.

Your Own Creativity

We sometimes confuse creativity with talent.

As adults, we sometimes confuse creativity with talent. It is important to remember that in addition to allowing us to make something new, creativity helps us explore new ways to do something, solve a problem, or achieve a goal. You don't have to be an artist to plan activities for children that encourage creativity. Understanding your own creativity and how you approach problems and new situations will help you become sensitive to creativity in children. Recognizing how you feel when you are being creative will help you support children's efforts at trying out new ideas.

Think about the satisfaction you feel when you solve a problem while cooking, gardening, using a new tool or appliance, visiting a new city, or helping a child master a new skill. That feeling is similar to the pride that children feel when they have figured out something for themselves.

Here are some exercises you can do to help stimulate your own creative thinking.

1. **Describe a new way to spend time with your family. How could you include your children and spouse in planning a special family activity?**

   _____

   _____

   _____

   _____

2. **List some unusual ways to use a common object—for example, an egg carton, a newspaper, a pencil, or a suitcase.**

   _____

   _____

   _____

   _____

3. **Write a new ending for a favorite story, movie, or book.**

   _____

   _____

   _____

   _____

4. Describe something you did with children that was creative.

_____

_____

_____

_____

These questions or similar ones can help you think of new ways to approach a problem. They can also be useful in helping children develop their creativity. Supporting children's creativity is part of being a provider. It is a role that gives much satisfaction in return as you watch children gain in self-confidence and explore their world enthusiastically.

When you have finished this overview section, you should complete the pre-training assessment. Refer to the glossary at the end of the module if you need definitions of the terms that are used.

PRE-TRAINING ASSESSMENT

Listed below are the skills that providers use to promote children's creativity. Think about whether you do these things regularly, sometimes, or not enough. Place a check in one of the columns on the right for each skill listed. Then discuss your answers with your trainer.

Skill	I Do This Regularly	I Do This Sometimes	I Don't Do This Enough
Arranging the Environment and Providing Materials to Encourage Exploration and Experimentation			
1. Setting up the environment so children can easily select, replace, and care for materials and equipment without adult assistance.			
2. Providing enough time in the daily schedule for children to explore, use their imaginations, and make plans and carry them out.			
3. Providing toys and materials that children can use to express their creativity in different ways.			
4. Providing and rotating a variety of materials and props based on children's interests, including some from the children's own cultures.			
5. Providing sufficient space for children's ongoing projects.			
6. Hanging interesting pictures and other objects at children's height for them to explore and enjoy.			
7. Arranging the indoor and outdoor environment so that children can move freely and safely.			

Skill	I Do This Regularly	I Do This Sometimes	I Don't Do This Enough
Offering a Variety of Activities and Experiences to Promote Creativity 8. Providing sensory experiences to stimulate children's imaginative and creative expression.			
9. Providing a variety of props and participating in children's dramatic play.			
10. Providing a variety of open-ended, age-appropriate art materials and activities that match children's skills and interests.			
11. Providing sand and water play, and a variety of props regularly.			
12. Avoiding the use of coloring books and craft kits.			
13. Including a variety of planned and spontaneous music, movement, and dance activities in the daily schedule.			
Interacting With Children In Ways That Encourage and Respect Creative Expression 14. Establishing a secure and trusting relationship with each child.			
15. Providing positive feedback about children's creative thinking.			
16. Recognizing that young children are more interested in the process of creating than in the product.			

Skill	I Do This Regularly	I Do This Sometimes	I Don't Do This Enough
17. Recognizing that older children care about the products that result from their creative endeavors.			
18. Displaying children's creative work attractively and where they can see it.			
19. Accepting and valuing each child's creative expression.			

Review your responses, then list three to five skills you would like to improve or topics you would like to learn more about to help you promote children's creativity. When you finish this module, you will list examples of your new or improved knowledge and skills.

_____

_____

_____

_____

_____

Discuss the overview and pre-training assessment with your trainer. Then begin the learning activities for Module 7.

LEARNING ACTIVITIES

I. Encouraging Children's Creativity Throughout the Day

> **In this activity you will learn:**
>
> - to interact with children in ways that promote creative thinking; and
> - to establish an atmosphere in your home that encourages creativity.

Let children know that you value creativity.

The environment you create and the ways that you interact with and respond to children can give them the message that you value and support creativity. What you say, how you ask and answer questions, and how you encourage learning through discovery all nurture children's creativity. It is crucial to carefully listen to each child and to recognize each child as an individual. Your enthusiasm for a child's efforts and successes will greatly encourage his or her creativity.

Encouraging Infants' Creativity

Infants are naturally curious. They have an amazing ability to concentrate. Infants use all their senses—touch, sight, hearing, taste, and smell—to play with objects and observe what is happening around them. However, this can happen only if infants feel safe and secure. A positive relationship between infant and provider is the key to encouraging an infant's creativity. When infants feel cared for and secure, they can turn their attention to explorations of their world. Creativity is encouraged by providers who talk with infants, let them learn by discovering things independently, and provide a consistent base of security.

Infants quickly learn that what they do attracts the attention of adults. When their cries are answered, they begin to realize that they can have an effect on their world; they can make things happen. They are experiencing cause and effect: I'm hungry so I cry, and my provider brings my bottle. When infants realize they can make things happen, they are eager to try again to bring about a change or a desired result. This sense of strength and effectiveness sets the stage for creativity in later childhood.

Try these suggestions.

Here are some suggestions for responding to infants in ways that encourage their creativity. Add your own suggestion at the end of the list.

- **Learn to interpret their babbling and attempts to communicate.** Jorge (16 months) brings the toy radio to Ms. Gonzalez. "Ah, ah, ah," he says as he sways back and forth. "What do you want, Jorge?" says Ms. Gonzalez. Jorge gives the radio to Ms. Gonzalez. She responds, "Oh, you want me to wind up the radio so you can dance. Here it is."

- **Learn to recognize nonverbal cues.** Peter (10 months) is whimpering in the book corner. He lies down, puts his thumb in his mouth, and gets up again. He crawls to his blanket, lies down again, and sucks his thumb. Ms. Lewis says, "Peter, are you sleepy? It's early, but I think you're trying to tell me you need a nap. Let me put you in your crib."

- **Give infants freedom to move, explore, and do things for themselves.** As infants begin to roll over, crawl, and walk, they gradually realize that they can make things happen. When they touch musical toys, the toys make a sound. When they roll over, infants can get from one place to the next.

- **Learn to watch and wait.** When Ms. Bates notices the look of concentration on Jian Guo's (5 months) face as he reaches for the mobile hanging over his crib. When he begins fretting, she goes over to him and says, "Are you finished with the mobile for now? How about if I take you over to the changing table to get a clean diaper?"

- **Talk with infants throughout the day to encourage their creativity.** Infants take pleasure in their growing communication skills. They feel good about being able to communicate with a trusted provider. Experiencing this pleasure regularly, they feel secure and thus free to explore and to learn from all their daily routines—feeding, diapering, napping, and playing.

- _____

  _____

  _____

  _____

Encouraging Toddlers' Creativity

Toddlers experience tremendous changes in the period from 18 months to 3 years. They are no longer infants, but they are not yet preschool children; and at times they act like both. Their back-and-forth behavior and striving for independence can puzzle and often exhaust the best-intentioned adults. Providers need to understand who toddlers are and what they need from adults so they can support their curiosity, creativity, and unique forms of self-expression.

Toddlers' creativity is promoted when you encourage learning by doing, respond to questions, and recognize a toddler's overriding need to "do it myself." Toddlers need many opportunities to learn firsthand through experimentation; they use their creativity as they begin to understand concepts such as in and out, up and down, and big and little. Toddlers need both space and time to be curious, to find out how things work, and to learn about what their bodies and muscles can do. Each of these experiences promotes creativity.

Try these suggestions.

Here are some suggestions of things you can do to encourage toddlers' creativity. Add your own suggestion at the end of the list.

- **Acknowledge and support toddlers' many attempts to do things independently.** Provide many opportunities for toddlers to do things for themselves even if they make mistakes. Recognize that each toddler will demonstrate the need for independence in different ways. When you observe toddlers' efforts to be independent, encourage them with your positive words. "Why Alison, you put on your sock all by yourself!" "It's okay if some juice spills, Craig. You are learning how to pour."

- **Provide many opportunities for toddlers to observe and experience cause and effect.** Provide toys and materials that toddlers can manipulate and experiment with. When you observe cause-and-effect relations in their play, help toddlers focus on what they are seeing. "Travis, your block tower was so high, it fell down." "Anita, look what happened when you pounded the playdough with your hand."

- **Provide materials and experiences that allow toddlers to do things over and over.** It seems that toddlers never tire of filling containers and dumping out the contents, only to fill the container again. They enjoy using their newly mastered skills to do tasks again and again. Be patient when toddlers want to wipe the table or wash their hands endlessly.

- **Encourage toddlers' developing language skills.** Toddlers' vocabulary increases rapidly, and they become increasingly able to express themselves with words. Take plenty of time each day to talk with toddlers about what they are doing. Share the pleasure and joy of language by telling stories about things the children do, reciting simple nursery rhymes, and having fun with sounds. "What kinds of noises does your truck make, Bruce? I hear it go vroom, vroom."

- **Realize that even though they want to be independent, toddlers still need help from adults.** Toddlers typically go back and forth in their moves toward independence. One day a child will refuse to let you help her eat, and the next day she may climb in your lap and ask to be fed. While this behavior can be confusing and tiring for providers, understanding toddlers' need for emotional reassurance will help. It also helps to verbalize this need for toddlers: "Let me help you with your jacket, Sherrie, and you can put your hat on all by yourself." "Can you help me wipe the floor with the sponge, Joy? The mop looks too big for you."

* _____
  _____
  _____
  _____

Encouraging Preschool Children's Creativity

Moving from toddlerhood into the preschool period, children continue to want to reach out and physically touch their environment. The rate of growth has slowed down in 3-, 4-, and 5-year-olds, so they have much more energy to use. Also, they don't tire as quickly and can stay involved for longer periods of time. They also have much greater control over their large muscles and as they move through the preschool period they continue to develop their fine motor skills and eye-hand coordination.

Along with preschool children's greatly expanding physical skills comes rapid intellectual development. As they move, dig, build, lift, climb, handle, taste, fill, empty, and manipulate, they begin to gather and use information about objects and events in their environment: "These things are different; these look and taste the same; when you put this color with this color, it looks different."

Language growth is also rapid as preschool children learn words and use them to describe what they are seeing and experiencing. When providers create an environment that allows for active exploration, provide a variety of materials, and plan the daily schedule so children have time to explore actively, children begin to develop attitudes about the creative process and their own abilities to create and learn. When children experience the challenge and joy of discovery, they also develop attitudes that allow them to stick to a task. When providers nurture these attitudes in preschool children, they will have lasting effects on every aspect of the child's development.

Try these suggestions.

Here are some suggestions of things you can do to encourage the creativity of preschool children. Add your own suggestion at the end of the list.

* **Help children solve their own problems** by asking children open-ended questions that cannot be answered with just a "yes" or "no." For example, when two children want to play with the

same doll, you might ask, "How do you think you both could play with the doll?"

- **Help children discover new concepts on their own** by providing new materials and asking open-ended questions. For example, you might bring a small pitcher of water to the sandbox and say to the children at play, "What do you think would happen if we added some water to the sand?"

- **Provide a wide variety of choices and opportunities for success.** It is best to avoid competitive activities with winners and losers. Give children raw materials with which to express their ideas—paints, crayons, sand, water, playdough, blocks, and dramatic play props. Give positive feedback for their original ideas for doing things and comment on their creative expressions.

- **Allow plenty of time for children to try things again and again.** Preschool children have their own ideas and want to carry them out themselves; however, they are beginners at doing things and may make mistakes. Be patient about children's "messes." Toying with objects and ideas is part of the creative process.

- _____

_____

_____

_____

Encouraging School-Age Children's Creativity

Like younger children, school-age children enjoy the process of creating—making up a dance, inventing characters for a story, hammering nails into a wooden board. They are, however, becoming increasingly interested in the products that result from their creative efforts. They take great pleasure in creating things that can actually be used (a potholder), displayed (a weaving), read (a poem), taught to someone else (a part in a play), and so on.

Some school-age children are highly critical of their products and will look to you for encouragement and approval. At times, even your approval will not convince them of the value of their creations, and they may destroy them or throw them away. In these instances, encourage the child to start again. These children are perfectionists and need your help and support to continue expressing their feelings and ideas in creative ways.

School-age children often go through stages when they are intensely interested and involved in a specific activity or topic. For example, you might care for a child who is loves building with small plastic blocks, spending every afternoon for three weeks building a city of the future. Or you might care for a child who loves to draw cartoon figures and spends every afternoon perfecting his version of Donald

Duck. In a month's time these same two children may have dropped their projects and thrown themselves into new endeavors. Providers need to observe school-age children to know when it's time to provide for their changing interests.

Try these suggestions.

Here are some suggestions of things you can do to encourage the creativity of school-age children. Add your own suggestion at the end of the list.

- **Teach children specific skills that they can use creatively.** School-age children enjoy learning skills such as knitting, sewing, tooling leather, wood carving, cake decorating, or painting with water colors. If you know of someone in the community who has a particular skill, ask him or her to visit your home to help the children learn the skill.

- **Provide space for children to store their long-term projects.** Many of the creative projects that school-age children undertake cannot be completed in a single day at your home. Instead, children may work on them for weeks at a time. Show them that you value and respect their work by providing a safe place for storage.

- **Introduce children to brainstorming so they can use it as a problem-solving tool.**[1] Select a familiar object to focus on, such as a three-ring binder, a ruler, a fork, or a paper towel. Set a timer for five minutes. Ask children to write down all the possible uses for the object they can think of. Explain that all ideas are to be accepted—none are right or wrong. Then ask children to share their suggestions. Once children understand how to brainstorm, you can ask them to use the skill to help you think of new ideas for snack, new activities, or new materials to include in the collage box.

- **Surround children with examples of creativity.** In addition to the children's own work, display Newbury award-winning children's books; reproductions of art from a variety of cultures; books on famous architects, musicians, and artists; and examples of a variety of excellent music—jazz, folk, classical, opera.

- _____

  _____

  _____

  _____

[1] Based on Department of Defense, _Creating Environments for School-Age Child Care_ (Washington, DC: U.S. Government Printing Office, August, 1980), p. 80.

Using Everyday Experiences to Encourage Creativity

Children are naturally curious. On their own they are constantly making discoveries as they investigate their world. Providers can encourage this natural process by giving children many varied opportunities to learn from ordinary experiences. Here are some suggestions.

- Place a new toy or interesting objects on the floor or table where children can reach them. Without saying anything, watch their reactions as children explore the toy or objects on their own.

- As you prepare a snack together, provide opportunities for children to explore with their senses. "How does that banana taste?" "Can you feel the soft fuzz on this peach?" "Did you hear that crunchy cracker?"

- Take advantage of how much children can learn as they help you with everyday chores. Give them enough time to complete what they are doing even if it isn't what you had planned. When Young Sim is helping you make a snack, be patient if she decides to arrange the fruit in a complicated spiral pattern.

- Use diaper-changing time as an opportunity to talk and sing with younger children. Help them become more aware of their bodies as you play "Where Are Your Toes?" or "Tickle Your Chin." Enjoy language together as you sing silly songs or say simple nursery rhymes.

- As children move around indoors and outdoors, talk with them about going around, under, over, through, in and out.

- When listening to a child's account of her day at school, ask questions about her feelings, interests, and ideas. "Who was your favorite character in *Henry Huggins*?" "How did you feel when your teacher asked you to read your story out loud?" "What could you do at recess the next time your friend Sadie is out sick?"

Provide opportunities for children to make choices.

One important way to encourage children's creativity is to provide opportunities for them to make choices. Making their own decisions allows children to feel important and helps them see themselves as persons apart from parents and providers. When offering choices to children, you need to be sure that you will be comfortable with whatever choice the child makes. Also, all the options should be ones that children can safely and capably handle.

You can offer choices such as these to the children in your care.

- **Which toys to play with and which activities to do.** Even infants can decide if they would like to hold the blue rattle or the red one. You can hold both rattles within a child's reach and let the child reach for the preferred one. Arrange toys and materials on low shelves so children can choose the ones they want without having to ask an adult. Allow older children to decide what they want to do and for how long.

- **Which snacks to eat.** Learn the children's favorite snacks and whenever possible, involve them as you plan nutritious and appropriate snacks: "Karl, what kind of pizza should we make next week?"

- **How to accomplish a new task.** Children can often figure out how to do things for themselves without adult intervention. For example, infants come up with many ways to accomplish the difficult task of using a spoon, toddlers find ways to get dressed or undressed without your help, preschool children learn to use scissors, and school-age children learn to read instructions for a craft project.

When offering choices to the younger children, remember that they like consistency and develop trust from knowing that their needs will be met. Toddlers in particular like to have their routines remain the same, and they like to know what is going to happen next. For this reason, choices that involve changes in daily routines or rituals are not recommended.

Coloring books, dittos, and adult-directed projects are not creative experiences.

Many providers wonder if it is a good idea to provide coloring books, dittos, or pre-cut models as part of their daily activities. The answer is simple: **no, it is not a good idea.**

For one thing, it's nearly impossible for young children to stay in the lines of a ditto or coloring book figure. This sets up children for failure. In addition, these types of experiences deny children an opportunity to use their imaginations, to experiment, and to express their individuality. They are not creative experiences. Although parents may find dittos and coloring books appealing, children often prefer open-ended materials. Even if children will use these items, they do not promote development or allow children to express their creativity.

What should you do if parents want their children to use these materials? Take the time to explain to parents why you know that these structured materials don't help children grow and learn. Most parents who look forward to seeing colored dittos and professional-looking artwork are really looking for signs that their child is doing well while at family child care. What they want to see is evidence of their child's progress. Completed dittos with their child's name on them seem to be proof that their child is accomplishing something during the day.

By sharing with parents your approach to encouraging children's creativity, you can offer them the reassurances they need. You can help parents understand that, even without dittos and coloring books, their children are doing important things during the day. It doesn't take long to convince parents that their child's green and purple version of a pumpkin is more of a treasure than a perfectly round orange pumpkin that an adult cut out and labeled with the child's name.

In this learning activity you will keep a log for three days of all the times you encourage the creativity of the children in your care. Focus on the small things you do throughout the day that help children solve problems, use their senses, express their feelings, try new ideas, explore their environment, and so on. Review the example that follows. Then use the blank form to record your words and actions.

Encouraging Creativity Throughout the Day
(Example)

Dates: *April 5-7*

What You Did	How This Encouraged Creativity
Alex (3-1/2 years) was finger painting, and his sleeve was slipping down and getting in the paint. I gently pushed up his sleeve and said, "Just look at the enormous circles you are making."	*Alex was absorbed in making circles, so I didn't interrupt his concentration. That's why I didn't ask him to stop and fix his sleeve. Instead, I tried to fix his sleeve without interrupting him. Also, I recognized his interest in the process of creating by commenting on what he was doing rather than the picture he was making.*
Yancey (9 years) hung his coat on one of the hooks by the door. His coat immediately fell down. I said, "Your coat is really too big for that hook. Where else could you and the other school-age kids hang their coats?"	*I let Yancey know that it wasn't his fault that the coat fell down, and I asked for his ideas about another place to put the coats.*
Stacey (21 months) picked up a pocketbook and said, "Me go Mommy's work." I responded, "Tell her I said hello."	*Stacey is beginning make-believe play. My comment helped stimulate her imagination.*
I gave Dirk (10 months) a piece of peach. He squished it, then put it in his mouth and made a funny face. I laughed and said, "Does that peach feel fuzzy on your tongue?"	*I let Dirk use his senses to explore his food. That is his way of being creative.*

Encouraging Creativity Throughout the Day

Dates: _____

What You Did	How This Encouraged Creativity

Discuss this learning activity with your trainer.

LEARNING ACTIVITIES

II. Using Music and Movement Experiences to Promote Creativity

In this activity you will learn:

- to recognize how music and movement experiences foster creativity in children; and

- to provide a variety of developmentally appropriate music and movement activities for children.

From infancy on, children respond to music.

From a very early age, children respond to music. Infants smile when adults sing to them. They begin to move their bodies when they hear music, and they respond to toys that make a noise. As children grow, their interest in music continues, and they begin to hum, sing, and make up chants.

As their coordination develops, they also begin to move to music: to sway, dance, bounce up and down, clap their hands, and stamp their feet. Older children may sing in the chorus, read music, play instruments, study ballet or tap dancing, or compose their own lyrics and music.

Music affects children's moods. Quiet, comforting music can lull children to sleep, while a march or very rhythmic music can encourage them to parade around the room and sing. Music gives children many opportunities to use their bodies and voices expressively.

Music and movement go well together.

Providers don't have to be talented to provide music and movement experiences for children. When young children sing, they aren't concerned with the quality of their voices or the provider's ability to sing; they respond to the enthusiasm and pure enjoyment of playing with sounds and moving their bodies. There are no wrong ways to sing, and children have a chance to express how they feel when listening to music. One child may find a song appealing; another may find it silly. One child may move his whole body to music while another may wave her arms while standing still. Because children naturally connect movement with music, listening to music invites them to explore what their bodies can do and to become aware of their bodies in space.

Listening to Sounds and Music

You can provide many opportunities throughout the day for children to hear and learn about various sounds and different types of music. Children can develop their listening skills as you point out sounds during the course of the day, play background music, or offer special "listening" activities.

Sounds are all around us.

Toys that make sounds are very appealing to infants—for example, rolling balls that chime or jingle, wind-up radios, and rattles. You can also make "sound boxes" by filling small containers with different types and amounts of dried beans and peas. (You can use film containers that have very tight lids or plastic yogurt containers that are securely sealed. Check these frequently to make sure children can't open them.)

Encourage children to become aware of the sounds around them. Ask them how different types of birds sing, what water sounds like when it drips or when it gushes, or how rain sounds. Play guessing games in which the children listen to sounds with closed eyes, or play music that includes various sounds that children can identify. Talk about sounds around the house such as the telephone, a bell, or a clock. Try pointing out sounds during walks: "Do you hear the birds singing, Kadija?"

Young children are also fascinated by sounds animals make. When reading to children, you can begin to identify and imitate various animal sounds. For example, you might point to the cat and say, "What does the cat say, Sheila? The cat says *meow*." By the time they are 15 to 18 months old, most children can supply the sounds themselves. Children will enjoy hearing songs that include animal sounds, such as "Old MacDonald."

Children enjoy many different kinds of music.

Listening to music can be both relaxing and enjoyable. Children should have many opportunities throughout the day to listen to different types of music, including children's songs, classical, jazz, marches, instrumentals, and folk songs. Many public libraries have a selection of children's records as well as other types of music that children will enjoy. Ask parents to tell you what kinds of songs or music their children like to listen to at home, and try to incorporate these into music experiences in your home. Each type of music has a different effect on children's moods: classical music or quiet children's songs might be relaxing at naptime, while a march or a jazz piece can prompt dancing.

You may want to promote older children's ability to concentrate by encouraging them to listen with you for a few minutes. The younger children probably will not be able to sit still and listen to music for very long, but they might enjoy listening while they do something else. For example, try playing music during an art activity. Ask the children who are painting or drawing to do so to the music: "What does the music make you think of?" "What kinds of colors do you think are in this music?" "Does this music make you feel like painting quickly or slowly?" Sometimes a child will stop what he is doing to listen to a favorite song or to a melody that is particularly appealing. Remember: play music selectively. If it is on all the time, it will become background noise rather than something to listen to and enjoy.

What music and sounds did you and the children listen to today?

_____

_____

_____

Singing with Children

You and the children will enjoy frequent, informal singing sessions as well as during a set singing time (if you have one). Make a list of all the simple songs you know and keep it handy to remind you of songs the children like to sing. Here are some suggested times for singing songs together.

- Use songs for transitions between activities—while getting ready for lunch or story time, for example. When children have to wait for a short time, reduce the frustration by singing.

- Use songs ritually. Start the day with the same song; use the same song for birthdays; use the same song regularly before brushing teeth or going outside or when greeting a new child. Some children need the security of certain events that they can count on, and they will be very quick to point out if you forget regular songs in their regular places.

- Use songs as singing games or have the children act out the stories in songs while they sing.

- Play games such as "London Bridge" and "The Farmer in the Dell." Encourage everyone to sing while they play. This may be difficult for some of the children at first.

- Act out story songs such as "The Old Woman Who Swallowed a Fly." You may want to make props for the children to use.

- Reinforce the importance of singing by making a tape of the children singing. They often love to listen to their own voices. Those who want to can sing individually as well as with the group.

- Sing the same song in different ways: loudly, softly, in a whisper, quickly, slowly, sitting, standing, marching, hopping, or with and without instruments.

- Make up your own songs with the children. They don't have to be long or complicated: "How are you? I'm fine, I'm fine" or "What do you like to eat? Ice cream!"

Infants and toddlers are a particularly good audience for providers who like to sing. They are responsive, clap their hands, and really don't care if you can carry a tune. They especially enjoy hearing their own names. Try making up rhymes or songs to a familiar tune and include the child's name. To the tune of "Alouette" you might sing "Jenny, penny, little Jenny penny" or "Edward, Edward, where is little Edward?"

When infants are learning to talk, their attempts at singing can be enjoyable for everyone. Their songs might consist of a sound repeated over and over, such as "B B B B" or "DADADADA." Gradually they can sing the words to a song, or half-babble, half-talk through a familiar song such as "Happy Birthday:" "Happy, happy, happy, BBBB."

It may be helpful to remember the following about children's singing abilities.

- They enjoy repeating songs they like.

- They tend to like singing quick, lively songs more often than slow ones.

- They enjoy funny songs and nonsense songs.

- We all have a speaking and a singing voice. You can help children become aware of this by saying the words to a song in your speaking voice, then using your singing voice for the same song.

- Children's ability to carry a tune improves with practice and good listening habits.

- Young children do not always understand what songs are appropriate for a given situation. If they want to sing "Jingle Bells" in May or "Good Morning" before going home, join them enthusiastically.

These ideas may be useful when introducing a new song.

- Allow children to play a tape recording you've made of the new song for several days. Younger children would probably rather hear your voice than a record of a professional singer.

- Tell a story about the new song. ("Once there was a little girl named Mary. She had a little lamb...") Use a flannel board when telling a story about the new song.

- Repeat the words for the song several times (break up the phrases if they are too long for some children to remember).

29

- Sing the song several times, encouraging children to join you.
- Let the children sing the song several times if they seem to enjoy it.
- You should not have to "drill" the children to get them to learn a new song. If they don't pick it up easily, come back to it at a later time or forget about it if it seems too difficult.

What are some of the favorite songs of the children you care for?

_____

_____

_____

Playing with Rhythm Instruments

Most children love to make their own music. You can begin by encouraging them to use their bodies as their first rhythm instruments. Start clapping and invite children to join you: "Let me hear you clap. How softly can you clap? How loudly can you clap? Can you clap slowly like this? Can you clap really fast?"

Toddlers and preschool children are ready to use simple instruments. When you first introduce them, give each child the same kind. When you bring out others, provide duplicates to help avoid conflict over sharing. The following are rhythm instruments that children enjoy:

- drums
- xylophones
- bells
- clackers
- rattles and maracas/shakers
- cymbals
- rhythm sticks
- tambourines
- sand paper blocks
- wood blocks
- pots and pans with wooden spoons
- triangles

Older preschool children and school-age children will also enjoy harmonicas, recorders, Jews harps, and stringed instruments.

Homemade instruments make interesting sounds.

Many instruments can be made by you or the children's parents. Because the primary purpose of instruments is to produce interesting and varied sounds, you don't need to invest in expensive, professional instruments. Drums can be made from oatmeal boxes; cymbals can be made using tin pie plates; and rattles can be made by filling containers with macaroni, rice, or buttons and closing them securely.

Allow plenty of time for children to explore the instruments. Remember that the youngest children are not interested in actually performing with the instruments. They probably won't march to music and play instruments at the same time. It's too difficult for them to do several things at once. Just making different sounds is exciting by itself.

Allow lots of time for the children to become familiar with the different instruments. What do they sound like? How do they make noise? Can the children make the same sounds the instruments make? Let the children know the names of the instruments. It can be fun to make up a song about the names; each child in turn can demonstrate how the instrument sounds.

Children of any age can enjoy marching in a band.

To have a marching band, each child can select an instrument and move around the room playing the instrument to different types of music. Try a march, then something slower. Put the instruments down and have the children clap to the beat or stamp their feet to the beat. You can march backward, in a circle, following a rope pattern on the floor, or in shapes. Have the children use the instruments as they stand in one place or sit in a circle on the floor.

What instruments are available for the children?

_____

_____

_____

What instruments would you like to add to your collection?

_____

_____

_____

Creative Movement

Even the youngest infants enjoy dancing and movement experiences. Try dancing with a child in your arms and moving to a song. When infants begin to stand and walk, you can hold their hands and move to the music. Some begin to move up and down as soon as the music begins. When they are able to walk well, you can play "Ring Around the Rosey." Some children enjoy sitting in your lap, facing you, and playing musical games such as "Row, Row, Row the Boat" while holding hands and rocking back and forth.

As they become steady on their feet and their balance improves, children often become very creative in their movements. They enjoy holding a provider's hands and moving to the music, and they also enjoy experimenting with what their bodies can do. You might ask them:

- "What can your feet do?"
- "How can you move your arms?"
- "What noises can your hands make?"

You might make suggestions such as these:

- "Let's bend our waists."
- "Let's wiggle fingers."
- "Let's stamp our feet really loudly."
- "Let's clap our hands softly."

Musical games are fun for children.

Older toddlers and preschool children will enjoy simple musical games such as "Bluebird, Bluebird" and "Ring Around the Rosey." If you do "The Hokey Pokey," remember to adapt it—"put one foot in," "put your other foot in" and so on—because some children won't know which is their left foot and which is their right.

Playing different types of music encourages children to move the way the music makes them feel. Use music that is fast and slow, loud and soft, happy and sad. Once the children feel comfortable moving to music, you can add props to further stimulate their imaginations: streamers, lightweight fabric, sheets, scarves, feathers, balloons, capes, ribbons, and hula hoops.

Older children will enjoy imitating the various ways that animals walk and move. They can crawl like a snake, waddle like a duck, kick like a mule, slither like a snake, or jump like a kangaroo. This can be done to music or without music.

Have the children pretend to be the wind, the rain, snow, or thunder especially on windy, rainy, or snowy days. How do they think a car moves, or a truck, a rocking chair, a weather vane? Some children enjoy using props such as hats when they are dancing. Have the children suggest other props to use.

Creative movement activities help children develop and refine their large and small motor skills in the following ways:

- Children become conscious of what their bodies can do. Providers have an important opportunity to accept and appreciate individual differences.

- Children develop and practice large motor skills, including hopping, skipping, jumping, trotting, swaying, swinging, and leaping.

- Children develop and refine their small muscles when they use rhythm instruments, imitate finger plays, and use props in movement activities.

How did you and the children move your bodies today?

_____

_____

_____

_____

Try these suggestions.

These tips may help you plan music and movement activities for the children in your care:

- Start with music that you enjoy. Your own enthusiasm and enjoyment will influence the children.

- Have all the materials you need ready ahead of time. Be sure the record or CD player or tape recorder is working; have the record, disk, or tape ready and the musical instruments nearby.

- Allow enough time for the activity, usually 10 to 20 minutes per planned experience. If the activity is particularly successful, allow more time to continue; if it isn't working the way you planned, cut it short.

- Look for cues from the children to see if the activity is developmentally appropriate; that is, can they do what you have asked, such as hopping or skipping? If not, try an easier movement.

- Be flexible. Give the children many opportunities to respond to the music in their own way. Encouraging children to "pay attention to your body and see what it feels like doing to this music" is more flexible than saying "everyone sway back and forth to the music."

- Encourage the children to come up with new ideas for music and movement experiences; ask them, "What else could we do to this music?"

- Provide time for music activities in small groups and for individual children to explore rhythm instruments alone.

- Encourage the children to be spontaneous with music and movement by setting an example. If you sing "will you clean up," they will begin to do the same. Model a creative way to walk to the neighborhood park.

- Maintain a balance between provider-planned music and movement experiences and those initiated by the children, such as singing while making playdough or rocking in the rocking boat.

- Plan music and movement activities to do outside as well as indoors.

Providing Music and Movement Activities for Children of Different Ages

From birth, infants are aware of the many sounds around them: the voices of their parents and providers, animal sounds, a doorbell ringing, or a clock ticking. They respond by turning their heads toward a sound, smiling, laughing, or moving an arm or leg. Some infants are very sensitive to sounds and may be startled or cry at unexpected or loud sounds. Others respond with curiosity and interest but may be afraid of a particular noise such as a vacuum cleaner or a siren.

Infants experience music and movement in different ways.

When planning music and movement experiences for infants, it helps to remember the following general characteristics of this age group:

- **They learn best when they are in charge of their own learning.** Infants will discover cause and effect on their own if you give them wooden spoons and pot lids to bang or bean bags to shake.

- **They learn by using their senses.** Infants are naturally drawn to music. They notice the music in their environment—the sound of wind chimes brushing together, the radio playing, the kettle whistling, and birds singing. Point out familiar sounds to infants: "Let's listen to the bird singing."

- **They learn through their interactions with others.** Help infants develop a sense of trust by responding to the child's moods with songs that reflect their feelings. For example, when an infant is quiet or uncomfortable, sing lullabies and folk songs. During active moods, play "Itsy Bitsy Spider."

- **They coo and babble.** Cooing and babbling are the beginning of language development. Respond to the sounds infants make with songlike conversation.

- **They enjoy being held.** Infants learn more about music when they respond to it physically. Movement is the natural partner of music. When infants listen to a song, they may turn their heads in the direction of the music, smile or laugh, or sway from side to side. Mobile infants typically move their arms or feet.

Think of an infant in your care. What kinds of music and movement experiences does she or he like?

_____

_____

_____

Toddlers use their skills to explore music and movement.

Toddlers, with their newly developed skills, can participate in a wide range of music and movement activities. You can sing songs, chant, or hum with toddlers throughout the day.

When planning music and movement experiences for toddlers, it helps to remember the following general characteristics of this age group:

- **They are discovering cause and effect.** Toddlers love to be the cause. Using their own voices to sing or making a sound with an instrument enables them to experience cause and effect firsthand: "I hit the drum and it makes a sound. I sing a song and my provider smiles and sings with me. I can make things happen with music."

- **They are sharpening their motor skills and coordination.** Toddlers can begin to use rhythm instruments to make their own music. In movement activities they enjoy exploring what their bodies can do.

- **They are striving to be competent.** They take pride in their ability to make sounds, sing, and move in different ways. Their self-expression takes many forms, and they are able to make choices during music and movement activities (what instrument to play, how to move across the room, and so on). You can reinforce that there are no right or wrong ways to sing, dance, or make music.

- **They are developing social skills.** Toddlers enjoy group music and movement activities—for example, dancing to a record, singing a song, and experimenting with ways in which bodies can move. Although the children are engaged in the same activity, they can express themselves in unique ways.

- **They are increasing their language skills.** Listening, making sounds, singing songs, and learning new words are all part of music experiences. These activities contribute to language development, which in turn promotes children's creative expression.

Think of a toddler in your care. What kinds of music and movement experiences does he or she like?

_____

_____

_____

Preschool children are beginning to develop rhythm.

Preschool children enjoy listening to music and are more aware of rhythm. They like to move, walk, or jump when someone claps rhythmically or plays an instrument. They can use musical instruments and like to repeat favorite songs over and over. They move their bodies creatively and enjoy props such as scarves, streamers, and hoops.

When planning music and movement experiences for preschool children, it helps to remember the following general characteristics of this age group:

- **They learn best by interacting directly with real-life materials.** Provide raw materials such as beans, jars, wires, rubber bands, and tin boxes, and invite the children to make their own musical instruments.

- **They are developing small muscle control.** Encourage preschool children to try all the instruments used in a marching band such as bells, tambourines, maraca, and triangles.

- **They are curious and love to experiment with materials on their own.** Give preschool children unfamiliar musical instruments (an auto harp or a kazoo, for example) to examine. Before you explain how the instruments are customarily played, let the children try out their own ideas of how to use the instruments.

- **They are able to express their feelings.** Encourage preschool children to make up their own songs or to change the lyrics to songs they already know how to sing.

- **They are developing control over their bodies, which also strengthens their self-images.** Lead preschool children in movement activities that will improve their coordination and balance, such as walking backward on a line, racing while carrying a hard-boiled egg on a spoon, dancing with a long streamer, and so on.

Think of a preschool child in your care. What kinds of music and movement experiences does she or he like?

_____

_____

_____

School-age children are developing their own music and movement tastes.

In general, school-age children are very interested in popular music and in doing the latest dances or exercises. Most will welcome opportunities to listen to music alone or with their friends. Music and movement activities allow school-age children to relax, unwind, and develop their personal music tastes.

Music and movement experiences for school-age children should be based on the following general characteristics of this age group:

- **They like to be in tune with their peers.** Encourage children to practice the latest dance steps. Let the children know that you respect them and their need to be part of their peer group.

- **They like to take on leadership roles.** Ask school-age children to lead the younger children in musical games such as "Hokey Pokey." They will delight in exaggerating their actions for the younger children.

- **They want to assert their independence.** Allow children to take out and put away records, tapes, and CDs on their own. Provide a special place for them to safely store music they bring from home.

- **They enjoy the satisfaction of seeing a project through from beginning to end.** Suggest that school-age children help you make some homemade instruments that the younger children can use—kazoos, drums, and tambourines, for example.

- **They might be interested in learning about different kinds of music.** Borrow a variety of music tapes or records from the library—show tunes, opera, blues, classical, jazz, and so on. Talk to children about the instruments they can hear and how popular music may include elements of many different kinds of music.

Think of a school-age child in your care. What kinds of music and movement experiences does he or she like?

_____

_____

_____

In this learning activity you will plan and implement a music or movement experience for some or all the children in your care. Begin by reading the example that follows.

Promoting Creativity with Music and Movement
(Example)

Child(ren): _Jill and Yolanda_   **Age(s):** _21, 36 months_   **Date:** _March 2_

Setting: _Free play_   **Experience:** _Listening to different kinds of music_

Describe the music experience:

One morning I asked Jill if she wanted to listen to music. We walked over to the tape recorder. I put on a tape.

What did the child(ren) do?

As soon as the music started, Jill pointed to the tape recorder and smiled. I said, "The tape recorder is playing music for us to listen to."

As we listened for a few seconds to a piece of classical music, Jill took my hand and began dancing—moving her hands in the air and swaying back and forth. Yolanda came over and began dancing, too. She took hold of Jill's other hand. We all danced, each in our own way, as we listened to the music.

How did this music experience encourage creativity?

The children are learning that listening to music is enjoyable. This will encourage them to listen to sounds and music around them.

Jill experienced cause and effect: when the tape recorder is turned on, there is music.

Each of us had the opportunity to respond to the music in our own way through our dancing.

Would you do this same music experience again? What type of changes would you make?

I will do this again. It is so simple, and I hadn't thought of it before. I will work on expanding our tape collection so we have different kinds of music to listen to.

Promoting Creativity with Music and Movement

Child(ren): _____   Age(s): _____   Date: _____

Setting: _____   Experience: _____

Describe the music experience:

_____

_____

_____

_____

What did the child(ren) do?

_____

_____

_____

_____

_____

_____

How did this music experience encourage creativity?

_____

_____

_____

_____

Would you do this same music experience again? What type of changes would you make?

_____

_____

_____

Discuss this activity with your trainer.

LEARNING ACTIVITIES

III. Planning Art Experiences That Promote Creativity

In this activity you will learn:

- to recognize how art experiences foster creativity in children; and

- to provide a variety of appropriate art experiences for children of different ages.

Art has no right or wrong result.

Art can take place at almost any time of the day and in nearly every area of your home, including outdoors. It is a relaxing activity for most children and stimulates all of the senses. Like most activities, art is most effective when FCC providers plan for it and have specific goals in mind. What and how much children get out of an art experience depends to a great extent on what you do to support their interest and involvement.

Most children love to paint, draw, glue things together, pound a lump of clay, or talk about the colors in a favorite picture. Art encourages children to use their imaginations and create something of their own. Through art experiences, children learn to be spontaneous in using a variety of textures, shapes, and colors. They can make choices and try out their own ideas without thinking that there has to be a right or wrong result.

A rich and varied art environment doesn't require a lot of money.

You don't need to spend a great deal of money to create a rich environment for art. Many of the raw materials are former throwaways, and other materials can be made from ingredients you already have on hand.

Almost any area of your home can be used for art activities, but most providers prefer to designate certain places for specific types of artwork. A child-sized table is a good place for children to draw, paste a collage, or play with clay. For messy art materials, set up an art space near a sink and away from carpeting and furniture that might get soiled. The kitchen or dining room table can also be used for art projects. Cover the floor under the table with a large piece of plastic such as a painter's heavy-duty dropcloth or an old vinyl tablecloth.

Easels should also be set up away from furniture, preferably over linoleum, tile, or wooden floors that can be protected with newspapers, a dropcloth, or an old shower curtain. In nice weather you can move the easel or table outdoors.

Try these suggestions.

Children will find it easy to find things if you arrange art materials according to how they are used. For example, store all the drawing materials in one container or section of the shelf, and store collage items in another. Here are some other storage suggestions:

• Use egg cartons for storing string, scissors, pencils, pens, or brushes. Tape each carton's edges together so it doesn't open when you or the children carry it.

• Use empty coffee cans for a variety of purposes. Make a scissors holder by punching holes in the plastic lid. Make a string or yarn holder by poking a hole in the middle of the lid and threading the string or yarn through the hole.

• Use baby food jars for individual portions of glue or paint.

• Stand up crayons in frozen juice cans.

• Make paint caddies from cardboard six-pack cartons. Cover juice cans with color-coded Contact paper, then fill the cans with corresponding colors of paint. Place a paint-filled can in each compartment. Painters can carry these caddies to indoor or outdoor painting sites.

• Use empty shoeboxes to store art materials. Cover the boxes with Contact paper for decoration or to color-code materials such as paper, yarn, fabric, or felt. Paste a picture label on the outside of each box so children can easily see what the box contains.

The charts on the following pages describe materials children can use for a variety of art experiences.

Item	Comments
Paper and cardboard	Provide a variety of papers—tissue, construction paper, sandpaper, wrapping paper—so children can experiment with texture, color, and absorbency. A local newspaper or printer may give away end rolls of newsprint, which works well as art paper. Ask hardware or wallpaper stores to donate outdated sample books. Used computer paper is available from offices. If you purchase paper, buy larger sizes (at least 12" x 18") so children can make bold movements.
Brushes	Offer a variety of sizes, depending on the ages of the children in your care. One-inch brushes with thick handles that are about 5" or 6" in length are easiest for young children to use.
Other painting tools	Provide sponges, potatoes, cotton balls, paper towels, marbles, ink stamps, feathers, leaves, tongue depressors, straws, strings, eye droppers, and anything else you or the children think of.
Easels	They are quite easy to make, or you can tack a piece of plastic to the wall to make a temporary easel.
Paint containers	Use glass furniture casters, muffin tins, baby food jars, Styrofoam egg cartons, juice cans, and yogurt containers.
Paint	Tempera paint comes in liquid and powdered form. The liquid version lasts a long time and produces vibrant colors; however, it is expensive. Powdered tempera is much cheaper, but it must be mixed to the right consistency. Add a few drops of alcohol or wintergreen to mixed tempera to keep it from going sour. Add a little soap flakes to improve the consistency and to make it easier to get out of clothes.
Finger paint	Make finger paint by combining 1 C liquid starch with 6 C water, 1-1/2 C soap flakes, and a few drops of food coloring. Another good recipe calls for mixing 3 T sugar with 1/2 C cornstarch in a sauce pan and then mixing in 2 C cold water. Cover the mixture and cook it over low heat until it has thickened. Add food coloring after the paint cools.
Building materials—any size scraps	Use linoleum, masonite, metal pieces, nails, tiles, wallboard, wire, wire mesh, wood scraps, large tapestry materials, and wooden dowels.

Item	Comments
Crayons and other drawing materials	Jumbo crayons are easiest for young children to grasp. Provide large, good-quality crayons that color evenly and steadily. Children respond to a lot of color; less expensive crayons are made with more wax and have less color. Using them might be frustrating and less rewarding for children. For more variety, offer white and colored chalk, pens, pencils, and washable markers. You can make soap crayons to use during water play by mixing 1/8 C water with 1 C soap flakes and adding food coloring. Pour the mixture into plastic ice cube or popsicle trays and allow it to harden.
Clay and playdough	Commercial varieties can be harmful if swallowed and are difficult to remove from carpets. To make playdough, combine and knead 2 C flour, 1 C salt, 2 T oil, 1 C water, and a few drops of food coloring. To make a smoother playdough, add 1 T cream of tartar to the above ingredients and heat the mixture in a pan, stirring constantly, until the dough pulls away from the sides of the pan and forms a lump. Then knead the dough. Store in plastic bags or containers in the refrigerator. To make dough that will harden, mix and knead 2 C corn starch, 1 C baking soda, 1 C water, and food coloring. The recipe for modeling clay is 1 C salt, 1-1/2 C flour, 1/2 C warm water, 2 T oil, and food coloring.
Paste or glue	White, store-bought varieties are inexpensive and effective. Older children may do projects that require different kinds of glue.
Scissors	Invest in good-quality scissors with blunt ends. Children are easily frustrated by poor-quality scissors that bend or tear the paper. If a child is left-handed, provide special left-handed scissors.
Natural items	Nature collectibles can be used in collages or for decorating. Collect acorns, feathers, flowers, pine cones, seashells, seeds, stones, pebbles, and so on.
Sewing items	Household items such as beads, braids, buttons, cotton balls, ribbons, shoelaces, snaps, hooks and eyes, and yarn can be sewn (or glued) onto felt or fabric. Purchase large plastic sewing needles, thick yarn, and plastic canvas at craft or "five and dime" stores.

Item	Comments
Fabrics	Children will use material of every color and texture for sewing projects, collages, puppetry, and so on. Save (or ask parents and neighbors to save) burlap, canvas, denim, felt, fake fur, lace, leather, oilcloth, and terrycloth scraps of all sizes.
Kitchen/laundry items	Save any or all of the following: aluminum foil, bottle tops, plastic wrap, parchment, corks, egg cartons, bleach bottles, empty food and beverage containers, boxes, Styrofoam packaging, cans, paper bags, popsicle sticks, paper towels, paper plates, paper cups, doilies, spray bottles, steel wool pads, string, and toothpicks. Food items such as eggshells, uncooked pasta, rice, potatoes, and beans can also be used in projects, although it's best to first check with parents in case they object to food being used in this way.
Other "artsy" items	Let your imagination take over—glitter, confetti, broken appliance parts, pipe cleaners, wooden beads, stamp pads and stamps, marbles, shredded paper, old business cards, hangers, and wires.
Clean-up items	Mops, sponges, brooms, and towels are needed to return your home to its "pre-art" status. Maintain a good supply so all the children can participate in clean-up. Store cleaning in locked cabinets.

Before going any further in this learning activity, take an inventory of your art supplies. Use the following charts to describe what you have on hand and how children use each item.

Art Supplies Inventory

Item	How Children Use This

What would you like to add to the above list?

_____

_____

_____

Plan and schedule art activities regularly.

Each day during free play, children should have the opportunity to select and use a variety of art materials. Keep paper, crayons, markers, collage materials, scissors, and glue available so children can get involved without your help. For some activities (for example, finger painting, weaving, making puppets, murals, or making collages with special glue or materials), providers need to plan and prepare. For example, if you want to offer the children the opportunity to paint, you may have to mix paint, put down a dropcloth, get out the easel, and so on. Also, such activities require closer supervision. If you care for children of different ages, scheduling a messy activity such as finger painting can be a challenge.

Follow these general guidelines when scheduling art activities.

- Individual, nonmessy art activities can take place at almost any time of the day. Many providers use the periods following breakfast or before parents arrive as ideal times for quiet art activities.

- It is best to schedule messy activities for times when infants will be napping. This will allow the older children to finger paint or make clay beads without being interrupted by curious babies. The mid-morning naptime is usually an ideal time for such projects. If the baby wakes up in the middle of a project, bring the child into the group. A baby can sit in a highchair and explore her own interesting materials (for example, a set of measuring spoons or a few pieces of squooshy banana). Schedule these activities to follow the mid-morning or mid-afternoon snack. Outdoor play time is another excellent time for group art activities. It is very stimulating to paint at an easel while the warm sun shines on your face.

- Plan activities that require your full attention such as finger painting or making plaster molds on days when you have lots of time and patience.

Try these suggestions.

Here are some tips for successful art activities. Add your own tip in the space provided at the end.

- Have everything you need for the art activity ready ahead of time, including dropcloths and smocks. Make sure you have enough materials so that each child has his or her own crayons, paper, brushes, and so on.

- Allow plenty of time for children to get used to the materials and enough time to use them.

- Have all clean-up supplies easily accessible, including a change of clothes when needed.

- Organize space for children's creations—a low shelf where children can put their pasted papers to dry flat, or a low clothesline and some clothespins where they can help you hang their paintings.

- Match art materials and activities to the children's abilities. Observe often to find out which children can cut with scissors, hold a small paintbrush, glue small pieces onto something else, or use the rolling pin to make a playdough pie. If children are having trouble or if you end up doing the activity for them, the activity is too difficult. Redirect the child to a more appropriate activity, or find some other way for them to participate.

- Be flexible. When an art experience doesn't turn out the way you planned it, adjust it to the children's interests. If they would rather punch holes all morning (to make confetti) than construct sewing cards, let them do that. Save sewing cards for another day.

- Continue a planned art experience for more than one day if the children are interested. A mural started on Monday can stay up until the end of the week or longer.

- Allow individual children to continue their art while others move on to other activities. Some children become very involved and need more time to experience the activity or to carry out their plans fully.

- _____

  _____

  _____

  _____

Drawing

All young children go through the same stages as they develop drawing skills. Children may begin drawing at different ages, but they all pass through the same stages in the same order. They develop at different rates and often repeat earlier stages as they are moving forward. A child's artistic ability develops as his or her physical and cognitive skills grow. Providers need to understand and recognize the stages of artistic development so that they can provide appropriate materials and art experiences and respond to children's work in ways that promote creativity.

The chart on the next page summarizes the developmental stages of children's art and suggests ways that providers can promote artistic development.

Developmental Stages of Children's Art

Stage	What Children Do and Why	Ways Providers Can Promote Artistic Development
Early scribbles	Children make random marks on papers, walls, table tops, or anywhere else they can reach. The marks go in many directions. Children cannot control which way the marks go, but this doesn't bother them. They enjoy the physical motions of scribbling.	Provide large pieces of paper so children can make wide arm movements and scribble in all directions. Store crayons, paints, markers, and chalk where children can select and use them during free play.
Later scribbles	Children learn that they can control the brush or crayon and the way they are scribbling. They enjoy being able to control their scribbling. They try circles, lines, or zigzags. They may cover the whole paper with scribbles.	Continue to provide children with a variety of art materials. Make only positive or neutral statements about their work. Children are not trying to draw pictures. Share the children's pleasure with their new skills.
Basic shapes	Children recognize circles and ovals in their scribbles and repeat them. They make rectangles and squares by drawing parallel vertical lines, then joining them with horizontal lines at the top and bottom. They combine straight lines to make crosses.	Have the easels set up with paints and brushes as often as possible. Whenever feasible, allow children to paint for as long as they want to. Continue to provide materials that children can use on their own such as paper, markers, crayons, and so on.
Drawing mandalas	Children combine two shapes they have already made to make mandalas—ovals or rectangles combined with crosses. They may make one or more mandalas combined with other shapes. This is the first step toward drawing representations of animals, people, buildings, trees, or flowers.	Include finger painting on paper, cookie sheets, or a table covered with vinyl. Observe children and comment on the shapes they make: "You put a cross inside your circle."

Developmental Stages of Children's Art (continued)

Stage	What Children Do and Why	Ways Providers Can Promote Artistic Development
Drawing suns	Children draw circles or ovals with lines coming from the outside. They don't call these suns, but adults think they look like suns. Children like the way these shapes look. They may add marks for human faces: eyes, nose, and mouth.	Continue positive comments. Don't ask "what is that?" or tell a child you like his or her "sun." Point out the shapes you see or comment on the color, size, or where they are placed on the paper.
Drawing humans	Children draw circles, then add lines from the bottom as legs and perhaps a line from either side as arms. Inside the circle, dots, lines, or small circles are used for eyes, noses, and mouths. They may add more features and perhaps clothes. They draw humans because they have learned from making mandalas and suns how to combine shapes and lines into a figure that represents a person. They are still developing a skill rather than drawing a picture.	Don't push children to reach this stage. They will develop this skill without your help. Just continue to provide materials, time to create, and your interest and approval.
Drawing animals and trees	Children apply the skills they use in drawing humans to drawing animals. Often the animals stand upright like humans. Later they will have bodies parallel with the bottom of the paper and four vertical lines for legs. Trees look like tall rectangles with circles on the top. Details such as branches or leaves appear later.	Don't push children to reach this stage; they will do so without your help. Just continue to provide materials, time to create, and your interest and approval.

Developmental Stages of Children's Art (continued)

Stage	What Children Do and Why	Ways Providers Can Promote Artistic Development
Making pictorial drawings	Children may draw several different objects on the same paper that may or may not be related to one another. They create pictures by using the shapes and figures they've already learned to draw. They teach themselves to use rectangles as doors, circles as suns, or a series of arcs as a rainbow. Size and color (if added) are not realistic, and objects are free-floating; for example, trees may appear at the top of the paper. Pictures may not be planned in advance; for example, a drop of red paint might become a sun. Children may also plan ahead, deciding to paint a picture of a boat or airplane.	Children reach this stage at the end of their preschool years. Ask children to tell you about their pictures. Listen carefully to what they are telling you, because these early pictures are the child's first use of art as communication. Be aware that the process of creating a picture is still very important, but the children are beginning also to care about their products. As children get older, they will plan what they are going to draw or paint and will develop the skills to carry out these plans. Also, they may become quite critical of their own work. Providers can support children's continued growth by encouraging them to experiment and use their creativity in new ways.

Painting

Painting requires smocks, easels, paintbrushes, paint, and paper. A low table is probably better than an easel for infants and toddlers. Older children generally prefer to paint at easels. Plan for a messy activity. Protect the painting area with newsprint or an old shower curtain taped to the floor. Put a small amount of paint in sturdy containers. Remember that young children like to paint both on and off the paper, and they like to paint their hands and fingers.

For beginners, paintbrushes with flat bristles and short handles (5" to 6") are recommended. They are easier to handle than brushes with longer handles. If you cannot find short-handled brushes, longer ones can be cut down and sanded. Sponges cut into shapes, small rollers, and straws can also serve as brushes.

Many first paintings look the same.

Children move through the same stages in painting as they do in drawing. In the beginning children are interested only in how it feels to paint. They love the way the brush feels when it slides across the paper and usually are not very interested in the color that results. This is why many first paintings look the same; they are generally a brownish-purplish color that results when the child brushes layer upon layer of color onto the paper, often using every inch of space available.

Very young children often start painting using only one color. They may start with the primary colors: red, yellow, or blue. When the children become more experienced, they will discover what happens when they combine colors. Put small amounts of paint in the jar; it's easier to control where the paint goes when there is not so much of it. It's also better for the brush because the paint shouldn't come over the level of the bristles.

Be available when children request help.

Children who haven't painted before may need help learning how to hold the brush or how to wipe the brush on the jar so that paint doesn't glob on the paper. Some children are not bothered by globs or enjoy holding brushes upside down. Be available to children who request help while allowing all children to experiment and learn through trial and error.

In your observations of children painting, you may have noticed that each has a particular style and approach. Some children prefer soft brushes; others like the hard ones. Some children fill the entire paper while others leave blank areas. Some will do many paintings during the day while others may do only one. The amount of time each child spends painting will vary, as will the intensity with which they work. Some children talk to themselves as they paint; others talk with other children who are also painting. Listening to what they say can provide valuable insights into the children's feelings about what they are doing.

Eventually, children plan what they want to paint.

Gradually, children become more purposeful in their painting. They ask for specific colors to use and want to place things on the paper in specific ways. They may become concerned with drips that disrupt what they are trying to do and may be very particular about the colors they select. Eventually, they reach the stage where they plan what they want to paint.

Most preschool children and school-age children enjoy a wide range of colors. They enjoy seeing what happens when colors mix or when white paint is used to create pastels. They like using colors such as purple and black as well as the primary colors. And they may still enjoy mixing every color available to create those brownish-purplish colors that adults find hard to name!

By combining different types of paints, papers, and tools for painting, providers can provide many new art experiences for children. Children enjoy painting on different types of paper, such as colored construction paper, sandpaper, wrapping paper, wallpaper samples, or Styrofoam packing pieces (on the table rather than at the easel). For variety, cut the paper into shapes such as circles or into long strips.

Have children experiment with a variety of painting techniques.

- blow painting (using a straw to blow a glob of paint across the paper);

- spatter painting (using a toothbrush and screen to paint stencils of leaves, feathers, shells, and so on);

- crayon-resist painting (painting with diluted paint over crayon designs); and

- folded painting (placing globs of paint on a piece of paper, folding it, then unfolding it).

Give children opportunities to explore different textures.

- Provide paper, tempera paint, and brushes.

- Put out in separate containers some sawdust, sand, salt, and tempera.

- Allow the children to experiment with what these substances do to the paint and paper. They can add a substance to the paint beforehand, or sprinkle it on the paper and paint over it, or sprinkle it on afterward.

- Ask children questions to stimulate their curiosity: "What will happen if...?" "What else could we add to the paint?" "What happens when you mix these two colors?"

Encourage children to experience different colors.

- Provide primary-colored paint (either finger paint or tempera).

- While the children are painting, add a container of white paint.

- Observe the children's reactions as they add white paint to create pastels.

- Encourage the children to try mixing other colors to see what happens.

Let children experiment with different types of tools.

- rollers,
- whisk brooms,
- straws,
- marbles,
- plastic squeeze bottles,
- sponges cut into shapes,
- stamps, and
- string.

Many children enjoy finger painting.

Finger paints are another kind of painting experience. Give children lots of room, and allow them to experiment with paint and fingers rather than making a picture. Children can paint on cookie sheets, cafeteria-type trays, or on a large piece of plastic or vinyl stretched across the table and taped in place. Painting directly on the table gives the child lots of room to experiment with paint rather than making a picture. If children want to have a picture of their finger paintings, any type of paper can be placed on top of their pictures and pressed down to create an imprint.

Give each child two or three tablespoons of paint, then put the paint containers out of reach of the younger children. It is best to begin with one-color paintings. Demonstrate for first-time painters how to make scribbly lines and how to use fingertips and hands to make different kinds of designs. Experienced finger painters develop their own finger-painting techniques.

Some children don't want to use finger paints because they don't like to get messy. Encourage these children by giving them just a dot of paint to begin with. If they are still reluctant, offer a different art experience and try the finger painting again in a few weeks.

Collages and Assemblages

Collage refers to the pasting of all kinds of things on a flat surface. An assemblage is a three-dimensional piece made by putting various things together. Assemblages and collages are wonderful opportunities for creative expression. Children can use a variety of materials to create something original.

Collages can include items such as fabric scraps, ribbon, wood scraps, Styrofoam, feathers, magazine pictures, and buttons. They can be created on a variety of papers, including cardboard, heavy corrugated paper, construction paper, or posterboard. Newsprint is not recommended because it is too thin. Computer paper can be used as long as the children are attaching only paper scraps.

Older children should have access to scissors so they can cut pieces of paper or thin materials, such as wallpaper samples or ribbon, to the size and shape they want.

When children are given a variety of items that can be put together in unusual ways, they create imaginative assemblages. Materials to provide include these:

- items that can poke into or hold together: toothpicks, wire, wooden dowels, straws, paper fasteners, yarn, nails, pipe cleaners;
- things that can be poked into or stuck on: cork, fabric, paper, Styrofoam balls, sponge fragments; and

- materials that attach to wood: tile pieces, Styrofoam, wooden clothespins, dowels.

The invitation to experiment develops the child's curiosity. Thinking of what to put with what leads to skills in planning. Learning that a big piece of cork is too heavy for one toothpick to hold up is a science discovery. Trying different ways to make an assemblage stand up is practice in solving problems. Looking around at other people's creations is part of developing a sense of what art is.

Clay and Playdough

Clay and playdough are yet another means for creative self-expression. Most children enjoy the feeling of manipulating clay and playdough—rolling it, pushing it, or pounding it. Older children begin to make things with clay or playdough and may enjoy using clay that hardens or can be baked into a permanent form.

Playdough introduces children to a new texture. Given a clump of dough for the first time, most children will smell it, taste it, poke it with a finger, or pat it. They need plenty of time to explore this new material and see what it can do and what they can make it do. The will feel its texture, push it around the table, and pound it with their hands. Helping to make the playdough becomes another creative experience.

Give children their own lump of playdough; don't expect them to share. They can play with dough directly on a tabletop. Some children like to stand at the table; others will want to sit down. Depending on their ages, they might enjoy using props such as wooden spoons, wooden mallets, rolling pins, and cookie cutters.

Older children will enjoy making objects that will harden when dried or baked. You can provide natural items such as shells or pine cones to use as decorations. Several recipes for this kind of modeling material were included in the chart earlier in this learning activity. Once the items have hardened, the children might like to paint them.

Printing and Etching

Even very young children can experiment with design printing. Mix a thick consistency of poster paint, then pour the mixture over a sponge until it is soaked with paint. Using the sponge as a "stamp pad," let the children experiment printing designs on paper. Printing tools might include slices of fruit and vegetables such as carrots, potatoes, apples, and corn on the cob. Cut the fruits and vegetables into chunks and wedges that are easy to hold. You can also print with nonfood items such as shape-sorter pieces, pieces of sponge, lengths of string, or odds and ends. Put out a variety of items from your junk collection and allow the children to select the items they want to experiment with. You and the children are limited only by your imaginations and your willingness to clean up.

Another fun and easy printing activity is to scratch out a design or picture on a printing "block" and then use this for making prints. Here's what to do:

- Give each child a printing "block" such as a Styrofoam food tray.

- Provide a variety of tools—forks, bottle caps, empty ballpoint pens, or nails (for older children only)—so the children can etch a design.

- Have the children paint over their "blocks" and then lay blank paper across the top. When the paper is carefully peeled off, it will carry a printed design.

For school-age children you could provide special fabric paint so they could design their own hand-printed T-shirts or fabric wall hangings.

Puppets

Puppets are not only fun to create, they're also useful for developing body awareness, language concepts, and spatial relationships. They lend themselves readily to dramatic play and can help a shy child participate in group activities. There are many styles and ways of making puppets. Here are some of the more popular materials:

- Sock collage puppets: Children can cut and glue collage materials onto a sock "head," forming facial features for people or animals. Alternatively, use gloves or paper lunch bags as puppet bases.

- Newspaper puppets: Children can make a puppet body by fastening rolled newspaper with rubber bands. Then they can decorate and dress the puppet body.

- Papier-mache puppets: Children can place strips of paste-drenched newspaper all over an inflated balloon. When dry, the papier-mached balloon can be painted to resemble a human or animal head. Clothing can be "sewn" around the "neck" of the balloon head to make a complete puppet or animal.

Weaving

Weaving is a challenging and rewarding activity for older preschool and school-age children. To weave, children need the following:

- Something to weave on, such as:

    Chicken wire
    Mesh vegetable bags

Scraps of pegboard
Berry containers
Styrofoam containers into which holes have been punched
Simple homemade looms (see below for several examples)

- Some thick and textured materials to weave with, such as:

Pipe cleaners
Straws
Rug and textured yarns such as mohair
Ribbon
Twine
Florist wire
Strips cut from colored plastic bags
Strips of cellophane
Weeds or grasses

- Tools for weaving, such as:

Stiffened yarn
Plastic needles
Tongue depressors with holes drilled in the ends

Older children will enjoy using homemade looms.

To make a cardboard loom you will need a rectangular piece of heavy cardboard (at least 9" x 12"), a ruler and a pencil, a sharp knife or scissors, and some strong yarn or string. Have children make a mark every 1/4" along each of the shorter ends of the cardboard. Help the children make 1/2" slits through each mark. Use strong string or yarn to thread the loom—bend the cardboard to make an arc, then wrap the string around from one end to the other, and underneath, securing the string in each slit. The finished loom will be bowed, like a stringed musical instrument. Children can make shuttles out of scraps of cardboard or paint stirrers. Have them wrap yarn or other weaving materials around the shuttle. Then they can use the shuttle to weave in and out as they go across each row. Finished products can serve as placemats, wall hangings, or potholders. Make knots in the strings at the end of the loom. Then trim them to make a fringe. Once the weaving is finished, the loom will be ready to be used again.

A deep-dish, paper or Styrofoam plate makes another kind of loom. Around the edges, have children cut an uneven number of slits 1/2" to 1" apart and 3/4" deep. Next, children push a thick piece of yarn or string into one of these slits, leaving a tail of several inches. They wind the yarn back and forth across the plate until all the slits are filled. To finish, children tie the two loose ends on the back side of the plate. Children then weave with strips of fabric or yarn, taking them under and over the strings of the loom. To lift off the weaving, children bend up the edges of the plate and gently slip it off.[5]

A simple frame loom can be made with a few pieces of wood stripping (or pre-cut frame pieces from a crafts store). You or the children can pound tall nails into the frame at 1/4" intervals on opposite ends. Thread the loom with a sturdy string. If the loom is a large one, two children can work at the same time, or children can take turns creating interesting rows. Hang the finished weaving where everyone can see it.

Providing Art Experiences for Children of Different Ages

Experiences with a variety of art materials encourage children to use their senses, to explore, and to be creative. The youngest children are most interested in the process of playing with art materials; they have little interest in the end products. Older children still enjoy the process; however, they are also proud and sometimes critical of their creations.

Infants use their senses in art experiences.

Infants approach art as they do all activities: by using their senses. They coo at the feel of velvet, delight in swirling pudding "paint" with their fingers, and find that playdough is even more fun to poke holes in than to chew. By allowing infants lots of opportunities to explore art materials with their senses, you help them learn about these materials and what happens when they use them in different ways. Your interest and encouragement sends infants the message that art experiences are important.

Art experiences for infants should be based on the following general characteristics of this age group:

- **They learn by using their senses.** Hang a patchwork quilt or piece of fabric on the wall at infants' eye level, make a mobile out of colorful pieces of terrycloth or felt, and provide different textures to explore: balls or bean bags, fabric pieces, books.

- **They learn through their interactions** with others and need to feel part of the group. Plan an art activity that you can do with an infant sitting in your lap. For example, you could give the infant some playdough to play with. When older children are doing an activity, think of a way for infants to participate. For example, while the older children are making potato prints, an infant could play with some potato shapes.

---

[5] Adapted from U.S. Department of Health and Human Services, *Doing Things* (Washington, DC: U.S. Department of Health and Human Services, Office of Human Development Services, Administration for Children, Youth, and Families, Head Start Bureau, 1978), p. 9.

- **They are learning to use language to communicate.** Point out pictures on the wall, and talk about the colors and things you both see. Discuss how pictures make you feel when you look at them. Encourage the other children to talk to infants about what they are doing.

- **They are developing fine motor skills** and need lots of practice to master them. Give an infant a large nontoxic crayon and a large piece of paper, anchored to the table with tape. Let the child explore and discover what the crayon can do. Give seated infants pieces of paper to tear; try magazines and junk mail, too. Collect a box of ribbons and large pieces (at least 5" x 7") of felt or other fabrics for infants to pick up and play with. Be sure all pieces are large enough so they won't be swallowed and short enough to avoid tangling.

- **They learn by exploring their environment.** Scatter a variety of different sized or brightly colored fabric or carpet pieces around an area of the room for infants to crawl to or over. Give them enough room to move about without causing problems.

Think of an infant in your care. What kinds of art experiences do you provide for her or him?

_____

_____

_____

Toddlers are ready to explore a variety of art materials.

For toddlers, art opens up a whole new world of experiences. At your FCC home, toddlers are introduced, many for the first time, to drawing, painting, and playing with dough. As their fine motor skills develop, toddlers gradually learn to make marks and scribbles with crayons, to hold paintbrushes, and to enjoy the sensation of using finger paint. For toddlers, the process of using art materials is far more important than the final product.

Art experiences for toddlers should be based on the following general characteristics of this age group:

- **They are exploring cause and effect.** Each time toddlers use art materials, they make a change and create something uniquely their own. Talk to them about what they are doing, focusing on the process rather than the product of their art.

- **They are increasing their fine motor skills and coordination.** Almost all art experiences enhance eye-hand coordination and fine muscle development—tearing paper, using a crayon, holding a paintbrush, finger painting with shaving cream, or poking a hole in dough. Some older toddlers might be ready for pasting. You

can give them a large piece of paper, a clump of paste, and some of the pieces they have torn. Show them how to put paste on the back of the pieces and attach them to the large piece of paper. Don't be surprised if they become more involved with how the paste feels and smells than with the process of pasting something. If they aren't interested in pasting something on the piece of paper, they probably are not yet ready for this activity.

- **They are striving for competence.** Art experiences should provide many opportunities for toddlers to make choices. Let them use and return nonmessy art supplies on their own.

- **They are developing social skills.** Through art experiences, toddlers can practice their emerging skills. They can trade crayons, talk about what they are doing, or work beside another child at an easel. Invite toddlers to join older children for group projects such as mural painting or making costumes for a play.

- **They are increasing their language skills.** Model the use of descriptive language: "I see you filled your paper with bright blue squiggly lines." Encourage toddlers to talk about their art experiences by asking them open-ended questions such as these: "How does the dough feel?" or "Tell me about your picture."

Think of a toddler in your care. What kinds of art experiences do you provide for her or him?

_____

_____

_____

Preschool children explore and manipulate art materials.

Like toddlers, most preschool children also are more interested in the process of creating than the products. They enjoy exploring and manipulating a variety of art materials. They want to discover what will happen if they use the side of their crayon to make scribbles, or if they finger paint with their fists or elbows. Many children simply enjoy the physical experience of scribbling. As they develop, they are pleased to discover that they can control what marks their crayon makes on the paper or how much glue comes out when they squeeze a bottle. As they learn to use different media, they like to experiment with colors, brush strokes, textures, and combinations of shapes.

Art experiences for preschool children should be based on the following general characteristics of this age group:

- **They need firsthand experiences manipulating objects** to learn about how things work, cause and effect, problem solving, and so on. Give children opportunities to use real materials in their work: buttons, wood chips, feathers, and Styrofoam packing materials, for example.

- **They have their own ideas and make plans that they want to carry out by themselves.** When you provide a rich supply of interesting and varied materials, children can decide how they want to use them. There is no right or wrong way and no good or bad result. Give positive feedback for children's original ideas for doing things as well as for ideas expressed in their artwork. Ask questions to help them elaborate on their ideas and extend their thinking.

- **They are beginning to represent real things in their pictures, but they are not yet adept.** Avoid focusing on what it is that the child has painted or drawn. It can be embarrassing and hurtful if you guess wrong. Your goal is to encourage the child to focus on how the painting was made, what colors were used, where it should be displayed, and so on. "Tell me about your picture" is always an appropriate comment.

- **They are curious and ask many "why" questions.** Preschool children are natural scientists. When you let them discover things for themselves (what happens when you mix two colors of paint, for example), they develop an understanding of the fundamentals of math and science.

- **They have a wide variety of interests and skills.** Provide for these differences in the daily schedule. One child can finish painting while others move on to do something else. Accept children's individual approaches and use of materials. For example, one child might make a collage using only one kind of material (torn paper); another will want to experiment with many different textures, colors, and objects.

Think of a preschool child in your care. What kinds of art experiences do you provide for her or him?

_____

_____

_____

School-age children use art to express themselves and to relax.

Most school-age children have developed the skills to begin and complete almost any art project. Children of this age enjoy undertaking challenging craft projects that show off their skills. At the same time, they view art as a means of relaxation. They will doodle or sketch in their notebooks as they chat with their friends or listen to music. School-age children begin to think of art in the same way that many adults do—as a way to express themselves and escape the stresses of their day.

Art experiences for school-age children should be based on the following general characteristics of this age group:

- **They like to follow directions that lead to an end result.** This is one of the reasons why school-age children enjoy craft projects. They take great pride in being able to make something—a macrame plant hanger, a tie-dyed T-shirt, a crocheted stuffed animal—by themselves. You can find pictures and directions in adult and children's magazines. Ask the librarian at your local library to help you find some craft books for children.

- **They like to take on leadership roles.** Ask the children to help you set up a group art activity and to help the younger children if necessary. A group activity such as a mural needs a strong leader to help the children decide what they are going to do and to delegate the different tasks.

- **They want to assert their independence.** Allow children to do art projects on their own without your help. Have on hand some materials that are just for the school-age children to use. Store these out of reach of the younger children.

- **They are interested in learning specific skills** such as knitting, origami, tie-dying, macrame, weaving, and so on. Many school-age children have the fine motor skills and interest to learn how to do something really well. They are motivated to reach higher levels of competence—for example, to learn more challenging knitting patterns or macrame knots.

Think of a school-age child in your care. What kinds of art experiences do you provide for her or him?

_____

_____

_____

In this learning activity you will observe one child participating in art experiences over a three-day period and record your observations. You will then plan and implement an art experience based on the child's interests and skills. Begin by reading the examples that follow. Then conduct your observation, plan your experience, try it out, and record what happens.

Art Experience Observation
(Example)

Child: _Kara_   **Age:** _3-1/2 years_   **Date(s):** _June 7-9_

Setting: _Free play, indoors and out_

Art Experience	Time	What Happened?
Marking with crayons on the easel	_5 minutes_	_Kara used a blue crayon at the easel. She made straight marks all over the paper. Then she moved her arm in circular motions to make large closed circles. Then she left her paper on the easel._
Easel painting outside	_10 minutes_	_Kara used a brush made from a small piece of sponge clipped to a clothespin. First she used blue paint to make more circles. Then she used red paint to make lines coming from the outside of the circles. The red and blue paint ran together, making a purplish color. When she was done, she asked me to hang the paper to dry._

Art Experience Plan
(Example)

Child: _Kara_   **Age:** _3-1/2 years_   **Date(s):** _June 10_

Setting: _Free play, indoors and out_   **Experience:** _Sponge painting—different shapes_

Why have you planned this experience?

Kara seemed to like painting with a sponge. I think she'd like to paint with sponges cut into different shapes.

What materials are needed?

Two pie pans, two colors of tempera paint, three sponges cut into assorted shapes, large pieces of paper.

Which other children might enjoy this experience?

Nadine (3-1/2 years) and Carter (4 years).

What happened during the experience?

I set up the activity and waited to see if any children would come over by themselves. Nadine came and had fun smearing paint on her paper. Then Kara came over. She used a square sponge to draw circles on her paper. Then she smeared them all together. I suggested that she might try to use the round sponge to make dots on her papers. She tried it but went back to using the square sponge. Carter stopped by to see what we were doing, but he wanted to play restaurant with Denise.

How did this experience promote creativity?

Kara had the experience of being the cause of a change in the paper by making circles and smearing the paint. I showed respect for her ideas by stepping back and letting her use the materials her way even though it wasn't what I had in mind.

Art Experiences Observation

Child: _____   Age: _____   Date(s): _____

Setting: _____   Experience: _____

Art Experience	Time	What Happened?

Art Experience Plan

Child: _____   **Age:** _____   **Date(s):** _____

Setting: _____   **Experience:** _____

Description of Experience:

_____

_____

_____

Why have you planned this experience?

_____

_____

_____

What materials are needed?

_____

_____

Which other children might enjoy this experience?

_____

_____

What happened during the experience?

_____

_____

_____

How did this experience promote creativity?

_____

_____

_____

Discuss this learning activity with your trainer. You might want to repeat it, focusing on the other children in your care.

65

LEARNING ACTIVITIES

IV. Using Sand and Water to Promote Creativity

In this activity you will learn:

- to plan developmentally appropriate experiences using sand and water; and

- to promote children's creativity as they play with sand and water.

Sand and water play are soothing and relaxing.

Children are naturally drawn to sand and water play. These activities let children be messy in a world that usually demands neatness and order. Think back to your own childhood. Can you remember how much fun it was to blow bubbles through a straw or bury your feet in cool, wet sand? These experiences were enjoyable, and they were times of learning as well. Sand and water invite creativity, exploration, and experimentation. These materials are pleasing to look at and touch, and playing with them can be a soothing, relaxing activity for children.

When splashing in a tub full of water, infants learn what water feels like and how it moves. By sifting, pouring, and poking sand, they also learn about sand's special qualities. As they grow and develop, toddlers apply their knowledge of what sand and water are like in their play. Instead of just splashing water, they create a rhythm of splashes to propel a toy boat through a tub of water. Instead of just filling and emptying pails of sand, they'll form the sand into a castle and in time will refine their activities to add such things as tunnels and a moat.

Preschool children like to experiment with water and sand. They find out what happens when sand gets wet and what happens when food coloring is added to water. There are many ways to pour sand and water, many things to observe. Most important, there are no right or wrong ways to play with sand or water. Playing with these media encourages children to ask questions, which enhances their creativity.

For school-age children, sand and water play usually focuses on projects. Many older children love to make elaborate sand creations that show off their skills. They might enjoy leading younger children in craft projects such as making bubble frames or making plaster molds. On a warm day, school-age children will enjoy an outdoor water-slide. They can take the lead in establishing the safety rules

for using the slide. School-age children can be careful research scientists. They will enjoy designing and carrying out experiments with sand and water. Remind them that professional scientists always document how they conduct their experiments and what the results are.

Children develop many skills through sand and water play.

The skills children learn through sand and water play help them develop language skills, expand their thinking, improve their physical prowess, develop problem solving skills, and get along with other children and adults. Some examples follow.

Language Development: Children naturally talk with one another and their provider when they are playing with sand and water. Their vocabulary expands as they learn to name what they are observing and to describe the many concepts they discover.

Cognitive Development: Through their play, children learn many things. By burying a shovel and digging it up again, children learn about object permanence. By pouring four cups of water into an empty quart-size milk carton, children gain a foundation for math. When children play with sand and water, they discover and observe many things, including these:

- how properties change (for example, when they add things to sand and water and how sand and water look when viewed through an object such as a magnifying glass or clear plastic cup);

- how water changes (it freezes, melts, cools things down, evaporates);

- how water changes other things (it makes sand soggy);

- water is absorbed by different material (blotters, cork, Styrofoam, paper towels, etc.) in different ways;

- some objects float in water and others don't;

- reflections and ripples can be observed in water;

- water doesn't stay in one place;

- water levels rise and fall;

- some things dissolve in water (salt, food coloring) and others don't (objects);

- sand does many things (pours, sifts, builds);

- sand has a distinct texture (it can be fine or coarse, dry or wet);

- sand and water can be measured;

- volume and capacity can be observed (containers hold different amounts of sand and water); and

- water takes the shape of the object it is poured into.

Physical Development: Almost everything children do with sand and water helps develop their small muscles. By pouring sand through a funnel, they learn coordination skills. Pouring, sifting, scooping, digging, and so on are all ways of refining small muscle skills. Active splashing and broad arm movements during outdoor water play contribute to physical development.

Social Development: Typically, several children will play at the sand and water together. They practice social skills such as sharing, cooperating, planning, compromising, and problem solving. Sand and water tables can also become settings for dramatic play:

- Soapy water leads to bathing dolls and washing doll clothes.

- Children make drinks and "potions" to sell or use in a variety of ways.

- Boats, water paddles, and tubing lead to play about boats and water travel.

- Children make sand castles, tunnels, mountains, and lakes.

- Transportation toys such as small cars and dump trucks encourage children to make roads, rivers, buildings, and volcanoes. For example, they might dig tunnels into sand hills and run their cars through the tunnels.

- Children make and sell or "eat" mud pies or cakes.

Sand and water play can take place indoors or outdoors. The easiest place to offer sand and water play is outside. A bare spot of ground can be used for digging, and buckets of water and large paintbrushes can lead to an activity of "painting" the house or fence. A windy day makes blowing bubbles a different and exciting activity.

For ongoing water and sand play, you can use plastic dishtubs or wading pools. Of course, sandboxes are ideal for sand play. Some providers use an inner tube or tractor tire as a sandbox frame.

Indoors, providers tend to use their kitchens and bathrooms for water play. These rooms have sinks that can be used for water play, and it's relatively easy to mop up the messes. Another option is to use plastic dishpans placed on a low table. For group water play, you can use a plastic baby bath.

Use a sheet of plastic, an oilcloth tablecloth, or an old shower curtain to protect the floor. A sheet placed under a sand table works well, as it is easy to fold up, carry outdoors, and shake out. Several layers of newspapers or old towels can be placed on top of the waterproof floor covering as further protection for spills. You can make children's smocks or aprons from old shower curtains, heavy-duty garbage bags, or old raincoats. Some providers have children wear rubber boots or plastic bags over their shoes to keep them dry. Of course, bare feet and swimsuits are always an option. Even with all these precautions, it's wise to have a change of clothes on hand for each child.

Before using the kitchen or bathroom for water play, child-proof these areas. Lock up all hazardous items such as razors or chemicals, cover electrical outlets, and remove electrical appliances such as hair dryers so that wet hands don't come in contact with electricity. Provide stepstools with rubber slats so children can reach tall sinks. So the children won't be burned by hot water, take special precautions to make sure that the hot water faucets cannot be turned on accidentally. Also, never leave children under age 5 alone during water play.

Describe how you provide indoor and outdoor sand and water play.

_____

_____

_____

_____

Provide a variety of props for sand and water play.

There are many props that children enjoy using with sand and water. You and the children's parents can collect many of the items listed below. Sand and water props should be safe for the ages of the children at play. For example, infants and toddlers who use their senses to explore everything might swallow small items such as seashells or marbles.

As you review the lists of props for sand and water play that follow, put a check next to the ones that you already have. Circle the props you would like to add to your collection.

Props for Sand Play

Buckets and shovels
Cookie cutters
Funnels
Ladles
Measuring cups and spoons
Pebbles and rocks
Rake
Rubber animals and people
Seeds
Sifter
Straws
Toy cars/dump trucks

Colander
Feathers
Gelatin molds
Magnifying glass
Muffin tin
Plastic dishes (regular and doll-sized)
Rolling pin
Seashells
Sieve
Sticks
String
Whisk broom

Props for Water Play

Bubble-blowing materials (straws, soap flakes, glycerine)	Sponges
	Squeeze bottles
	Buckets
Egg beater	Corks
Food coloring/vegetable dye	Eye dropper
Ladles	Funnels
Measuring cups and spoons	Paintbrushes
Plastic or rubber bottles (with and without holes punched in them)	Scale
	Scoops
	Soap (bar, liquid, flakes)
Siphon	Strainer
	Whisks

Many of the items suggested for water play can also be used for sand play and vice versa. In addition, you'll probably have many other items to add to these lists.

Introduce sand and water play to infants and toddlers.

You can introduce infants to the pleasures of sand when they will play with it rather than eat it, usually at 15 to 18 months. While most infants will end up tasting sand at some point, infants who want only to eat sand and not to play with it are too young. As children play with sand, talk to them about how it feels. If they taste it, you might say, "This is sand, Rebecca. We don't eat it, we play with it. Here, give me your hand and we'll touch the sand." Or you could say, "I don't think that tastes very good, Alex. Let's see what else we can do with the sand. Try poking your fingers in it."

When infants are able to sit independently and manipulate toys—at around 6 to 9 months—they may begin to enjoy water play. Here are some suggestions for infant and toddler water play.

- Place the infant on a large towel on the floor or on the grass. Put a shallow plastic tub filled with about 2" of water directly in front of the infant. If you care for more than one infant, have a separate tub for each child.

- When infants can stand independently and maintain their balance (usually at 14 to 18 months), they can try water play in a shallow plastic tub placed on a low table.

- Give children lots of time just to explore the water—to see how it feels and sounds. Later on you can introduce water toys to stimulate play.

- Toddlers enjoy water play with two or three other children, watching and talking about what they and the others are doing.

- For toddlers who no longer put everything in their mouths, let them add soap to the water so they can discover what happens.

Sand and water play help older children learn new concepts.

After giving older children many opportunities to experiment with sand and water, providers can create learning experiments that encourage children to discover new skills and concepts.

- Present materials to children sequentially; for example, first dry sand and then wet, or first clear water and later colored or soapy water.

- Provide different surfaces that children can pour water on, such as wax paper, a blotter, a sponge, or plastic.

- Provide objects that can be used to conduct sink or float experiments.

- Provide a series of cans with holes punched in them so that children can see how long it takes for the different cans to empty.

- Provide materials that are proportional, such as measuring cups or nesting cups.

In this learning activity you will plan, implement, and evaluate a sand or water play activity that can be enjoyed by all the children in your care. Begin by reviewing the example that follows.

Sand and Water Play Activity
(Example)

Children: _All of them_   **Ages:** _8 months to 8 years_   **Date:** _August 24_

Setting: _Outdoors in the yard_   **Activity:** _Blowing bubbles_

What materials did you provide?

Liquid detergent, pail, measuring cups, bubble frames made from coat hangers, pipe cleaners, and berry baskets.

What did you and the children do?

First we mixed the bubble solution: 1/2 cup of liquid detergent mixed with 2/3 cup of water. Maggie (5 years) and Leah (8 years) took charge of the mixing. They used the 1/4 cup two times to measure 1/2 cup of detergent. They used the 1-cup measure and poured water in up to the 2/3-cup line. Then they looked in the pail and said that there wasn't enough mixture. They asked if they could make another batch. I said sure. I picked up Janna (8 months) and let her feel the soapy water. Then the children took turns making bubbles. Maggie and Leah used the coat hanger frames, and Keenan (30 months) used the bubble baskets. There were bubbles everywhere. Keenan chased them across the back yard. I said to Janna, "Look at all the bubbles we made! Would you like to blow bubbles?" She laughed. I dipped a pipe cleaner frame into the solution and held it up close to her face. I showed her how to blow and helped her blow a bubble. She was very excited. "Can I play with her?" said Leah. I said okay, so Leah put Janna on the ground and waved a berry basket to make small bubbles for Janna to catch. "Waving this berry basket makes even more bubbles than blowing does," said Leah. Leah showed Janna how to clap her hands to catch the bubbles.

How did this activity encourage creativity?

By making their own bubble solution, Maggie and Leah got to see what happens when you mix soap and water together. Leah tried waving instead of blowing the berry basket to see what would happen. Janna used her senses—touch and taste—to explore the soapy water. Keenan found a way to enjoy physical activity as well as bubble making.

Would you do this same activity again? What changes would you make?

Yes. And I liked doing it outside. Next time I'll ask Leah to write down the measurements for soap and water when we double the recipe. Everyone seems to like the berry baskets best. I'll ask the children's parents to start saving them for us.

Sand and Water Play Activity

Children: ———————— **Ages:** ———————— **Date:** ————————

Setting: ———————— **Activity:** ————————————————

What materials did you provide?

_____

_____

What did you and the children do?

_____

_____

_____

_____

_____

How did this activity encourage creativity?

_____

_____

_____

_____

Would you do this same activity again? What changes would you make?

_____

_____

_____

_____

_____

Discuss this learning activity with your trainer.

S U M M A R I Z I N G   Y O U R   P R O G R E S S

You have now completed all of the learning activities for this module. Whether you are an experienced FCC provider or a new one, this module has probably helped you develop new skills in promoting children's creativity. Before you go on, take a few minutes to review your responses to the pre-training assessment for this module. Summarize what you learned, and list the skills you developed or improved.

Discuss your response to this section with your trainer. If there are topics you would like to know more about, you will find recommended readings listed in the Introduction in Volume I.

Your final step in this module is to complete the knowledge and competency assessments. Let your trainer know when you are ready to schedule the assessments. After you have successfully completed these assessments, you will be ready to start a new module. Congratulations on your progress so far, and good luck with your next module.

Promoting Children's Creativity

Arranging the Environment and Providing Materials to Encourage Exploration and Experimentation

1. **How did Ms. Rizzi arrange the environment to promote children's creativity?**

   a. She provided an interesting variety of construction materials and fasteners.

   b. She prepared an inviting open space near the materials.

   c. She provided space for storage of partially finished, ongoing projects.

2. **How do unstructured (or open-ended) materials promote creativity in children?**

   a. There is no right or wrong way to use the materials.

   b. The children may use the materials in a variety of ways—for example, simply enjoying the process of connecting pieces, creating moving parts, or creating representational structures such as buildings or space shuttles.

   c. Children use their imaginations, creating expressions that are unique and relevant to their own lives.

Offering a Variety of Activities and Experiences to Promote Creativity

1. **Why are cooking activities such as making playdough good opportunities to promote creativity?**

   a. Children feel proud to participate and make something real.

   b. Children can use their senses to explore ingredients.

2. **How did Ms. Vaughn support creative thinking?**

   a. She asked the children to think and express their ideas about special ingredients.

   b. She let the children know that all of their suggestions were good ones. She asked them if they could use one now and the other the next time they make banana bread.

Interacting with Children in Ways That Encourage and Respect Creative Expression

1. **How did Ms. Sanchez encourage the girls' creativity?**

   a. She provided the time, space, and equipment the girls needed to practice their song and dance.

   b. She told the girls that she and the other children would like to see their performance.

2. **How did the way Ms. Sanchez responded to Bryanna's idea create an atmosphere that supports creativity?**

   a. She made time in the daily schedule for the performance.

   b. She made space in the environment for the performance.

   c. She acknowledged Bryanna's idea for the children to wear their pajamas by saying that she would ask their parents to pack pajamas in their bags.

G L O S S A R Y

Closed question	A question for which there is only one right answer.
Creativity	An attitude or way of looking at things that involves being willing to try out new ways of doing something and realizing that there is more than one way to solve a problem.
Flexibility	A willingness to change the way one does something or to try a new approach when making something or completing a task.
Open-ended question	A question that can be answered in many ways; there isn't one right answer.
Problem solving	The process of thinking through a problem and coming up with one or several possible solutions.
Self-esteem	A sense of worth; a good feeling about oneself and one's abilities. Someone with strong self-esteem feels respected, valued, and able to do things successfully and independently.
Unstructured materials	Materials that can be used in many different ways.

Module 8:
SELF

OVERVIEW

Building children's self-esteem involves:

- developing a positive and supportive relationship with each child;
- helping children accept and appreciate themselves and others; and
- providing children with opportunities to feel successful and competent.

People with self-esteem feel good about themselves.

Self-esteem is a sense of one's own worth. People with self-esteem are proud of who they are and what they can do. People who have self-esteem feel:

- **powerful**—able to do things on their own;
- **connected** to others—to friends and to their families; and
- **respected** and **valued** by others.

Our self-esteem comes from daily experiences that confirm who we are and what we are capable of doing. If most of these experiences are good, our self-esteem grows. If most of these experiences are bad, we wonder if there is something wrong with us. Our self-esteem is lowered.

Children's feelings about themselves affect their adjustments to life.

From birth, children begin developing a sense of self. Some of their feelings toward themselves may be positive, and some may be negative. These feelings will affect their entire adjustment to life—their ability to play, to relate to others, and to learn. And these feelings are strongly influenced by their relationships with other people—such as family members, friends, and FCC providers.

You are a very important person to the children in your care. In the course of daily life in your home—as you help a child complete a puzzle or share the task of setting the table for lunch—you are helping children develop positive feelings about themselves. The children you care for are developing an understanding of who they are and learning to feel good about themselves. Through your positive interactions with the children in your care, you can support the development of self-esteem that will help children succeed throughout their lives.

Listed on the next page are examples of how providers demonstrate their competence in building children's self-esteem.

Developing a Positive and Supportive Relationship with Each Child

Know what each child is able to do and show that you think each child is special. "Danny, will you be my helper today and carry the cooler outside?"

Understand that it's hard for children to say goodbye to their parents and be there to ease the pain. "It's hard to say goodbye to Daddy. He feels sad too. He'll be back to get you later."

Identify and deal with children's feelings. "I understand that you want to go over to Sarah's house after school. We need to discuss it with your mom. If she says it's okay, then you and Sarah can play together tomorrow."

Use gentle contact—a hug, a touch, a lap to sit on—to show children of all ages that you care for them.

Helping Children Accept and Appreciate Themselves and Others

Express surprise and joy when a child makes a new discovery. "Look at what you can do! When you kick the mobile, the horses move."

Show by what you say and do that you respect each child. "Martha, I see you used four different colors in your picture."

Include in your home pictures, toys, and books, and serve foods that reflect the ethnic backgrounds of the children.

Avoid making biased remarks concerning gender, handicapping conditions, race, ethnic background, and so on.

Providing Children with Opportunities to Feel Successful and Competent

Encourage children to dress themselves even if this takes a long time. "You worked hard to tie your shoes."

Accept mistakes as natural. "Oh, the paint spilled. Let's get a sponge and clean it up."

Select materials that children are ready to master. Comment on their success. "You put that puzzle together all by yourself! I bet you feel good."

Repeat activities so children can master skills and experience success.

Building Children's Self-Esteem

In the following situations, FCC providers are building children's self-esteem. As you read each one, think about what the providers are doing and why. Then answer the questions that follow.

Developing a Positive and Supportive Relationship with Each Child

It's free play time in Ms. Neuberger's FCC home. Ms. Neuberger, with Kyle (5 months) in her arms, is walking around the room to see what the children are doing. She stops at the easel where Shawn is painting a picture. Shawn is smiling and seems very happy with his work. He steps back from the easel to look at his picture. Ms. Neuberger says, "Shawn, would you like some help hanging your picture?" "Okay," he answers. She gently sits Kyle on the floor. Then she and Shawn each hold one side of the picture and hang it in the picture gallery (the front hall). Ms. Neuberger points to the picture and says, "I see you have used a lot of blue paint. You painted a blue picture last week, too." Shawn smiles and says, "Yeah, I like blue. I'm going to paint another blue picture." He goes back to the easel to start another picture. Ms. Neuberger picks up Kyle, and they walk over to see what Theresa and David are building with the blocks.

1. **How did Ms. Neuberger build a positive and supportive relationship with Shawn?**

_____

_____

_____

2. **How did Ms. Neuberger build Shawn's self-esteem?**

_____

_____

_____

Helping Children Accept and Appreciate Themselves and Others

As Mariah (9 years) arrives from her after-school gymnastics class, 4-year-old Pam greets her at the door: "Show me what you did today—please!" Mariah tells Pam, "Leave me alone. I need to get my snack." Mariah walks into the kitchen, where she says a quiet hello to Ms. Nunes. Ms. Nunes has overheard the conversation between the two girls. She knows that Mariah is usually happy to show Pam her gymnastics skills, so she thinks to herself, "Something must have happened today to make Mariah feel bad. I'll try to find out what it was." She says to Mariah, "Hi. I'd like to hear about your day if you'd like to tell me about it." Mariah responds, "There's nothing to tell. What's for snack? I'm really hungry." Ms. Nunes decides to try a less direct approach. "Well, we have fruit and yogurt. I'll help you cut up some fruit if you like." "Okay," says

83

Ms. Nunes takes some apples and pears from the refrigerator, along with the container of yogurt. She puts them on the counter and asks Mariah to get a couple of knives. Mariah and Ms. Nunes stand at the counter cutting up the fruit. Mariah turns to Ms. Nunes and says, "I'm so uncoordinated. Everyone else could do a front flip but me." "Everyone else?" says Ms. Nunes. "Well, not everyone," Mariah replies. "But I want to be able to do one. It's not fair. I try really hard, but I just can't do it." Ms. Nunes puts her hand on Mariah's shoulder and says, "I know that must make you feel bad. Let's think for a minute, though. You're new to the gymnastics class, and you've learned a lot in the short time you've been there. Sometimes it takes a long time to learn to do something really well." "I know," says Mariah. "But I want to be able to do it now!" She sits down to eat her snack. "I know what I can do," she says. "I'll ask my next door neighbor Tracy to help me. She's been taking gymnastics for 3 years. Maybe she can help me learn to do a front flip." "That's a good idea. She can help you with the front flip, and she might also help you understand that even a super gymnast like you needs to work hard to learn a new skill." Mariah smiles. "Yeah, even a future Olympic champion like me has to practice!" she says.

1. **What feelings did Mariah have after her gymnastics class?**

_____

_____

_____

2. **How did Ms. Nunes help Mariah learn to accept and appreciate herself?**

_____

_____

_____

Providing Children with Opportunities to Feel Successful and Competent

After several rainy days, Ms. Kent and the children are very excited to see the sun again. "Can we go to the park today?" asks Amber. "Yeah, to the park," echo Darnell and Ian. "That's a great idea," says Ms. Kent. "Would you like to pack a picnic, too?" The children jump up and down, squealing, "Yes, yes." Janine crawls over and holds her arms out so Ms. Kent can pick her up. "I see you want to join in the excitement too," says Ms. Kent. She lifts up Janine and carries her into the kitchen. "Come on, everybody, let's make the lunch, then we can decide what toys we want to bring with us." The children gather in the kitchen. Ms. Kent puts Janine down and hands her some mixing bowls and cups to play with. She asks the other children, "What shall we put in our picnic lunch?" The children offer several suggestions: "Apples." "Sandwiches." "Carrots." "Cheese." "Lemonade." "Those are some good ideas," says Ms. Kent. "Let's look in the refrigerator and see what kinds of sandwich fillings we have. Then we can all work together to make a great picnic lunch." "I'll peel the carrots," says Amber. Darnell bends down and says to Janine, "We're going on a picnic. I'm going to push your stroller all the way to the park." Janine looks up at him with a big smile. "She'll like that a lot, Darnell," says Ms. Kent.

1. **How did Ms. Kent's response to the children's suggestion help them feel successful and competent?**

_____

_____

_____

2. **How did Ms. Kent continue to interact with children in ways that supported their self-esteem?**

_____

_____

_____

Compare your answers with those on the answer sheet at the end of this module. If your answers are different, discuss them with your trainer. There can be more than one answer.

Your Own Self-Esteem

Our experiences in life shape our self-esteem.

Self-esteem is very important to all of us. Growing up, we have many experiences that help shape our feelings about ourselves. Often, we learn to value who we are and what we can do. Yet in each new situation, our self-esteem is tested. In situations where we feel capable and trusted, we do well. Our self-esteem is high. In other situations we may feel less skillful. We are unsure of what support we will get. If we fail, our self-esteem may suffer.

Think of times when you've felt really good about yourself. Perhaps you had some of the following feelings:

- You felt good about an accomplishment. "Look at this closet. It took me all day, but now I know where to find everything."

- You were ready to accept responsibilities. "I'll organize the block party."

- You were independent. "I haven't been there before, but I have a map so I'll be able to find my way."

- You didn't give up easily. "This reading assignment is really hard to understand. I think if I take notes, I'll get the important points."

- You weren't afraid to express your feelings. "I felt hurt when you questioned my word."

You can also probably remember times when you felt bad about yourself. Your self-esteem was at a low. Perhaps you had some of these feelings:

- You put yourself down. "Oh, I'm so stupid. I can never get it right."

- You felt powerless. "I don't have any idea what I'm supposed to do. I'm hopelessly lost."

- You avoided difficult situations. "I'm not going to the club dance if she's going to be there."

- You blamed others. "I couldn't help it! He didn't tell me where the paint was."

- You felt that no one valued you. "They'll never pick me."

A provider with low self-esteem may tend to pass on these feelings to the children in her care. As we have been taught, so we tend to teach. "I'm stupid" and "I can't" easily become "you're stupid" and "you can't."

Who helped you develop self-esteem?

As you focus on building your own self-esteem, try to remember people who have helped you develop self-esteem. How were you helped to feel sure of yourself and able to try new things? And how can you pass on those positive feelings to the children you care for? Many different people in your life have encouraged your self-esteem. Think back to a teacher you had in school who made you feel especially good about yourself. Picture yourself in the classroom. Then respond to the following questions.

What did the teacher do or say to build your self-esteem?

_____

_____

_____

_____

How did you feel about yourself at the time?

_____

_____

_____

_____

How has this experience affected how you feel?

_____

_____

_____

_____

Your positive feelings help children feel good, too.

Self-esteem makes people happier and more productive. Your feelings about yourself influence your behavior as you care for children each day. The more capable and positive you feel about your skills as a provider, the more rewards you will have from your profession. The children you care for will sense that you are a positive person, and that will help them feel good also.

When you have finished this overview section, you should complete the pre-training assessment. Refer to the glossary at the end of this module if you need definitions of the terms that are used.

PRE-TRAINING ASSESSMENT

Listed below are the skills that FCC providers use to build children's self-esteem. Think about whether you do these things regularly, sometimes, or not enough. Place a check in one of the columns on the right for each skill listed. Then discuss your answers with your trainer.

Skill	I Do This Regularly	I Do This Sometimes	I Don't Do This Enough
Developing a Positive and Supportive Relationship With Each Child 1. Observing children to learn about each child's needs, strengths, and interests and providing appropriate materials and activities.			
2. Talking to children about their feelings so they can learn to understand and express their emotions.			
3. Showing children in many ways that they are cared for.			
4. Spending individual time with each child every day.			
5. Planning the day's activities so each child can use and practice new skills.			
6. Helping children feel comfortable about making the transition from their homes to the FCC home.			

Skill	I Do This Regularly	I Do This Sometimes	I Don't Do This Enough
Helping Children Accept and Appreciate Themselves and Others			
7. Expressing pleasure and interest in words and actions to help children feel good about who they are and what they can do.			
8. Including in your home pictures of families and providing space for children to store their personal belongings.			
9. Helping children learn to use words to let each other know what they want and how they feel.			
10. Modeling positive ways to talk and act to show other people that you care about them.			
11. Letting children know that you care for them even at times when they are unhappy or angry.			
Providing Children With Opportunities to Feel Successful and Competent			
12. Offering help to children learning new skills until they let you know that they can manage on their own.			
13. Allowing children to learn from their mistakes and encouraging them to solve their own problems.			
14. Repeating games or activities so children can master skills and feel successful.			

Skill	I Do This Regularly	I Do This Sometimes	I Don't Do This Enough
15. Including a wide variety of materials in the home to meet the diverse needs of different children.			
16. Letting children do as much as possible for themselves, providing help only when asked or when a child is very frustrated.			

Review your responses, then list three to five skills you would like to improve or topics you would like to learn more about. When you finish this module, you will list examples of your new or improved knowledge and skills.

Discuss the overview and pre-training assessment with your trainer. Then begin the learning activities for Module 8.

I. Using Age-Appropriate Approaches to Build Children's Self-Esteem

In this activity you will learn:

- to recognize some typical behaviors of children; and

- to use what you know about children to build their self-esteem.

How Infants Develop Trust

The work of Erik Erikson identifies stages in the lifelong process of developing self-esteem. In the first stage of development, **trust**, infants are introduced to the world. At first, they do very little for themselves; they are totally dependent on adults to care for them. Although they are very dependent, infants are still interested in what they can see, hear, taste, and smell in their environment. They are good observers and respond to everything around them.

During the first months of life, infants learn if they are valued or only tolerated by experiencing how people care for them. They pick up messages from:

- how they are held—stiffly or softly and warmly;

- how they are diapered—quickly because diapering is an unpleasant task to be done fast, or leisurely, because diapering is a time to talk and play together; and

- how they are fed—to keep them quiet or to give them pleasure as well as nourishment.

Providers should meet infants' needs consistently, promptly, and lovingly.

The most important way you can nourish the self-esteem of an infant is to meet the child's basic needs in a caring way. When these needs are met consistently, promptly, and lovingly, infants learn to trust themselves and the world around them. Infants have very basic needs:

- to be fed when hungry and burped after feeding;

- to be held and loved often, not just when they cry;

- to be changed when soiled or wet and uncomfortable;

- to be comforted when upset;

- to sleep when tired;

- to be given interesting objects to look at and play with when awake; and

- to be talked to in caring and soft tones.

As infants become more mobile, they develop new abilities and interests. Their needs change and providers must respond to them in new ways. Infants learn as they grasp, pull, push, let go, crawl, and move on their own. By providing a safe environment and interesting things to see and do, providers can help infants learn to trust their own bodies and invite them to move out into their world.

The chart that follows shows several typical behaviors of infants and age-appropriate responses that can encourage them to develop self-esteem. In the blank spaces at the bottom, add an example of the behavior of an infant in your care, and the support you offered to help the child develop self-esteem.

Typical Behavior	Provider Support
Justin (4 months) wakes up crying.	Pick up Justin promptly and comfort him to let him know that you care about his feelings and can be trusted to meet his needs.
Hannah (12 months) holds on to the side of the sofa and pulls herself up to standing.	Praise and applaud Hannah's new skill. Tell her that she worked hard to learn how to stand up.
Francie (14 months) gently pats Daniel (6 months) on the back as he cries loudly.	Thank Francie for helping to make Daniel feel better. Pick up Daniel and try to find out what is making him cry. Talk to Francie about what you are doing for Daniel so she can learn to show concern and kindness too.

How Toddlers Develop Autonomy

The development of trust in infancy sets the stage for the development of **autonomy** in the toddler years. Autonomy means independence, learning to do things for oneself and to make decisions. When toddlers feel secure in their environment and trust the important people in their lives (such as you and their parents), they are able to venture out to explore the world. These explorations are expressions of their growing independence.

Toddlers spend much of their time testing limits and asserting themselves. They like to be in charge, and they see things from their own point of view. When they want something, they don't understand that someone else might want it too. "My" and "mine" are words that toddlers often use to express their feelings. One of their favorite words is "no." They don't say this to make you or their parents angry; they say it to try out their independence and to let you know that they can make decisions for themselves.

Their growing abilities and independence leave toddlers facing a dilemma. Although growing up has its advantages, it also means leaving many good things behind. Drinking from a cup is exciting, but doesn't provide the comfort of being nursed or sucking on a bottle. Wearing underpants, even if they are decorated with dinosaurs, means taking responsibility that diapers don't require.

If toddlers could put their feelings in words, they would probably tell you, "We want to be big and we want to be little." Because growing up doesn't work that way, and because they can't always use words to express their frustration, you will see their struggle in their behavior. When Jamie (27 months) screams "me do!" as he refuses to let you help put on his socks and then, five minutes later, breaks into tears of frustration and heads for the comfort of your arms, you can see the push and pull he is experiencing.

Remember that toddlers are struggling to grow up.

It is easier to cope with toddler behavior if you understand that toddlers are not being naughty but rather are struggling with growing up. The ways you respond to toddlers' behavior can help toddlers develop self-esteem. It may help to remember the following:

- When a toddler hurts another child, he needs your help to learn how to control his behavior.

- When a toddler wets her pants, be sympathetic: "Sometimes it's hard to get to the potty on time." Then ask yourself, "Is this child really ready to be out of diapers?"

- When a toddler cries and wants to be held, pay attention to this need: "I can hear that you need a hug. Let me finish diapering Tanya, then we can sit in the rocking chair."

The chart that follows shows several typical behaviors of toddlers and age-appropriate responses that can encourage them to develop self-esteem. In the blank spaces at the bottom, add an example of the behavior of a toddler in your care, and the support you offered to help the child develop self-esteem.

Typical Behavior	Provider Support
Ginny (22 months) spreads peanut butter on her crackers at snack time.	Acknowledge Ginny for her hard work. Let her participate in routines so she can feel good about doing things for herself. Provide a sturdy stepstool she can use independently.
Carl (32 months) often says "no" when asked to do something.	Realize that this is Carl's way of asserting independence. Sometimes offer two "yes" choices for him to select a food, activity, or toy. Play games where the answer is a laughing "no."
Terry (24 months) asks lots of questions about how to use the toilet.	Recognize that Terry might be ready for toilet training. Work with her parents to ensure that all of you use a positive, developmentally appropriate approach to help Terry learn this exciting self-help skill.
Kenny (30 months) pours juice from the small pitcher into his cup, however, he spills the juice.	Praise Kenny's efforts and help him clean up the spill (without scolding) so he will feel good about trying new things.

How Preschool Children Develop Initiative

Initiative is the term Erikson used to describe the preschool years. It's a good word for preschool children who tend to be active, talkative, and creative; they initiate a lot. Preschool children seem to have endless energy. They are eager for new experiences and have gained many skills that help them learn. They can build, draw, mold, paint, put things together, climb, and swing with increasing skill.

Preschool children are increasingly social. They play with other children and may develop strong friendships. They notice how people are alike and different, and they are curious about these differences. They are learning to cooperate and play with others, and they want to be liked. Dramatic play is a favorite activity. You can learn a lot about how children feel about themselves and what is important to them by watching them play.

Sometimes adults try to push children into academic learning too early. They teach letters and numbers so children will be "ready" for first grade. If preschool children are pushed to do things before they are ready, they will experience failure and their self-esteem will suffer. Instead, they should have many opportunities to learn through play. Preschool children need activities that allow them to succeed easily and feel good about themselves. In this way they develop self-esteem.

Allow preschool children to do many things for themselves.

Sometimes adults aren't aware of how capable preschool children are. They may continue to help children eat, dress, and use the toilet even when children can do these things for themselves. When you let children do as much as possible for themselves, this helps them feel good about their skills. It's important to provide help only when asked or when adult assistance would calm an anxious child and lead to success. These suggestions may help you build preschool children's self-esteem.

- Set up a system in your home so children can use the toilet with little supervision. Post a sign using pictures and words to remind them to flush, wash their hands, and throw away the used paper towel.

- Be patient when it takes time for children to say something. Preschool children have large vocabularies and feel good when they can use words to express themselves.

- Allow preschool children to try new things safely and praise their efforts. At this age children feel confident in their skills and are eager to take risks.

- Give preschool children many opportunities to make decisions for themselves such as what art materials to use or how to move their bodies to music. They are beginning to feel a sense of control over their lives, which contributes to the development of self-esteem.

The chart that follows shows several typical behaviors of preschool children and age-appropriate responses that can encourage them to develop self-esteem. In the blank spaces at the bottom, add an example of the behavior of a preschool child in your care, and the support you offered to help the child develop self-esteem.

Typical Behavior	Provider Support
James (3-1/2 years) wants to pull the wagon that Kim (4 years) is using. He grabs the handle and pushes her out of the way.	Give James words to use when he wants a turn. Observe to see when he is reaching his limit and step in before he lashes out physically. Provide outlets such as playdough or clay or dramatic play so children can manage their strong feelings.
Sarah (4 years) sees you using a screwdriver to fix a broken shelf. She says, "My daddy knows how to use a screwdriver. I don't know how."	Help Sarah feel good about being a girl. Read books that reinforce the belief that gender doesn't determine what a person can and cannot do. Set up a woodworking center so Sarah can learn to use a screwdriver.
Mark (4-1/2 years) follows you into the kitchen as you get ready to serve lunch. He wants to help.	Ask Mark if he wants to help you. Suggest several tasks and let him pick which ones he would like to do. As he gains new skills, ask him to do more difficult tasks. Let him know that his help is needed and valuable.
Janet (4-1/2 years) and her family are going on a plane to visit her grandmother. Janet talks a lot about the upcoming trip.	Provide props and dress-up clothes so Janet can act out getting ready for a trip and going on the airplane. Encourage her to act out her feelings about this important event in her life.

How School-Age Children Develop Industry[1]

When children enter school, Erikson says that they begin the stage of **industry**. During this period (approximately 5 to 12 years of age), children focus on developing the skills they need for their work in school and life. They are refining their physical skills and can become quite good at sports and athletic activities. School life and friends are very important to this age group. They feel less need for supervision, yet they are still dependent on adults. Your FCC home can provide a safe and welcoming place for children before and after school and during school vacations.

Children in middle childhood want to try new things. They enjoy working on real projects and care a lot about how well they perform a skill or complete a task. As preschool children they might have been content to experiment with all the different colors at the easel; now they want to create a "good" picture. At this age, children begin to evaluate their performance against accepted standards, and they begin to compare themselves to their peers. These comparisons can be damaging to self-esteem: "Marta was moved to a higher reading group, but I wasn't, so I must be stupid." Often children view themselves in terms of extremes—smart or stupid, good or bad. To develop a realistic sense of their own skills, children may need some adult assistance. As a provider you can help children recognize their many strengths and help them to understand that while it's nice to have a special skill or talent, how one uses the talent is what makes a person a valuable human being.

In middle childhood, acceptance by friends is an increasingly important source of self-esteem. Some children want to develop friendships and join in group activities, but they don't know how. If a child in your care has trouble making friends, talk to the child to help him or her develop strategies for entering a game or group conversation. Social relationships are very important, and the ability to make and keep friends has a great impact on the development of self-esteem.

School-age children have developed prosocial skills and are able to use words instead of their fists when angry. But when school-agers do lash out at a friend, the attack may be quite hostile, directed at the person rather than to accomplish some other goal (such as getting a turn on the tricycle). Most children understand and accept each other's bad behavior as being a normal part of friendship; however, these personal attacks can be quite painful for children who are not able to take them in stride. They may need adult assistance to understand how a friend can be nice one minute and hurtful the next. (It may help to remind them of a time when they said or did something that hurt a friend even though it was unintentional.)

---

[1] Based on Nancy E. Curry and Carl N. Johnson, *Beyond Self-Esteem: Developing a Genuine Sense of Human Value* (Washington, DC: National Association for the Education of Young Children, 1990), pp. 67-87 and 129-148.

Try these suggestions.

There are many ways that providers can help school-age children develop self-esteem. Some suggestions follow:

- Encourage children as they tackle a difficult homework assignment, write a story, or build a clubhouse. Make sure that your comments provide information that will help them be successful: "Use a pencil to sketch your map. When you're sure that it's accurate, you can use the markers."

- Give children age-appropriate responsibilities. Show them how to do a task (washing the cooler after a picnic, for example), then allow them to do it without assistance.

- Plan activities that will allow children to be totally involved over a long period of time. Allow the children to determine when they are finished rather than setting a predetermined time limit. "Raoul and Andrew have been working on their space station for three weeks. Every day they get out their project and make more space ships and creatures."

- Help children think about the consequences of their actions. "How do you think Albert felt when you made fun of his new haircut? Is there something you can do so the two of you can be friends again?"

The chart that follows shows several typical behaviors of school-age children and age-appropriate responses that can encourage children to develop self-esteem. In the blank spaces at the bottom, add an example of the behavior of a school-age child in your care, and the support you offered to help the child develop self-esteem.

Typical Behavior	Provider Support
Raoul (7 years) and Andrew (6-1/2 years) are writing and illustrating a book about dinosaurs.	Provide a place to store the book out of the reach of the younger children. Ask them if they would like some clay to use to make models of the dinosaurs. When they seem ready, ask them to show their project to the other children.
Gillian (7-1/2 years) works on a painting all afternoon. She is unhappy about the way it looks so she tears up the picture.	Praise Gillian for her efforts to let her know that you recognize her hard work. Help her understand that she has unique abilities and achievements and that her painting skills will develop as she paints more pictures.
Ellen (5 years) has a lot to say about her day when she comes home from kindergarten.	Be available to listen to Ellen's account of her day at kindergarten. Talk with her about her interests, feelings, and ideas. Provide many opportunities for her to use her growing language skills.
Tracy (11 years) thinks she is too old for family child care.	Involve Tracy in planning the kinds of materials and activities that will be available in family child care. Give her a blank schedule and ask her to plan what she wants to do each afternoon. Show her that you recognize her capabilities.
Mitchell (10 years) wants to play with his friend who lives on the next street.	Talk with Mitchell's parents about having his friend visit him at family child care (if the provider won't be over the legal capacity of children in care) or spending time at his friend's house.

Discuss with your trainer the different approaches you use to help children develop self-esteem.

LEARNING ACTIVITIES

II. Getting to Know Each Child

In this activity you will learn:

- to understand children's individual differences; and

- to foster self-esteem by getting to know individual children.

Providers can help children respect and appreciate themselves.

Children learn to respect themselves when they are respected. Each of the children you work with is a unique human being. By getting to know each child and responding to his or her individual needs, you help children respect and appreciate themselves. This is the essence of self-esteem.

While all children pass through the same stages of development in the same order, there are still many differences in the ways they approach and respond to people and situations. Individual personality traits that are evident in infancy may continue throughout childhood and even into our adult years.

Your own experiences as a child, as a parent, and as a provider will affect your expectations of children's behavior. For example, you may have strong memories of your own school years and how you and your friends felt and behaved in different situations. Or your own children might have been very challenging during their toddler years. As a provider, you may have cared for an infant who was very adaptable or one who was fussy. All of these experiences influence how you view the children in your care.

It's important to learn what makes each child unique.

To get beyond preconceived notions of how a child might feel or need, it is important to get to know each child as an individual. Here are examples of the ways in which individual children can differ:

- **Adaptability**—Rico (6 months) is happy to try mashed sweet potato for the first time. Amy (6 months) spits it out and knocks the spoon away. Tiffany (3-1/2 years) adjusts easily when you have to postpone the picnic, but Leona (4 years) keeps asking when the picnic will take place.

- **Sensitivity**—Mai (4 months) is sensitive to light, sound, texture, and temperature and may get upset when something startles her, such as a slamming door or a rush of cold air. Dennis (5 months) can sleep regardless of what is happening in the environment. Starr (7-1/2 years) bounces right back when a friend is unkind to her; Katie (8 years) has hurt feelings for a long time.

- **Consistency**—Owen (3 months) follows a regular schedule for eating, sleeping, and diapering. With Jay (3-1/2 months), you are never quite sure what he will need and when he will need it. Fern (3 years) is always eager to use the playdough. Andrew (4 years) joins in with enthusiasm one day, but the next day he has no interest in the activity.

- **Activity levels**—Stuart (5 years) is constantly moving. He runs more often than he walks and throws his whole body into every activity. Barney (4-1/2 years) is usually content to play with his toys while he watches what's going on around him.

- **Intensity**—Some children express their emotions quietly, others with great expression. For example, Lynn (2 months) whimpers while Tracy cries loudly. Some children express their happiness by laughing with glee; others smile quietly.

Try these suggestions.

Here are several suggestions to help you understand individual children's behavior so you can develop positive relationships with all the children in your care.

- **Respect individual differences.** Every child is a person who needs to be respected in order to learn to respect himself or herself and to respect other children and adults.

- **Be aware of your own style.** Are you a person who likes a lot of physical contact? Do you prefer quiet times, or do you enjoy excitement? Do you get angry easily? Are your feelings hurt easily?

- **Observe children, especially those who you find it hard to work with or feel you do not understand.** Record their behavior for five minutes, several times a day for a week. Ask yourself what these children seem to be feeling and thinking. Look for patterns to give you insight into their behavior.

- **Ask another provider, your trainer or an FCC staff member to observe a child** whose behavior you feel you do not understand or whose behavior you are having trouble handling. Compare notes. Often a fresh perspective gives insight.

Remember that some children will be harder for you to get to know than others. Building relationships with children is part of being a professional. Although it's easy to spend lots of time with your favorite children, make a point of spending individual time with every child each day. Chances are that as you get to know each child, you will discover something interesting or appealing about the child that you didn't see at first.

In this learning activity you will focus on one child in your care whose behavior you feel you don't understand or whom you find it hard to work with. The activity asks you first to answer some questions about that child's behavior. Then you'll plan three strategies for getting to know this child, try your strategies for a week, and see what you've learned about the child that will help you in supporting her or his self-esteem. First read the examples that follow.

Getting to Know a Child
(Example 1)

Child: _Cathy_   **Age:** _26 months_   **Dates:** _January 10-14_

What is it about this child that is hard for you to understand or deal with?

Cathy rarely shares with other children. She holds onto her things and shouts "mine."

Think about yourself. Is there something about you that might make it hard for you to understand or deal with this child?

In my family we were encouraged to share our belongings with each other and with our friends. It's hard for me to understand selfishness.

List three strategies to help you get to know and deal successfully with this child. Use each strategy over the next two weeks, and record brief observations of what happens.

Strategy	What Happened
I will spend time with her.	_Cathy helped me wipe off the table before snack. She helped put the blocks back in the dishpan._ _Cathy sat and rocked with me in the rocking chair. We talked about the baby her mother is expecting. She said that the baby can't sleep in her crib._
I will observe her.	_When Larry (25 months) slipped and fell, Cathy looked very worried._ _Cathy played in the sand box with Becky (3-1/2 years). Then both girls played dress-up. Cathy screamed "mine!" when Becky reached for the red pocketbook._
I will read about toddlers.	_I learned that this is typical behavior for toddlers. Maybe Cathy isn't ready to share yet._

Summarize what you learned about this child:

Cathy knows that her mother is going to have a baby but isn't sure how she feels about getting a baby sister or brother.

She likes to help do "real work" such as cleaning up.

Cathy was worried when another child tripped and fell.

Cathy enjoyed playing in the sandbox and playing dress-up with Becky.

Cathy screams "mine" because she hasn't learned to share yet.

How will you use what you learned to support the development of this child's self-esteem?

I will keep spending time with Cathy. I didn't know I could enjoy being with her.

I won't force her to share. Instead, I will help her protect her things until she begins feeling secure about really having what she needs.

I will talk to her parents about the comment she made about the crib. Perhaps they can put off moving Cathy out of her crib until she is ready to give it up. Also, I will work with her parents to help Cathy understand what it will be like to have a new brother or sister.

Getting to Know a Child
(Example 2)

Child: _Deena_   **Age:** _5-1/2 years_   **Dates:** _January 10-14_

What is it about this child that is hard for you to understand or deal with?

Deena is very bossy to the younger children. She wants them to do things her way and doesn't let them make suggestions.

Think about yourself. Is there something about you that might make it hard for you to understand or deal with this child?

I was the youngest in my family, and my older sisters used to boss me around. I am probably remembering how I felt when I hear Deena telling the others what to do.

List three strategies to help you get to know and deal successfully with this child. Use each strategy over the next two weeks, and record brief observations of what happens.

Strategy	What Happened
I will help Deena feel competent and responsible.	_Deena took charge of organizing the dress-up clothes. I let her do it by herself so she could feel proud of her accomplishments. She told her mother about her hard work when she came to pick her up._ _I asked Deena to help me think of some new ideas for snacks. She came up with some good ideas._
I will observe her.	_When Heather's father came to get her Deena helped her find her lost mittens._ _Deena played school with Michael and Leigh. She made them sit at the table and draw pictures. She told them what they could draw and what colors to use._
I will read about 5-year-olds.	_I learned that many 5-year-olds tend to be bossy at times. I also learned that starting school can be stressful for children even when they appear to be adjusting well. They may keep their worries to themselves._

Summarize what you learned about this child:

Deena is ready to take on responsibilities and complete tasks on her own. She feels good about herself when she can work hard and do a good job.

She has good ideas and wants to share them.

She likes to help others, as when she volunteered to look for the lost mittens.

She seems to be expressing her feelings about school when she bosses the other children (as when she made them sit at the table). She may be having some anxieties related to school.

How will you use what you have learned to support the development of this child's self-esteem?

I will keep giving Deena responsibilities and allow her to do jobs by herself if she chooses.

I will talk to her parents about what she might be feeling about school.

I will get some children's books about starting school from the library and read them with Deena. Reading about other children's experiences in school may encourage her to talk about how she feels about school.

Getting to Know a Child

Child: _____ **Age:** _____ **Dates:** _____

What is it about this child that is hard for you to understand or deal with?

_____

_____

_____

_____

_____

_____

_____

_____

_____

_____

_____

Think about yourself. Is there something about you that might make it hard for you to understand or deal with this child?

_____

_____

_____

_____

_____

_____

_____

_____

_____

_____

_____

On the next page, list three strategies to help you get to know and deal successfully with this child. Use each strategy over the next two weeks, and record brief observations of what happens.

Getting to Know a Child

Strategy	What Happened

Summarize what you learned about this child.

_____

_____

_____

_____

_____

_____

_____

How will you use what you learned to support the development of this child's self-esteem?

_____

_____

_____

_____

_____

_____

_____

Discuss what you learned with your trainer.

L E A R N I N G   A C T I V I T I E S

III. Helping Children Deal with Separation

In this activity you will learn:

- to observe how individual children react to separation;

- to communicate with children in ways that help them deal with their feelings about separation; and

- to provide an environment that helps children deal with their feelings about separation.

Dealing with Separation: A Lifelong Event

Each day in your FCC home begins with parents and children saying goodbye to each other. This can evoke deep feelings in parents and children. Think about how you feel when you have to say goodbye to someone you love. Sad? Angry? Guilty? Afraid? Parents and children have these feelings too. It can be tempting to want to get separations over with as quickly as possible.

Separation is a lifelong process and an important part of growing up. It deserves the same careful planning as every other aspect of your program. When children are supported as they handle their feelings about separation, their self-esteem grows. They learn that they can handle their painful feelings and that you, someone they trust, are there if they need help.

How children handle separation is closely tied to their stage of development. Looking at the world through their eyes can help you understand behavior that can seem baffling at times.

Infants, at about age 4 to 5 months, begin to learn that they are separate human beings. By about 8 months of age, they show that they have become attached to their parents and other special adults such as providers. They now know the difference between people they know and strangers. At this age, infants may have a difficult time saying goodbye to their parents.

As children learn to walk, the world opens up to them. Infants between 10 and 16 months are joyful explorers who appear to be in love with the world around them. One week they are upset when their parents leave. Two weeks later they are so busy doing and exploring, they don't seem to notice their parents. This is not the case, however. They are very aware of their parents and glad to see them. The presence of parents fuels their love for exploring the world.

Toddlers, at about 18 months, may return to being clingy and very upset about being left. They are increasingly aware that the world is very big and they are very small. At about 24 to 26 months, children's responses to separation can be very intense. Toddlers are aware of the importance of their parents and may be scared when their parents are away. Different children may express their fear in different ways; one may kick and scream while another withdraws and whimpers.

Preschool children are better able to understand and accept separation. They can understand their provider's explanation of where their parents have gone and when they will be back to pick them up. They often express their feelings about separation—in their art or other play activities or in the books they chose to "read." Providers can support these healthy ways of coping with separation by scheduling lots of time for art and for books such as *Goodnight, Moon* and *The Runaway Bunny* by Margaret Wise Brown, or *Ira Sleeps Over* by Bernard Waber—three favorites.

School-age children are used to being away from their parents during their days at school, but they may still have difficulty separating from their parents from time to time. Occasions such as the beginning or end of the school year, moving to a new home, or having a good friend move far away may stir up painful feelings of loss. School-age children need someone to listen to their feelings and help them find ways to become comfortable with their new situations.

Strategies for Helping Children Handle Separation

Here are some suggestions for helping children handle separation in ways that also promote their self-esteem.

- **Build a partnership with parents.** Get to know each other and learn to work together. Encourage parents to spend time in your FCC home. If parents feel good about you and your program, their children will sense this and feel more secure. "Delante was so glad to see you at lunch time. He was sad for a little while when you left, but then we talked about what we could make for lunch the next time you come. He says that your favorite is pizza!"

- **Help parents foster their child's trust by saying goodbye.** Some parents may find it tempting to sneak out of your home while their child is looking the other way. Though it may seem the easiest thing to do, imagine how you would feel if the most important person in your life disappeared with no warning. Saying goodbye gives children the security of knowing they can count on their parents to let them know what is happening. "I'm sure it feels really bad to say good-bye to Tyler when he has tears rolling down his face. But when you give him a big hug and tell him you will see him soon, he feels sad, but he knows that you love him and will come back for him."

- **Encourage parents to develop goodbye rituals with their children.** The familiar actions of walking to the front door or having a giant love hug are reassuring and can give children a sense of control. "Gina likes to watch you walk to the car, then blow kisses and wave goodbye."

- **Listen to children's feelings.** Sharing feelings makes them more manageable. No one likes to hear complaining or crying, but by listening, you show respect. You help children learn that you will always be available to listen to their feelings. "I know you feel sad because your Mom is going to be away for a while. Sometimes it helps to talk about your feelings."

- **Examine your own feelings about separation.** What good and bad separation experiences do you remember from your childhood? How do you feel about parents saying goodbye and leaving their children with you for the day? How do your feelings influence your responses to parents and children? "When Brenda says she really misses her dad while he's away on business, it reminds me of how much I missed my parents when they went on trips without my brother and me."

- **Include many items from the children's homes in your environment.** Encourage parents to bring a child's special blanket or stuffed animal from home. Provide private spaces for children to store their possessions. Hang pictures of families to help children feel connected to their parents even when they are away. Have children make a parent mailbox so they can "write" letters to their parents during the day. "Is that the cuddly puppy your grandma sent you? Is he going to play with us today?"

- **Encourage children to help with daily routines and activities.** As they pour juice, set tables, clean up, tie a younger child's shoes, and so on, they gain self-confidence. They also learn to cope with separation. They will feel important and valued where they are, even though their parents are absent. "Nancy and Marcus really like the way you read *Where the Wild Things Are*. The three of you make the best 'roaring' and 'gnashing' sounds."

- **Talk with children about their parents during the day.** Look at family pictures. Encourage children to make pretend calls (or real, if parents can receive calls at work) to their parents. Comments such as "did your mommy put that bow in your hair?" or "was your dad able to get to your swim meet on Saturday?" can help children feel connected to their absent parents.

- **Encourage play that helps children gain a sense of mastery over separation.** With infants and toddlers, play "peek-a-boo" and hide-and-seek games. Provide dress-up clothes and props such as hats, briefcases, and empty food boxes so children can role-play situations where people leave and come back such as going to work and the grocery store. These make-believe activities help them handle their fearful feelings. "Ms. Rojas, what time will you be back from work today?"

- **Help parents understand confusing end-of-day behavior.** Reunions are the other side of separating. Some days children run gleefully into their parents' arms because they feel ready to go home. Other days their feelings may be ambivalent. They may burst out in tears, have a tantrum about getting their coat on, or complain about an event at school—something they didn't mention to you all afternoon. Help parents understand that sometimes children save their deepest feelings for them—the people they trust most.

- **Remind all the children about the routines of their days at your home.** A predictable order of events gives a sense of security, and by understanding this order, children are better able to understand when their parents will return to take them home. "When you wake up from your nap it will be snack time. Then we'll play outside for a while. When we come in it will be almost time for your dad to come."

- **Understand that it is normal for children to occasionally revert to younger behaviors in reaction to being separated from their families.** Thumb-sucking or wetting are typical of such behaviors. You don't need to pay undue attention to them; criticizing or focusing heavily on these habits will only make children feel bad about themselves.

In this learning activity you will think of ways to help individual children cope with separation. First review the example that follows. Then choose two children in your care whom you think are very different from each other. Use the suggestions in this module and what you know about these children to complete the questions on the blank chart.

Helping Children Deal with Separation
(Example)

	Child: Tony Age: 2-1/2 years	Child: George Age: 4 years
How does this child say goodbye to his or her parents in the morning?	*He holds on to his mother for a few minutes. She helps him hang up his coat and sits with him on the couch until she leaves for work.*	*His father asks him what he's going to play with first. George usually says "blocks," and they both get the blocks out of the closet. His father watches for a few minutes, then says goodbye.*
What kinds of make-believe do you see this child playing?	*Usually scenes from home— cooking, cleaning, eating.*	*He likes to be a police officer, directing traffic. Sometimes he dresses up as a daddy.*
How does this child use art materials to express his or her feelings?	*He likes "soothing art"—he finger paints carefully and smoothly.*	*He's quick. He makes broad brush strokes up and down and side to side when he's angry or sad.*
How do you know this child is thinking about his or her family?	*He points at the photo of his parents and him. He pretends to call them on the phone. He strokes his stuffed bunny.*	*He doesn't talk about his family very much. When we talk about families at lunch, he joins in.*
How does this child help with routines in the home?	*He likes to sweep—he's very serious about his work.*	*Sweeping does not interest George—he gets bored before he's done. He does well with clearing the dishes from the table.*
How could you help this child deal with separation?	*Read to him after his mother leaves and at the end of the day. Get him to try water play when he's sad.*	*Ask him about things he does with his parents and sisters. Use family pictures to talk about them— where they are when George is with me.*

Helping Children Deal with Separation

	Child: _____ Age: _____	Child: _____ Age: _____
How does this child say goodbye to his or her parents in the morning?		
What kinds of make-believe do you see this child playing?		
How does this child use art materials to express his or her feelings?		
How do you know this child is thinking about his or her family?		
How does this child help with routines in the home?		
How could you help this child deal with separation?		

Discuss your responses with your trainer.

LEARNING ACTIVITIES

IV. Using Caring Words to Help Build Self-Esteem

In this activity you will learn:

- to use caring words to let children know they are respected and understood; and
- to use caring words to help children learn to accept themselves and others.

FCC providers are models for children. Children listen to what you say and try to understand your meaning. The words you use teach them a lot about who they are. When those words are caring, they help build a child's self-esteem. Your "language environment" is as important as your physical environment.

Caring words begin with good listening.

Talking with children in ways that build self-esteem requires two special skills. First, a provider must listen carefully and determine what the child is really saying through words and/or actions—and what he or she is feeling. By looking at and listening to a child and thinking about your own experiences, you can often tell how the child feels. Second, a provider must respond so that the child knows that he or she is understood and respected.

For example, Ms. Ferraro watched and listened to 8-year-old James, who was new to her FCC program. James looked at the children's paintings hanging on the kitchen wall and said, "These sure are baby pictures." Ms. Ferraro said, "We let children paint all kinds of pictures here. Everyone paints in their own way, and everyone can hang their pictures if they want to. When you want to paint, you can use the paint in the jars or you can use the water colors that are stored on the top shelf."

Ms. Ferraro guessed that James was worried about how his paintings would turn out, and whether his pictures would be acceptable. His way of expressing his worry was to call the pictures on the wall "baby pictures." He might also have wanted Ms. Ferraro to know that he isn't a "baby" like the other kids; he is a big kid who goes to school. In this situation Ms. Ferraro listened carefully to what James said and tried to figure out what he was feeling. She responded to him in a way that showed that she understood that he was feeling worried and that she respected his concerns.

If Ms. Ferraro had not developed skills in listening and talking with children, she might have said, "These aren't baby pictures. It isn't nice to say that about the other children's work." This statement would have made James feel bad. It would have left him still worried about his own ability to paint pictures and whether Ms. Ferraro would recognize that he was a big kid.

Use caring words throughout the day.

When you greet children each morning and after school, you set the tone for their day. By saying something special about each child, you show that you notice and care for each one. Your caring words are also important to the parents who bring their children to your home. Here are some examples of what you might say when greeting children and their parents.

- "You're the first one here this morning. You and I can spend some quiet time together. Would you like to pick out a book for us to read?"

- "Robin, I see you smiling this morning. Maybe you're feeling more comfortable staying here while your daddy goes to work."

- "Good morning to you, Wendall. This must be your Grandpa Fred that I heard so much about last week. I know you're happy he came to visit."

- "Sandy and Jerome, it's great to have you back from school. After you put your things away, I'd like to hear about your day."

- "Your mommy told me that you went camping over the weekend. I'd really like to hear about what you saw and did."

Using caring words takes some practice. It may be a while before new ways of talking to children feel natural. You will be rewarded when the children you care for let you know how much better they feel because of your understanding and care.

During the day you have many opportunities to talk to the children you care for. In this learning activity you will read an example of how providers can use caring words in different situations. Then you will write down what you might say in typical situations to build a child's self-esteem.

Using Caring Words
(Example)

What do you say when comforting a cranky infant?

"Katie, you're having a hard time. I can tell by your tears that you're feeling sad. Let's sit here in the rocking chair and we'll rock a while. I'll help you feel better."

What do you say when an infant is trying to master a new skill?

"You crawled under the table, Keith, and now you're stuck. You backed yourself in. I'm here if you can't get out by yourself. I can help you, but you try first."

What do you say to a toddler who says "no" when you ask him or her to help put away the toys?

"I heard you say that you didn't want to put away the blocks now. It's hard to stop when you're having fun. Let's do it together, Todd. You hand me the blocks and I'll put them on the shelf."

What do you say to a toddler who climbs up on the shelves?

"I have to take you down from the shelves, Betsy. The shelves are for holding our toys and books—not for climbing on. It's not safe. Come here to the pile of pillows. This is where you can climb. That's what the pillows are for."

What do you say when a preschool child calls another child or an adult a name, such as fat or stupid?

"We don't call people names here, Carol. We just use each other's real names. Kevin is not stupid, and neither are you. Kevin is playing in his own way. You may play in your own way. Both ways are fine."

What do you say when a preschool child has a new sibling in the house and expresses jealousy?

"Sometimes it's hard to have to share Mommy and Daddy with a new baby. Maybe you think they love the baby more than you because they have to do all those things for the baby, like changing diapers. When you were a baby, Mommy and Daddy did these same things for you. They still love you, too, as 4-year-old Justin. You don't have to be like a baby for them to love you. I bet you feel good about being able to do so many things because you are 4."

What do you say when a school-age child's parent is away traveling for work?

"Your dad's job needs him to work somewhere else for a while. He won't forget you while he is gone. He'll love you no matter where he is. Let's look on the calendar so you can see when he will be back."

What do you say when a school-age child wants your attention and you are busy?

"Gail, I know you want me to read your new poem, but right now I have to change Terry's diaper. You need to wait five minutes until I am ready to read the poem, or you can come read it to both of us while I get Terry changed."

Using Caring Words

When a child doesn't want to go home:

_____

_____

_____

_____

When a child is upset or angry:

_____

_____

_____

_____

When a child has trouble completing a task:

_____

_____

_____

_____

When a child (who can use the toilet) wets his or her pants:

_____

_____

_____

_____

When a child is upset about failing a test in school:

_____

_____

_____

_____

Share your words with your trainer. You could also display your caring words on a bulletin board to help you get used to using them.

V. Providing the Right Kind of Support for Children

In this activity you will learn:

- to use what you know about each child to predict how he or she will approach a new situation; and

- to use what you know to help them experience success.

Children need opportunities to feel successful and competent.

As a provider you spend much of your day doing things for children that they cannot do for themselves. It is important, however, to recognize when children are ready to help themselves and to provide many opportunities for them to be and feel successful and competent. A provider does this by letting 6-month-old Sheila hold her own bottle, encouraging 2-year-old Arturo to use the toilet, helping 3-year-old Sara climb up the slide while holding her hand, or allowing school-age children to decide what game they want to play. Children feel good about themselves when they can practice skills they already have and learn new skills in a safe and accepting environment.

Each child develops according to a personal clock and has his or her own style, capacity to learn, and fears. As a provider you need to create an environment that both challenges and supports each child in your care. You use your knowledge of children's individual capabilities and limitations to provide the right kind of support and guidance as children approach new tasks. This allows children to acquire new skills in a way that builds their self-esteem.

Observe closely so you will know when children do and don't need your help.

One of the hardest things to know is when to offer help to a child learning a new skill and when to withdraw this support gradually so that the child can manage on his or her own. Providers need to observe children closely so they can learn who needs his hand held, who needs words of encouragement when tackling a new project, and who simply needs a provider to wave or smile at the child as she practices a new skill.

In this learning activity you will focus on two children in your care. During the next five days, keep a diary of the times when you provide support to these children and when you step back to let the children do things without your assistance. First read the example that follows.

Providing the Right Kind of Support
(Example)

Dates: *November 5-9*

Child: *George* **Age:** *12 months*	**Child:** *Janine* **Age:** *9-1/2 years*
George was standing by the shelves, trying to reach a pie tin someone had put on a high shelf. He couldn't reach it. He kept trying until he was able to grasp it. He held it with one hand and banged it with his other hand. Then he put it on his head and laughed. I laughed with him and told him he worked hard to reach the pie tin. *George was looking at a book but he couldn't turn the pages. I brought over some books with thicker pages. He explored the books and found one that had pages he could turn.*	*Janine was reading a book for her next book report at school. She stared at one page for a long time. Then she asked me where the dictionary was. I told her it was on the shelf in my bedroom. She went to get it and looked up a word. "Now I get it," she said. "The dictionary is there for you whenever you need to use it," I said.* *Janine and Bradley (7 years) were arguing about a game they were playing. Janine grabbed Bradley's pile of money. I walked over and asked, "Do you two need some help?" They each explained what they were arguing about; then I asked if they had any ideas about how to solve their problem. They agreed to start the game over. That seemed to solve their problem.*

Providing the Right Kind of Support

Dates: _____

Child: _____ Age: _____	Child: _____ Age: _____

Providing the Right Kind of Support
(continued)

Dates: _____

Child: _____ Age: _____	Child: _____ Age: _____

Discuss your completed chart with your trainer.

VI. Providing an Environment That Builds Self-Esteem

In this activity you will learn:

- to recognize how the physical environment affects the development of self-esteem; and

- to choose materials, toys, and activities to help build self-esteem.

A provider is the most important part of the environment.

As a provider, you are the most important factor in the environment. Your caring relationship with each child is what promotes self-esteem. The children who grow to trust you will be free to explore and learn from their environment—and to trust themselves as well. The environment of your FCC home—its furniture and toys, along with the activities you plan—can also help build children's self-esteem.

How can the environment itself build self-esteem? First, the furniture and equipment children use must be the right size, sturdy, and safe. If children can't reach the things they need—puzzles, crayons, and so on—they will feel frustrated and angry. If a climber is too large for children to use safely on their own, you will constantly have to be there to help. The children will learn that they have to depend on an adult, and this will not help their self-esteem. The more they can explore the environment on their own, the more proud they will be of themselves. Their self-esteem grows with their increasing independence.

Provide age-appropriate toys and materials.

Toys and materials should be appropriate for the ages of the children in your care. If the toys are broken or too simple to be of interest, the children will become frustrated or bored. Too many toys can make children confused. Too few can lead to fights or boredom. The key is to provide enough challenging (but not so challenging that they are frustrating) toys that will interest the children in your care. Children's self-esteem grows when they have many opportunities to experience success with materials and toys.

Everything should have a place in your FCC home. Each place can be labeled with a picture and/or words on low shelves so that the children can find and return the things they need. This helps children learn to make choices for themselves and to take care of their environment.

Plan activities of interest to children.

The activities you plan can also help build self-esteem. Knowing what will interest children at each stage of their development will help you plan activities that are right for them. Because you know each child, you have discovered the special interests of each one. When you plan activities you know will interest a child, you are saying to that child, "You are important to me and I know you will like this."

Children develop skills in many areas.

Every day the children in your care are learning new skills and developing new interests. To build self-esteem, you will need to change the environment, materials, and activities as children learn to:

- comfort themselves so they can fall asleep;
- hold their own spoons and bottles;
- roll over;
- start a "peek-a-boo" game;
- use the toilet;
- zip up their jackets;
- tell you what they want;
- climb the stairs;
- put puzzles together;
- paint and draw pictures they can name;
- solve problems with blocks;
- enjoy listening to stories;
- make up their own stories;
- make plans and carry them out;
- turn a cartwheel;
- look up a word in the dictionary;
- follow the directions for making a model;
- ride a bike to a friend's house (with parent's permission); and
- share their feelings and experiences.

Children develop self-esteem through successes, not failures.

Sometimes adults expect more from children than the children are capable of doing. When they see a child scooting along on a riding toy, they buy a tricycle with pedals. When a child can paint at the easel with one color, they think he can handle five colors. When a child learns to kick a ball, they make plans to sign her up for a soccer team. If you provide toys and materials that are too difficult, children are likely to fail. This lowers their self-esteem. Materials and activities must be selected with care to ensure success.

It is always a good idea to build on the skills of a particular child—to help him or her achieve success in new areas on the basis of skills he or she has already mastered. Of course, all children fail at some tasks or activities at some point; no child does everything right the first time or even the second time. The environment should be set up to encourage experiments so that children will want to keep trying. Their efforts should meet with success often enough that they will respond favorably to new challenges, confident that they can succeed.

In this learning activity you will think about how the children in your care develop self-esteem by using materials in the environment. Review the example and complete the blank chart that follows.

Providing an Environment That Builds Self-Esteem
(Example)

Typical Toys or Materials	What Children Do	How This Builds Their Self-Esteem
Plastic stacking rings that can be stacked in any order	*Take them on and off the ring* *Roll them* *Put them on their arms* *Chew on them* *Stack them*	*They are trying out ideas on their own* *They feel grown up when wearing a "bracelet"*
Wagon	*Load it up with toys and pull it around* *Sit in it and ask me to pull it around the yard* *Pull a younger child around the yard*	*They feel powerful* *They enjoy one-on-one time with an adult* *They feel good about doing something for a younger child*
Books	*Use all of their senses to explore books* *Listen to stories being read to them* *Read to themselves* *Read to younger children* *Look up a word in the dictionary* *Learn about something new*	*They feel good about their explorations* *They enjoy feeling close to another person* *They are proud of what they can do* *They feel "smart"*
Playdough	*Pound it, roll it* *Make impressions in it* *Make things with it (meatballs, snakes, cookies, cake)* *Mix colors together*	*It feels good* *It is soothing to play with* *They can easily succeed with it* *They like to show others what they can make with it*
Box of scrap materials	*Sort the materials into categories* *Plan and make a collage* *Work with a friend to make puppets* *Pick up, chew, rub, and otherwise explore the materials*	*They feel good about their hard work* *They enjoy a friend's company* *They use their senses to explore and learn about the world*

Providing an Environment That Builds Self-Esteem

Typical Toys or Materials	What Children Do	How This Builds Their Self-Esteem

Discuss your chart with your trainer.

S U M M A R I Z I N G   Y O U R   P R O G R E S S

You have now completed all of the learning activities for this module. Whether you are an experienced provider or a new one, this module has probably helped you develop new skills for building children's self-esteem. Before you go on, take a few minutes to review your responses to the pre-training assessment for this module. Summarize what you learned, and list the skills you developed or improved.

_____

_____

_____

_____

_____

_____

_____

_____

_____

_____

_____

_____

_____

_____

_____

Discuss your responses to this section with your trainer. If there are topics you would like to know more about, you will find recommended readings listed in the Introduction in Volume I.

Your final step in this module is to complete the knowledge and competency assessments. Let your trainer know when you are ready to schedule the assessments. After you have successfully completed these assessments, you will be ready to start a new module. Congratulations on your progress so far, and good luck with your next module.

ANSWER SHEETS

Building Children's Self-Esteem

Developing a Positive and Supportive Relationship with Each Child

1. **How did Ms. Neuberger build a positive and supportive relationship with Shawn?**

   a. She took time to talk with him as she and Kyle walked round the room.

   b. She stated that she liked the color blue without making judgments about his work.

2. **How did Ms. Neuberger build Shawn's self-esteem?**

   a. She gave him individual attention while they hung his picture.

   b. She let him know that she remembered he had used blue paint last week, too.

Helping Children Accept and Appreciate Themselves and Others

1. **How did Mariah feel after her gymnastics class?**

   a. Angry

   b. Frustrated

   c. Discouraged

   d. Incompetent

2. **How did Ms. Nunes help Mariah accept and appreciate herself?**

   a. She made herself available in case Mariah wanted to talk.

   b. She acknowledged Mariah's feelings.

   c. She reminded Mariah that she was new to the class.

   d. She told Mariah that it takes hard work and practice to learn new skills.

   e. She told Mariah that it was a good idea to ask for her neighbor's help.

Providing Children with Opportunities to Feel Successful and Competent

1. **How did Ms. Kent's response to the children's suggestions help them feel successful and competent?**

   She told them that their suggestion of going to the park was a great idea.

2. **How did Ms. Kent continue to interact with the children in ways that supported their self-esteem?**

   a. She asked them what they would like to bring for the picnic lunch.

   b. She encouraged them to help make lunch.

   c. She gave Janine some mixing bowls and cups to play with so she could feel like she was helping, too.

   d. She told Darnell that Janine would like him to push her stroller to the park.

GLOSSARY

Autonomy　Independence; the stage when children develop the ability to make choices and to have control over their own actions.

Environment　The complete makeup of the parts of your home and yard in which you care for children, including furnishings, toys, and planned activities.

Industry　Productivity; the stage when children develop and use their skills to accomplish tasks in school and in life.

Initiative　Self-motivation; the stage when preschool children display high energy and newly acquired skills to explore their world actively.

Observation　The act of watching systematically what a child says and does to learn more about that child. The information gained from observation is used to plan activities that address the child's needs, strengths, and interests.

Self-esteem　A sense of worth; a good feeling about oneself and one's abilities. Someone with strong self-esteem feels connected to others, respected and valued, and able to do things successfully and independently.

Separation　The process children go through as they grow up and become independent from their parents. Children often have strong feelings about separating from their families, and providers can help children understand and express these feelings.

Temperament　The nature or disposition of a child; the way a child responds to and interacts with people, materials, and situations in his or her world.

Trust　The stage when infants develop deep feelings of comfort and confidence because their basic needs are met promptly, consistently, and lovingly.

Module 9:
SOCIAL

O V E R V I E W

Promoting children's social development involves:

- helping children learn to get along with others;

- helping children understand and express their feelings and respect those of others; and

- providing an environment and experiences that help children develop social skills.

Most children enjoy playing with others.

Social development refers to the way children learn to get along with others and to enjoy the people in their lives. As children develop socially they learn to share, cooperate, take turns, and negotiate with other children and adults. Children's social development is strengthened when they have secure relationships with their parents and other adults, when they have many opportunities to play with other children, and when they feel good about themselves. Although they may argue and fight, most children really enjoy playing with others. They negotiate, make compromises, and cooperate with each other so that play can continue.

Social development begins when an infant responds to a familiar voice or the special touch of a parent or provider. It continues as toddlers enjoy playing alongside each other, as preschool children learn to play in groups, and as school-age children make up their own games on the playground. Children spend a lot of time engaged in dramatic play. They develop social skills as they try out different roles, invent complex scenarios, and learn to take turns being the cook, the firefighter, the police officer, or the baby.

Children learn how to behave from being with adults.

FCC providers play an important role in promoting children's social development. Through their relationships with adults, children learn what behaviors are accepted in society. As a provider, you let children know that they are loved and accepted; you meet their needs as consistently and promptly as possible. This helps children feel good about themselves, which in turn allows them to appreciate, respect, and get along with other children and adults. (Because children's feelings about themselves will determine how they develop socially, you may want to review the material in Module 8, Self.) In addition, you provide an environment where children can spend time alone or play with others. You also help children learn to respect the rights of others so that everyone can enjoy the benefits of being part of a group. And you help children understand their feelings and show them acceptable ways to express those feelings.

In addition to relationships with their parents and providers, children need to make friends with their peers. Part of your job is ensuring that children have many opportunities to choose what they want to do and who they want to play with during their days at your FCC home.

Listed below are examples of how FCC providers demonstrate their competence in promoting children's social development.

Helping Children Learn to Get Along with Others

Encourage children to help each other. "Peter, I think Todd might need your help to carry the table outside."

Include enough time for free play in the daily schedule so children can choose to play with special friends. "Jane, I see you and Carla are working together in the sandbox."

Model positive ways to interact with others. "Mrs. King, thank you for saving those old magazines for us. Gillian and the other children will enjoy using them for collages and special projects."

Encourage young children's awareness of others by talking about what they are doing. "Jamie, I see you are playing peek-a-boo with Donna. She really likes it when you play with her."

Help children find solutions to their conflicts. "You are angry because you both think the other person cheated. How can you work out your differences so you can still play checkers together?"

Help children of different ages appreciate and value each other. "Brian will be home from school soon. Then you can tell him about your weekend camping trip."

Helping Children Understand and Express Their Feelings and Respect Those of Others

Share some of your own feelings when appropriate. "I'm excited because my sister and her family are coming to visit us next week."

Accept children's feelings while helping them control their actions. "I know you feel angry when John knocks down your building. You can tell him you're angry but I can't let you hurt him."

Encourage children to be aware of how their peers are feeling. "Karen is happy now because you let her use some of your crayons."

State what you think children are feeling when they are having trouble expressing their emotions. "I wonder if you are feeling sad because you miss your mom a lot when she goes away on a trip. Maybe you'd like to write a poem or draw a picture to send to your mom."

Respect children by listening to their feelings and responding appropriately. "It feels bad when two good friends are fighting with each other. Tell me what happened when you asked both girls to spend the night at your house."

Encourage children to use words to express how they feel. "When Michael teases you, it makes you feel bad so you cry. Tell Michael that you want him to stop teasing you."

Read stories that help children deal with their feelings about friendship, sharing, handicaps, and other similar topics. One good book is *Alexander and the Terrible, Horrible, No-Good, Very Bad Day* by Judith Viorst. "Can you think of a time when you had a 'terrible, horrible, no-good, very bad day'?"

Providing an Environment and Experiences That Help Children Develop Social Skills

Plan activities that encourage cooperation. "The plants in our garden are very dry. Joan and Nancy, can you please help carry that long hose over to the garden? "

Provide activities for two or more children to enjoy together, such as digging in a sandbox or playing a board game. "Heather, you can ask Corinna if she wants to play Parcheesi with you. You had a good time playing together yesterday."

Include infants at mealtimes even if they have already eaten. "Here, Cordell. You can sit here in your infant seat and be with us. Then we'll all be together."

Establish and maintain rules that help children learn social skills. "Derek, there's only room for two children at the easel. What would you like to do while you are waiting for the other children to finish their painting?"

Extend children's dramatic play by joining in for a while. "Dr. Jones, thank you for fixing my broken arm. I'll see you next month when you take off the cast."

Help children see how they are the same and different. "Lottie has a long, curly pony tail and Martina has a long, straight one."

Encourage cooperation rather than competition. "Let's help the block builders clean up. Then all the toys will be back on the shelves and we can go outside together."

Provide duplicates of popular toys so that children who cannot yet share can play together peacefully. "Here is a jeep for Tasha and one for Miguel."

Provide a variety of props that children can use for dramatic play. "Jackie and Kia, that was a good idea to use the muffin tin in your bake shop. Would you like to make some baker hats to wear while you're at work?"

Promoting Children's Social Development

In the following situations, FCC providers are promoting children's social development. As you read each one, think about what the providers are doing and why. Then answer the questions that follow.

Helping Children Learn to Get Along with Others

Ms. Waxler is sitting at a table encouraging Paula to try a more difficult puzzle than the one she usually does. While Paula picks another puzzle from the shelf, Ms. Waxler stands up and looks around the room to see what everyone else is doing. She sees Sally and Gina, two good friends, playing in the corner. They are each waving their arms and looking very angry. Ms. Waxler walks over to listen to the argument. The children are playing restaurant, and both girls want to be the waitress. Ms. Waxler says to them, "I ate in a restaurant last week. There were so many customers they needed two waitresses." Then she steps back. The girls look at each other; then Sally says, "Let's sit the dolls in the chairs. Then we can both be waitresses." Ms. Waxler said, "That's good thinking, girls. You found a way to have fun together." Ms. Waxler then goes back to see how Paula is doing on the puzzle.

1. **How did Ms. Waxler help the girls learn to get along with each other?**

_____

_____

_____

_____

2. **How did Ms. Waxler help the girls feel good about solving their problem?**

_____

_____

_____

_____

Helping Children Understand and Express Their Feelings and Respect Those of Others

Ms. Brown and the children are outside engaged in a variety of activities. She walks around the yard to watch and listen to the children at play. Maddie and Peter are at the bottom of the ladder to the slide. Maddie begins to climb the ladder, then stops. Peter, who is next in line, tells her to "hurry up," puts his hand on her back, and pushes her. Maddie turns around and pushes him back. Ms. Brown quickly walks over near the slide and says, "Maddie, I think you might be feeling a little scared about going down the slide, so you are taking your time climbing up the ladder. Peter, I think you might be feeling impatient because you want to have your turn on the slide.

I can't let you push each other. You can both use your words to tell each other how you feel. Maddie, you can go first, tell Peter how you feel." Ms. Brown stays with the children while they tell each other how they feel. Maddie steps down off the ladder so Peter can have his turn while she takes a little more time to conquer her fears. As Ms. Brown walks away, she turns back and hears Peter encouraging Maddie to come down the slide. "It's really fun, Maddie. You won't hurt yourself!"

1. How did Ms. Brown let the children know that she understood and respected their feelings?

_____

_____

_____

_____

2. How did Ms. Brown help the children express their feelings?

_____

_____

_____

_____

Providing an Environment and Experiences That Help Children Develop Social Skills

Ms. Sequoia announces that it's almost time for lunch. "This chicken noodle soup smells really tasty," she says. "Before we sit down to enjoy our soup and sandwiches, I need some helpers to get the table ready." "I'll help," says Leroy. "Me too," says Melissa. Ms. Sequoia thanks the children, then says, "First we need to get the table ready." "Okay," says Leroy, "I'll wipe it clean." He goes over to the sink to get a soapy sponge. "Me too! " says Melissa as she toddles after Leroy. "You're too little," he says. "Only big kids who go to kindergarten can reach the sink." Ms. Sequoia waits until Leroy gets his sponge, then says, "Our table is pretty big. Even someone as big as you are might need some help. If you help Melissa reach the sink, she can get a sponge too. Then you can work together to get the table clean." Leroy gets the stepstool and holds Melissa while she stands on tiptoes to reach the sink. The two children wipe the table and return their sponges to the sink. "That looks great," says Ms. Sequoia. "Now we need some napkins, bowls, spoons, and cups." "I'll get the bowls and spoons and cups," says Leroy. "Melissa can fold the napkins." Ms. Sequoia turns to the children and says, "That sounds like a good idea. Thank you both for your help."

1. How did Ms. Sequoia turn the daily routine of getting ready for lunch into an experience that helped the children develop social skills?

_____

_____

_____

_____

2. What social skills did the children learn as they got the table ready for lunch?

_____

_____

_____

_____

Compare your answers with those on the answer sheet at the end of this module. If your answers are different, discuss them with your trainer. There can be more than one answer.

Your Own Social Development

Adults use the social skills they learned in childhood.

Adults use social skills every day. When you yield to another car in traffic or wait for a turn to offer your opinion at a training workshop, you are using the social skills you learned as a child and will continue to use throughout your life.

Sometimes you find yourself in situations where you need to use your social skills to adapt to a new group of people. Perhaps you just joined a choir or started a new exercise class. In both of these situations, you use social skills to get to know the other group members and to adjust to the group's accepted ways of doing things.

Some adults find it very difficult to adjust to new situations. Although this difficulty may stem from their personalities, perhaps these adults never really learned, when they were children, how to get to know new people.

You can model positive social behaviors.

Young children learn about how society expects them to behave by watching adults interact with each other as well as with children. Children need to see the important adults in their lives working cooperatively, sharing feelings and ideas, having friendly conversations, and enjoying each other's company. You model social behaviors for children when a neighbor drops in to borrow some milk and you gladly help her out, when you warmly greet the children and their parents in the morning, or when you welcome your spouse home for lunch or at the end of the day. The children can gain a more complete picture of you when they see you using your social skills to work out problems, share happy experiences, and cooperate with others.

Think about how you use and model social skills. Give some examples below.

Sharing:

_____

_____

_____

Cooperating:

_____

_____

_____

141

Taking turns:

_____

_____

_____

Solving problems:

_____

_____

_____

Helping:

_____

_____

_____

Appreciating others:

_____

_____

_____

Showing concern:

_____

_____

_____

What social skill do you find most difficult? Why?

_____

_____

_____

What does this tell you about your work with children?

_____

_____

_____

Social development is an ongoing process. As adults, we continue to learn about ourselves and ways of relating to others. Your social skills help you enjoy working with children and their families.

When you have finished this overview section, you should complete the pre-training assessment. Refer to the glossary at the end of this module if you need definitions for the terms that are used.

PRE-TRAINING ASSESSMENT

Listed below are the skills that FCC providers use to promote children's social development. Think about whether you do these things regularly, sometimes, or not enough. Place a check in one of the columns on the right for each skill listed. Then discuss your answers with your trainer.

Skill	I Do This Regularly	I Do This Sometimes	I Don't Do This Enough
Helping Children Learn to Get Along With Others 1. Observing and listening to learn how each child relates to the others in your care.			
2. Talking, making eye contact, and playing with children to let them know how it feels to interact with another person.			
3. Encouraging children to help each other.			
4. Encouraging children to solve their own conflicts.			
5. Modeling positive ways to cooperate, share, and interact with others.			
6. Providing toys, materials, and activities that can involve more than one child at a time.			
7. Including enough time in the daily schedule for free play so children can decide with whom they would like to play.			

Skill	I Do This Regularly	I Do This Sometimes	I Don't Do This Enough
Helping Children Understand and Express Their Feelings and Respect Those of Others			
8. Helping younger children learn new words to express their feelings and reminding older children to tell others how they feel.			
9. Providing a variety of props so children can use dramatic play to work through their fears and other feelings.			
10. Identifying your own feelings when appropriate so children can learn to express their feelings.			
11. Verbally expressing feelings for infants when they are crying, laughing, gurgling, and so on, and for older children when necessary.			
12. Meeting young children's needs according to their personal schedules for eating, sleeping, and so on.			
13. Talking with children about what they are doing to show your respect and appreciation for their accomplishments.			

Skill	I Do This Regularly	I Do This Sometimes	I Don't Do This Enough
Providing an Environment and Experiences That Help Children Develop Social Skills			
14. Arranging the environment so children can spend time alone or with one or two others.			
15. Planning special group projects such as painting a mural so children of different ages can play and work together.			
16. Providing duplicates of favorite toys so children can play together without having to share.			
17. Creating prop boxes with materials related to children's interests that can be used for dramatic play by children of different ages.			
18. Providing duplicates of certain dramatic play props, such as firefighters' hats, to encourage group play.			
19. Providing toys and materials such as beads and string that children can use when they want to play alone.			

Review your responses, then list three to five skills you would like to improve or topics you would like to learn more about to help you promote children's social development. When you finish this module, you will list examples of your new or improved knowledge and skills.

_____

_____

_____

_____

_____

_____

Discuss the overview and pre-training assessment with your trainer. Then begin the learning activities for Module 9.

LEARNING ACTIVITIES

I. Using Age-Appropriate Approaches to Promote Social Development

In this activity you will learn:

- to recognize some typical behaviors of children from infancy through school age;

- to use your knowledge of child development to promote children's social development; and

- to use age-appropriate approaches to promote children's social development.

A child's social development begins at birth. Young infants are entirely dependent on the adults who care for them. Through their interactions with the adults who diaper, feed, comfort, and talk to them, infants learn to trust their parents and providers. This trust is the beginning of the child's social development.

When young children don't experience having their needs met and don't learn to trust people, they may have difficulties relating to others later in life. As older children or adults, they may be insecure and have low self-esteem. Adjusting to new situations such as moving to a new home and school may be more difficult for children who did not receive consistent, loving care during infancy. They also may find it hard to make and keep friends. When FCC providers understand how children of different ages learn social skills, they can use age-appropriate approaches to help children learn positive ways to interact with others and to develop and maintain friendships.

How Infants Develop Socially

During the first 3 months of life, infants relate to others by crying, smiling, grasping a finger, and cuddling. They turn their heads when someone speaks, focus more and more steadily on faces and objects, and make noises in response to sounds and words they hear around them. As they get older, infants who receive loving and consistent care respond to their FCC providers by smiling, hugging, and showing that they feel good. They want to be around others and may cry when left alone.

Infants may be afraid of strangers.

As infants become more mobile, they show their increasing awareness of being separate individuals as they put their hands in your mouth, touch your hair, and pull your earrings or glasses. They imitate sounds and gestures. They become attached to their

149

providers and show this by being curious about, and sometimes frightened of, strangers. Some children may scream or try to hide from an unfamiliar person. Children at this age are becoming more interested in the world around them, including other children.

Mobile infants are becoming more independent.

Mobile infants (approximately 9 to 18 months old) have clear likes and dislikes and show you how they feel. They are becoming more independent, are able to crawl and walk where they want to go, and are eager to explore. They enjoy watching other children and may imitate what they see others do. They can crawl after you and climb up on your lap. They point to things they want and begin saying a few words.

FCC providers can develop nurturing, loving relationships with infants as they diaper, feed, comfort, and talk with them throughout the day. Through consistent, responsive attention to their needs, infants learn to feel that someone else respects and cares for them. Often a provider is the first person outside the family who has a relationship with the infant. When it is a positive one, this relationship communicates to the infant, "There are other caring people for you to meet in the world."

Infants are active communicators.

As you get to know an infant, you will discover an active participant with many ways of interacting. Young infants use facial expressions and sounds to connect with others. When a baby and provider are in tune with each other, they are like dancing partners. They take turns talking and looking into each other's eyes. When they are not in tune, their interaction is likely to be bumpy and uncomfortable for each of them. If, for example, a provider is talking too loudly, an infant may turn away. Unless the provider knows what the infant is communicating, she may feel rejected.

Playing with infants and encouraging the other children to play with them also support social development. A 3-year-old can hold a rattle near an infant and encourage her to reach for it. A school-age child can push the stroller when you go for a walk around the neighborhood. Older infants enjoy playing Peek-a-Boo and rolling a ball back and forth. These simple games teach them how to respond and be responded to. They learn to have a good time with another person, and they discover that relating to other people is fun. Eventually they will initiate these kinds of games themselves.

If you care for infants, you may recognize some of the examples of social development in the situations described on the next page. As you read about how the FCC provider, Ms. Harvey, might respond, think about what you might do in a similar situation. In the blank box at the bottom, write down what you might do in the situation described in the left column.

Situation	What Ms. Harvey Might Do
Ms. Harvey is reading with the other children when Timothy (3 months) wakes up crying.	Although she is reading to the other children, Ms. Harvey knows that Timothy needs a quick response to his crying. She says to the children, "Timothy is crying because he needs something. I'll be back after I help him feel better."
Beth (6 months) squeals with delight when she sees Marci (3-1/2 years) arrive in the morning.	Ms. Harvey can use words to describe Beth's feelings: "I can see that you really like Marci. She really likes you, too." Later, she might encourage the relationship between the two girls by asking Marci to hand Beth the rattle that she dropped on the floor.
Nicky (8 months) crawls after Ms. Harvey when she goes into the kitchen.	Ms. Harvey can acknowledge Nicky by saying, "Hi, Nicky. I see your smiling face. I'm going to pick you up now so I can give you a hug."
Bryce (10 months) is holding onto the side of the low climber. He turns, looks at Ms. Harvey, and says "Aah, aah."	

How Toddlers Develop Socially

Toddlers work very hard to figure out who they are. When they run, climb, jump, test limits, and shout, "No! Me do!" they are saying, "This is me!" The experiences of being loved, cooperated with, and cared for help toddlers feel good about themselves and let them know what it means to love and care for another person.

Toddlers are very curious about other children and very observant. In an FCC home, toddlers quickly learn whose mommy and daddy, bottle, and shoes belong to whom. Their curiosity often leads them to establishing friendships with other children.

Because toddlers are trying to make sense of a world that can seem very big and confusing to them, they need providers to set clear limits. If toddlers can depend on the fact that an adult is in charge, they feel free to explore and learn about themselves and other people.

Toddlers may talk non-stop.

Toddlers are rapidly learning to use language to communicate with others—an important social skill. Just as some toddlers are very interested in practicing their physical skills by constantly moving, others want to practice their language skills by talking nonstop. You can foster language development by listening to toddlers, talking with them, asking them questions, and answering their questions. In short, providers can engage toddlers in conversations to model for them the give-and-take involved in communicating with others.

To foster toddlers' social interactions, providers need to give them many opportunities to interact with other children. Toddlers tend to have strong feelings and often don't know how to express them. They might hit, bite, pinch, or push instead. Providers should be prepared to respond to these negative behaviors. If you watch carefully, you will recognize the signs when a child is going to lash out at another, and you can step in before any harm is done. Some toddlers show tremendous sensitivity and ability to work things out with each other without adult assistance.

Most toddlers are not yet ready to share.

Toddlers are beginning to understand what personal property is, but they are not yet ready to share their own belongings. You can model and encourage sharing and provide duplicates of favorite toys and materials.

Toddlers are also beginning to enjoy playing with other children. They may enjoy rolling a ball with a younger child or going down the slide with an older one. You can encourage toddlers to interact with other children by providing activities such as sand and water play that involve more than one child at once. (These types of activities are also very appropriate for a multi-age group because children of different ages will find different ways to enjoy them, based on their skills and interests.)

If you care for toddlers, you may recognize some of the examples of social development in the situations described on the next page. As you read about how the FCC provider, Ms. Harvey, might respond, think about what you might do in a similar situation. In the blank box at the bottom, write down what you might do in the situation described in the left column.

Situation	What Ms. Harvey Might Do
Greg (22 months) reaches for the baseball cap that James (3 years) is wearing. James holds the cap tight and says, "no!" Greg pushes James and yells, "My hat!"	As soon as she hears the "no!" Ms. Harvey should move quickly toward the two boys. She probably won't reach them in time to stop the pushing, but she can take Greg's hand and lead him away. When James gets up and goes back to playing, she can say to Greg, "James is wearing that hat. You can get another hat from the shelf."
Laura (20 months) and Ned (28 months) are getting ready to go outside. Both children can get their coats on without Ms. Harvey's help, but Laura can't get hers zipped.	Ms. Harvey might say to Ned, "Can you please help Laura zip her coat? Then you'll both be ready to go outside." Then she can thank Ned for helping her and for helping Laura.
The children have just finished their afternoon snack. There are a lot of crumbs under the table. B.J. (23 months) wants to help clean up.	

How Preschool Children Develop Socially

By the time children are 3 and 4 years old, they have learned a lot about accepted behaviors and are ready to develop friendships. Most are eager to imitate how adults get along with each other, and they enjoy being with other people. As preschool children develop socially, they become less dependent on adults. They usually want to spend time with children their own age. It's important to allow lots of time for free play so children can choose their own playmates.

Preschool children spend a lot of time playing with their peers and want to be well-liked. They use their rapidly developing language skills to engage in real conversations with each other—you will hear all kinds of interesting discussions. Listen carefully to these conversations to find out how the children are getting along, whose ideas are listened to, who needs help learning to get others to listen, and what their interests are. You can use this information for planning to meet individual needs.

Dramatic play builds social skills.

Most preschool children enjoy pretending to be someone else. By pretending to be a mother, a baby, a television character, or a firefighter, children are trying to make sense of their world. These dramatic play opportunities also help children develop social skills. To play with others, they must take turns, negotiate, share, and cooperate.

The preschool years are also characterized by exclusion. You may notice that some children tend to be those doing the excluding while others tend to be the ones excluded. It doesn't work to force the children to play with each other. This will not help them learn social skills. You can observe to see how often a child is excluded and help the child learn ways to get included in the other children's play. You might give him or her a special prop to share or suggest a role to play.

Preschool children like to make up rules and are even willing to follow them. They might enjoy playing simple games that stress cooperation rather than competition. If you care for school-age children as well as preschool children, an older child might be willing to teach a younger one to play a simple card or board game.

In a family child care setting, preschool children are likely to play cooperatively with each other and with children who are older than they are and those who are younger. They might enjoy leading younger children in dramatic play and other activities, although they might be a little bossy. When allowed to join in, they also like to participate in the older children's play.

If you care for preschool children, you may recognize some of the examples of social development in the situations described on the next page. As you read about how the FCC provider, Ms. Harvey, might respond, think about what you might do in a similar situation. In the blank box at the bottom, write down what you might do in the situation described in the left column.

Situation	What Ms. Harvey Might Do
Patty (4-1/2 years) and Shaundyce (almost 5 years) are taking their babies for a walk around the yard. Brenda (4 years) pushes her carriage over to them and asks, "What are you doing? Can I come, too?" Patty turns around and says, "Go away. You can't play with us." Shaundyce pipes in, "Yeah. You can't play."	Ms. Harvey should watch to see how Brenda will handle the situation. She shouldn't intervene unless it is necessary. If Brenda does not seem to know how to join the play, she might step in to model how to get included. For example, she might say, "Hi, girls. Where are you going with your babies? My baby has a little cough, so we're going to the doctor."
Dennis (3-1/2 years) is sitting on the couch quietly watching the children at the easel. He turns to watch the block builders for a while, then he looks to see if anyone is in the reading corner.	Ms. Harvey can first watch to see if Dennis needs her assistance. It may be that Dennis just wants to spend some time alone for a while. Because preschool children need opportunities for solitary play, Ms. Harvey can be sure there are enough toys and materials that can be used by a child alone—beads and string, puzzles, books, paints, and so on.
Sandy (5 years) sits watching Margaret (7 years) and Tyrone (6 years) playing checkers.	

How School-Age Children Develop Socially

Between the ages of 6 and 12, children continue to develop and refine their social skills. They become increasingly independent yet are still emotionally dependent on adults. They need the important adults in their lives, such as teachers, parents, and their FCC provider, to be there to provide assistance and support.

Younger school-age children may hide their feelings.

Younger school-age children (from about 6 to 8 years old) have learned to control their emotions and may hide their feelings from adults. Although they appear on the surface to be calm and happy, they may be dealing with unexpressed fears and concerns. Their needs may change daily, often because of events that you know nothing about. FCC providers need to be sure to talk with children often to keep in touch with what is happening in their lives. Let them know that you accept and value them just as they are and that they can take their time growing up. Above all, be a good listener rather than offering unsolicited advice. Encourage children to talk about their school activities, their relationships with classmates, and how they feel about themselves.

School-age children want to do things well.

In the preschool years, these children were content just to be doing things; now they want to do things well. For example, they now like to work on models, crafts, and woodworking because they feel good when they have accomplished a difficult task.

Children of this age still rely on their families as sources of security, but they are capable of complicated and extensive peer relationships. They like to do things together and are fascinated by rules. They make up their own games with very specific rules and rituals.

For some children the competitive nature of school and sports activities may be overwhelming. Typically they are very sensitive to criticism. While they want to perform well and do things right to please adults, they may fear failing and being rejected by their parents and friends. Try to make your FCC home a place where there are plenty of opportunities to play cooperative games and engage in noncompetitive projects. You and the children might think of ways to change the rules on board games so that there isn't just one winner. Allow children to play just for the pleasure of playing, to do something just because it's fun.

Most children want to be with their friends.

By the time they are 8 years old most children want to spend time with their friends. They like forming clubs and may include and exclude other children, sometimes on the basis of gender. You can help them set up clubs based on shared interests and provide a place for the club to meet and a place for them to store their club-related materials. When you observe a child being excluded, resist your first inclination to step in to insist that the child be included. These children are becoming very good at problem solving. You can encourage them to use democratic principles to work out their own arguments.

Toward the end of the school-age years (approximately 9 to 12) children are generally secure in their feelings about themselves. They show initiative, are usually cooperative, and appreciate others and their accomplishments. This is an uneven time for the sexes. In this age group, girls may be up to 2 years ahead of boys in their progress toward maturity.

As important as friends are in the early school-age years, they become even more important as children grow older. A child looks to the peer group for acceptance and may base his definition of himself on how his friends feel about him. Older school-age children are more content in FCC homes where there is at least one other child of the same age.

School-age children are interested in what goes on in the world.

Children of this age are aware of and interested in events outside their communities. They are developing opinions and enjoy discussing their perspectives on topics such as saving the environment and helping the homeless. They can also experience empathy—they can imagine how they might feel if they lived through an earthquake or what they might do if they won the lottery. They are often willing to talk to you about their feelings and want to know how you might feel in similar situations.

Some FCC providers fall into a pattern of using the older school-age children to help with caring for the younger children and to do household chores. A limited amount of this helps children develop a sense of responsibility and allows them to feel competent while they do a "real" job. It is important to remember, however, that these children need your attention as much as the younger ones. You need to provide activities and materials that meet these children's interests.

If you care for school-age children, you may recognize some of the examples of social development in the situations described on the following page. As you read about how the FCC provider, Ms. Harvey, might respond, think about what you might do in a similar situation. In the blank box at the bottom, write down what you might do in the situation described in the left column.

Situation	What Ms. Harvey Might Do
Dennis (8 years) just got a magic set for his birthday. He's been telling Carlos (6-1/2 years) about all the new tricks that he's been learning.	Ms. Harvey can encourage Dennis to share his talent with the other children. He could bring his magic set to the FCC home to share with Carlos. The two boys could practice their magic tricks until they were ready to put on a show for the younger children.
When Raoul (9 years) comes to Ms. Harvey's FCC home after school, the first thing he does is eat his snack. He usually sits alone at the kitchen table for about half an hour before he comes to tell Ms. Harvey about his day at school.	Ms. Harvey probably knows that Raoul needs to spend some time alone after being in a large group of children all day at school. She might need to add some more toys or materials such as interesting magazines (*World* from National Geographic or *Ranger Rick* from the National Wildlife Federation) that school-age children can use alone.
Sherrie (6-1/2 years and Lianna (7 years) are becoming very close friends. They like to use the big pillows to create a private space in the corner of the living room. They sit in their "clubhouse" drawing pictures and reading books together.	

Discuss this activity with your trainer.

II. Creating an Environment That Supports Social Development

> **In this activity you will learn:**
>
> - to set up the environment so that children are comfortable being in a group all day; and
>
> - to plan the environment so that children are encouraged to play with others.

Making Group Living Comfortable

Depending on how it has been set up, the physical environment of your FCC home can make it easy or hard for children to be part of a group all day. It is important for you as a provider to arrange furniture and display materials in your home in ways that make children feel comfortable interacting. By doing so, you are promoting their social development.

Children in a family child care program have to learn to adjust to group living. No matter how interesting and comfortable your environment is, it is *not* the children's home. A child who comes to your FCC home may have a number of concerns.

- Do I belong here?
- Will the things I make and the things I bring here be protected?
- Do I have to share the things I want to play with?
- How will I know when it's my turn?
- How will I know what to do?
- Will I have friends?

If you have completed Module 3, Learning Environment, you will probably remember several ways in which providers can arrange the environment to help children with these concerns:

- Provide a space for each child to store personal belongings and to keep artwork and other projects safe until they go home.

- Provide duplicates of materials whenever possible so younger children who are not yet ready to share don't have to.

- Give children a concrete way to know when their turn will come—a sign-up sheet, a clock, or a timer with a bell.

- Display materials neatly on low shelves, and put materials that are used together on the same shelf.

- Provide a separate storage area for school-age children to keep their materials out of reach of the younger children.

159

- Put some toys out on the floor or table to encourage reluctant children to use them.

- Offer occasional special projects or activities such as mural painting or making up a dance that may stir the interest of a passive child. Such projects give children a chance to switch roles or change their usual behaviors.

The environment offers social choices.

The physical environment can also be organized to offer children a variety of social choices. Sometimes children want to be alone. They need "time out" from group living. You can support this need by providing:

- earphones connected to a tape recorder or a record or CD player;

- small enclosed spaces—a comfortable chair designated as a special place where a child can be alone, a large cardboard box, or a small area defined with pillows; or

- a small table and chair for one child.

Sometimes children want to play with just one or two other children. They need spaces that can contain a limited number of people. When pieces of furniture are used as dividers, the room can be organized to create spaces for a few children. Outdoors, a large tire swing can hold two children. Large cardboard boxes are ideal for children who wish to build their own spaces. A tractor-tire sandbox is a cozy place for a small group.

Take a few minutes to look around the environment of your FCC home and answer the following questions:

What spaces do you have for children who want to be alone?

_____

_____

_____

In addition to the places you identified above, what other changes can you make in your environment to give a child a place to be alone for a while?

_____

_____

_____

Planning the Environment to Encourage Children to Play with Others

There are many ways in which the physical environment can encourage children to play with others. The play materials themselves can invite social interaction. Some materials, such as sand, water, playdough, and finger paint, are inviting and soothing. These materials are ideal for a multi-age group because children of a wide range of ages can experience and use them in many different ways. Children are drawn to them and feel relaxed when they play with these materials. As they play, they are likely to begin to share and talk to each other. When additional props are added, children often begin to pretend and make up play episodes with each other. Providing rolling pins, cookie cutters, plastic knives, and cups and saucers along with the playdough can lead to lots of dramatic play about cooking, baking, and serving.

Some materials encourage two or more children to play together. A rocking boat is most fun with a partner, as is a two-sided easel. A tunnel or a large cardboard box provides opportunities for many kinds of group play. Baskets of blocks or pop beads can be shared by two or three friends. Prop boxes and a rich variety of dramatic play items will encourage children to play together.

Small group projects also draw children into cooperative play. The group might even plan such a project together, collect the materials needed, and then carry out the project. Examples of special projects include:

- cooking a special meal;

- painting a group mural of something the children have experienced;

- planting and caring for a garden; and

- planning a party.

The more interesting and varied the environment, the more children will be drawn into play. If you offer the same things day after day, children will be bored and lose interest. But if the environment changes regularly, they will be eager to try out new ideas. Changes can be quite small and still make a difference.

Creating Space for Dramatic Play

Although dramatic play can take place anywhere, you will see more of it if you also create a special place for storing props and dress-up clothes. The most common theme in children's dramatic play is family life because this is what they are most familiar with. You can create a setting for playing house by making a corner of the living room or play room the make-believe area. A shelf or chest can hold props such as dress-up clothes, plastic dishes, pots, and pans, empty food boxes and cans, and so on. The more enclosed the area, the more real it will seem and the more children will like it. An enclosed

161

area gives them the feeling of being someplace else, away from the rest of the activities. This is why children like to crawl under a table or behind the sofa to play and use their imaginations.

Furniture in the make-believe area should be child-sized. You can paint a cardboard box or wooden crate to be used as a stove, a sink, or a bed for the doll baby. A small table and two child-sized chairs will set the stage for a variety of dramatic play. In addition to playing house, you may also witness customers being served in a restaurant, office workers writing important memos, or doctors examining sick babies.

For several reasons, it's a good idea to organize your dramatic play materials:

- **It makes your job easier.** When materials are always stored in a specific place and that place is labeled with a picture to show where each item belongs, it is much easier for you to get the children to help clean up after play time.

- **Children feel invited to play with materials when they can reach them without adult assistance.** A good storage system allows children to find the things they need, make independent choices, and begin their play without delay.

- **It helps if you keep props and toys clean and intact.** Children quickly lose interest when the dolls' arms and legs keep falling off or when the dress-up clothes are torn or have missing buttons or fasteners. An orderly arrangement of materials tells children that you value their toys and materials and will help them take care of them.

The following storage suggestions might work for your FCC program.

- Wooden pegs on a board for hanging clothes, hats, scarves, ties, and bags.

- A shoe rack or hanging shoe bag for shoes and other small items.

- A small coat tree at a child's height, for hanging clothes and bags.

- Three-tiered wire baskets that hang from hooks for storing plastic food, ties and bags, costume jewelry, and doll clothes.

- A piece of pegboard for hanging dress-up clothes, pots and pans, cooking utensils, and mops and brooms.

Encouraging Play Through the Use of Prop Boxes

Children's social development is further encouraged when the materials offered encourage them to play different roles. Consider children's interests as you select materials. Because you know that young children still are very tied to home, you can provide props that encourage them to play family roles. As they get older and more experienced in play, you will want to respond to their expanding interests. The props you put out may relate to an experience the group has shared, such as watching a puppet show. After a trip, help children recall what they saw and use the props to recreate their experiences. Props may also relate to something important that has happened in the children's lives—a child in your care going to the hospital or a fire in the neighborhood that the children witnessed.

One way to extend play is to create prop boxes. Select a theme—for example, a hospital prop box or one for a shoe store—and think of what children would need to engage in dramatic play around the theme. Then collect the materials you will need and store them in the prop box until you are ready to bring them out. Prop boxes are particularly effective in FCC homes. They are inexpensive and easy to store and allow for rich and varied dramatic play. They are also ideal for a multi-age group of children. The older children will probably be the planners and directors, but they will find ways to include all the others.

In this activity you will learn about preparing prop boxes to encourage children's dramatic play and social development. Begin by reading "Dramatic Play Kits or Prop Boxes." Then decide on a prop box that would be of interest to the children in your care. After making one, try it out for a few days and note the results. Think about what (if anything) you might do differently next time.

Dramatic Play Kits or Prop Boxes[1]

The suggestions listed below are possibilities for the contents of dramatic play kits or prop boxes. You may want to use a few or many of the suggested items.

Open-Ended Props Have on hand a collection of props that can be used by the children in their dramatic play in a number of ways. Examples include swatches of fabric, shells, stones, string, wire, cardboard cylinders, colored cubes, brown paper bags, staplers, tape, construction paper, magic markers, pipe cleaners, paper plates.

Dress-Ups Shoes, big boots, handbags, tote bags, briefcases, coats, sweaters, capes, dresses, skirts, shirts, aprons, scarves, helmets or hats (nurse, fire fighter, police officer, cowboy, astronaut, construction worker, fancy and frilly, washable sun and rain hats), clip-on ties, raincoats, umbrellas, galoshes, old graduation gowns, wedding clothes, a grass skirt, jewelry, watches, sunglasses, eyeglass frames.

Baby Things Diaper bag, diapers of suitable size, baby clothes, baby blanket, baby back-pack or front carrier, empty baby powder containers, baby bathtub or basin, cotton balls, Q-tips, towels, baby food, spoons, bottles, rattles.

Cooking/Bakery Pots, pans, muffin tins, pie tins, rolling pins, cake pans, mixing bowls, cookie sheets, spatula, eggbeaters, spoons, pitchers, salt and flour shakers, medicine bottles with colored water, tablecloths, aprons, hats, playdough.

Cleaning/Laundry Small brooms, mops, dust cloths, feather dusters, cake of soap, sponges, towels, plastic spray bottle, plastic basin, clothesline (hang it up between two chairs), clothespins, doll clothes to wash, laundry machines made from cardboard boxes, empty detergent box, play iron and ironing board, aprons, clothes basket.

Human Figures Collections of various types of "people" (including both adults and children) to use as needed for dramatic play activities. These could include a variety of sizes, materials, expressions, and roles. Be careful not to have stereotypical figures—women nurses, men doctors, etc. Some can be miniature plastic figures that you can buy by the hundreds. Others can be wooden cutouts that stand up, pictures from magazines mounted on cardboard and covered with clear Contact paper, or miniature dolls. The human figures should represent various ethnic groups.

---

[1] Adapted with permission from Cheryl Foster, *Competency-Based Training Module #24: Dramatic Play,* Supplement 5, "Dramatic Play Kits or Prop Boxes." (Coolidge, AZ: CDA Training Program, Institute of Human Development, Central Arizona College, 1982), pp. 41-46.

Doctor

Tongue depressors, real stethoscope, Bandaids, cloth for bandages, gauze, red finger paint for blood, cotton balls, eyedroppers, play thermometer, stop watch, scale, height-weight chart, beds and dolls, paper and pencils, prescription pads, telephone, small suitcase or shelves for medical supplies, table, white or green shirts (to wear as doctor and nurse uniforms), hospital gown, stretcher or cot, white sheet.

Veterinarian

Stuffed animals, scale, dog/cat boxes, leash, cat/dog food dishes, other items from doctor list above.

Post Office/Mail Carrier

Index card file, stamp pads, rubber stamps, crayons, pencils, old Christmas seals, gummed labels, envelopes, money, mailbox made from a cardboard box painted to resemble a real mailbox (arch piece of cardboard over a carton with slot cut in carton), mailbags (large paper bags with "shoulder strap" attached or old shoulder strap purses), rubber bands, writing pads, small postal scale, mail carrier hat, mail center badge, counter or table, collection of junk mail.

Supermarket

Cash register (could be made from a box), play money, paper pads, pencils or crayons, paper, shopping bags, empty food cans and boxes, plastic fruits and vegetables, boxes for shoppers to use for their food.

Jewelry Store

Old jewelry, boxes, sales slips, pencils, bags, money, cash register.

Shoe Store

Shoes (in shoe boxes if possible), foot measure or ruler, bags, pencils, sales slips, money, cash register, shoe-shine kit with clear polish or rags. Children can arrange several chairs along one wall for customers with a smaller chair or stool facing them for the salesperson.

Office

Table and chair for desk, old typewriter, old adding machine or calculator, pencils, pencil holder, paper, stapler, wastebasket, rubber stamp and ink pad, telephone, brief case, paper clips, assortment of junk mail, discarded business forms of many types.

Train/Plane/Bus

Tickets (a roll of expired theater tickets or remaining sections of used plane tickets), paper punch, rubber stamp and ink pad, small chairs lined up to resemble mode of transportation, old small suitcases.

Restaurant

Table, chairs, tablecloths, napkins, dishes, silverware, trays, sales slips, pencils, menus (paste food pictures on pieces of paper), pictures of food or play food to serve to customers, uniforms, aprons.

Picnic

Blanket, picnic basket, dishes, food pictures, empty cans, or boxes).

Beach

Blankets or beach towels, sunglasses, empty suntan oil bottles, beach bags, umbrellas, beach toys.

Hairdresser	Mirror, rollers or curlers, hairpins, hairnets, hair dryer and curling iron without cords, aprons or large bibs, towels, empty shampoo bottles (plastic), basin, easy-to-wash brushes, clean wide-toothed combs, small hand mirrors, bobby pins and hair clips, scarves, headbands, barrettes, wigs mounted on wig stands, manicure set, emery boards, magazines, pencil, paper, money.
Barber Shop	Old-fashioned shaving soap in a jar, shaving brush, toy plastic razor or real non-disposable razor without a blade, stand-up mirror, paper towels, plastic "barber clothes" to place around shoulders while "shaving."
Birthday Party	Hat box as cake, small boxes wrapped with paper and ribbon as gifts birthday candles, table, chairs, dishes, birthday hats, party rollers, party horns.
Firefighter	Hats, raincoats, boots, short lengths of garden hose.
Farmer/Gardener	Shovel, rake, hoe, wheelbarrow, seeds, gardening gloves, hat.
Painter	Buckets, paint brushes and rollers to be used with water on a variety of indoor and outdoor surfaces, painters' caps.
Gas Station Attendant	Shirt, hat, tire pump, boxes for cars, short lengths of garden hose.
Automobile Repair Person	Used (and washed) motor parts (spark plugs, filters, carburetors, cable sets, gears, etc.), tools such as hammers, pliers, screw drivers, oil funnel, empty oil cans, flashlights, wiring, air pump, windshield wipers, key carrier and keys, rags, old shirts, gloves, automobile supply catalogues.
Forest Ranger/ Camper/Cowboy/ Cowgirl	Canteen, flashlight, rope, mosquito netting, canvas for tent, knapsack, food supplies, nature books, compasses, small logs, grill, binoculars, old saddle, hats, vests, and boots.
Astronaut/Space Play	Rocket or space capsule made from a large box, space helmets made from empty ice cream containers, broken computer for space panel, homemade telescope, boots, headphones, camera, walkie-talkie, plastic tubing, silver garden gloves.

Creating and Using a Prop Box

Think about what kind of prop box would be interesting to the children in your care. Your imagination, what you know about the community, and what you know about the children's interests will help you think of ideas. Use the space below to list the items you collect.

Theme: _____

Items collected:

_____

_____

_____

_____

Next, decide how you want to introduce the new theme and the prop box. Try it out for a few days and complete the following.

How you introduced the prop box:

_____

_____

_____

_____

Results:

_____

_____

_____

_____

What (if anything) you would do differently next time:

_____

_____

_____

_____

Share your experiences with your trainer and discuss what other prop boxes you might make. Parents can be a big help in collecting props. Develop a plan with your trainer to start collecting items for two other prop boxes. You can use the form on the next page to help you plan.

Plan for Prop Boxes

Theme: _____   _____

Items to Collect

Items to Collect

LEARNING ACTIVITIES

III. Encouraging Children's Play

In this activity you will learn:

- to observe how children acquire concepts and skills through play; and

- to provide guidance as children play in order to promote their social development.

Play is a child's work, and it helps children develop in all areas. As they play, children have fun, try new things, make friends, pretend, and learn about the world. Through play, children develop physically, learn how to think and solve problems, find ways to express themselves in acceptable ways, and develop self-esteem. Play is also one of the most important ways in which children develop social skills. They learn to take turns, share favorite things, understand how a friend is feeling, and express their own feelings. In addition, play helps children try out grown-up roles and overcome their fears.

Infants' Play

Children begin playing during infancy, when playing and learning go hand in hand. For an infant, play can be almost anything—smiling back at a provider, kicking a mobile, crawling over a big pillow, beating a pan with a spoon, or reaching out and touching an older child's pigtail. Throughout the day there are numerous natural opportunities for play. Dressing an infant can be the perfect time to point out different body parts: "Where's Bobby's nose? Here it is!" An infant crawling across the room may find a bell to ring, another child to stop and touch, and a ball to bump and send rolling. One day Sarah (6 months) may discover her toes and find that playing with them is a lot of fun.

At times during the day, you can do special activities with one or more infants. You might sit on the floor with a child and roll a ball back and forth, or you might introduce a game such as Can You Do What I Do? to help a child become more aware of what other people are doing. Both planned and unplanned play times can be valuable opportunities for fostering an infant's social development.

As infants grow, they develop new social skills that influence how they play. For example, from a very young age, infants respond to Peek-a-Boo games that adults initiate. It doesn't take long for them to learn to keep a game going by peeking out from behind the doorway one more time. And in their second year of life, they may

169

learn how to begin the game by ducking behind the door or covering their faces with their blankets. Being able to take turns and knowing how to begin a game are skills that infants need for the more complex play of their toddler and preschool years.

Older infants are keen observers and enjoy imitating adults and pretending. By the time a child is about 18 months old, he or she has learned to pretend in more complex ways, such as pretending to feed a doll or put it to bed, just like a real baby.

Toddlers' Play

Toddlers spend their days playing alone, next to other children, occasionally with one another or with older children, and with providers. The more opportunities they have to interact with others, the more complex and positive their interactions become. Through play, toddlers learn about themselves, other people, and the world. They develop skills that they will use in more complex play when they are older.

You may observe that toddlers find the other children in your care very interesting. The presence of other children encourages toddlers to explore. A bell ringing in the hand of another child is much more interesting than a bell lying still on the shelf. The motion, the sound, and, most important, the fact that another child is making something happen all spark the toddler's interest.

Toddlers spend a lot of time doing the same things over and over again. This is how they learn to master a skill. A toddler may play alone with toys that are different from those used by others in the group. Although other children may be nearby, a toddler may not talk to them or move toward them. This kind of play is called solitary play. As children get older, they begin playing alongside each other using the same kinds of toys. This is called parallel play, and it may involve some talking between two children. For example, when Emily (32 months) and Eric (28 months) sit at opposite ends of a sand box, both using shovels, and chatting with one another, they are involved in parallel play. They are enjoying each other's company but are not yet ready to engage in cooperative play, such as building a home in the sand together.

Preschool Children's Play

Most preschool children play in groups cooperatively. The children organize their own play, assign roles, make up rules, give out specific tasks, and often work toward a common goal. For example, several children may decide to build a town with the blocks. Through discussion and negotiation, they decide who will build roads, who will build houses, and who will build stores. They resolve any conflicts that come up by finding a compromise that everyone agrees on. The result, a complete town and the process of working on it together, is more rewarding for the children than building independently. Children at this level of play really enjoy working and playing together. Liking to be with other people is an important part of their social development.

Preschool children enjoy dramatic play—pretending to be real or make-believe characters and making up stories and situations to act out. Dramatic play occurs in the backyard, while playing house, during block play, or on a neighborhood walk. Through dramatic play, children learn to share, listen to each other, take turns, compromise, and see somebody else's point of view. They can learn to control how they express their own feelings and emotions. They can try out being mean and nasty because it doesn't really count; it's only pretend. They can also overcome fears, such as the fear of going to the dentist or doctor or of moving to a new house.

What preschool children do during dramatic play differs according to their age and stage of development. Three-year-olds may not really understand that they are consciously deciding to pretend. They may spend a lot of time expressing fear, running away from monsters or another child who is pretending to be a scary creature. At this age children do a lot of collecting and gathering, packing suitcases, filling purses, planning trips. Sometimes the planning is all they have time for.

Four-year-olds may also run away from scary monsters or ghosts. They often create a safe place to hide out where the monster can't get them. They run and jump a lot, enjoy dress-up clothes and other props, and develop more roles than they did when they were younger. Now they can tell the difference between fantasy and reality. They understand that they have *decided* to pretend to be someone or do something.

The dramatic play of 5-year-old children is more involved. They develop complex sets of characters and situations and may pretend to be real people or fantasy figures from stories or television. Children this age may use dramatic play to practice doing something they are afraid of, such as getting a shot at the doctor or going on an airplane trip. They also may use dramatic play to work through anxieties about situations in their lives, such as a new baby at home or a parent about to go on a business trip.

Dramatic play is an important way for preschool children to learn how to get along with their peers. Playing with each other, they share information, offer suggestions, and sometimes tell each other how to behave. Children who are naturally shy may find that it is easier to be a part of a group when they can pretend to be someone else. The social skills developed through dramatic play are used in almost all the other situations a child encounters. The child who learns to follow the rules established by the group will be able to use this skill when he or she gets older and plays organized games that involve rules.

School-Age Children's Play

School-age children come to your home after a full day of school where most of their activities are planned and controlled by adults. Your home needs to be a place where they can relax, be themselves, make their own decisions, do things with the other children, and do things by themselves. Their play may include using their imaginations, organizing and leading the younger children, exploring special interests, making collections, playing board games, doing puzzles, working on crafts, or listening to music.

Many school-age children enjoy planning and putting on their own plays and shows. They will put the dress-up clothes and dramatic play props to good use. The older children may involve the younger ones, or they may put together a show that they will perform for the rest of the group. Writing a script, providing background music, and creating elaborate costumes can all be part of their dramatic play. Such projects may last from an afternoon to several weeks.

Depending on a child's temperament, he or she may enjoy playing board games with a friend. Some school-age children just enjoy the game, while others are driven to win. They may fight over the rules, and they may have difficulty accepting when they lose. An FCC provider can help children work through their disagreements and can provide cooperative games that don't lead to winners or losers.

School-age children will probably arrive at your FCC home with a lot of energy. After a long day at school, they are ready to use their bodies actively. They don't necessarily need to participate in organized sports. Children will enjoy playing hopscotch, jumping rope, playing catch, doing handstands, riding bikes, and so on. They may engage in physical activities with a friend, or they may choose to play alone.

Encouraging Children's Play

Providers play an important role in helping children play. By observing children's play, you can see which children get along with one another and what problems or anxieties different children are experiencing. You then can use this information to plan for children's individual needs. Observation also lets you know what is going on in the play situation and when your guidance is needed. You can provide a suitable prop that may help a child get involved in the play: "Kia, here is some money to give the storekeeper. I think he has run out of change." When it's almost time for lunch and the play must stop for a while, you can use reminders within the context of the play setting: "The baby needs to finish her bottle now so Daddy can have his lunch."

Try these suggestions.

The following ideas can be used to encourage and extend children's play.

- Let the children know that you think their play is important by providing, in an organized environment, enough time, space, and materials for the play.

- Refer to children in their role names. "Doctor, could you move your patient over here? Your examining table is in the way of the construction crew."

- Help children think about something they did in the past that they might want to recreate. "Do you remember last week when you went on the trip to the beach? You all had a lot of fun."

- Model playful behaviors yourself. "I could smell your bread baking from way over by the easel."

- Help children get started playing, but learn when to step back. "I really enjoyed my dinner, but I have to run to get my bus."

- When you do have to interrupt to remind children about a rule, try to offer guidance within the context of the play. "I think this grocery store can only hold two customers. Susan, can you and Tony take a walk around the block until these customers are finished with their shopping?"

- Reinforce positive social behaviors when you observe them. "I liked the way the two campers took turns wearing the backpack."

- Include school-age children in activities you have planned for the younger ones and give them responsibilities that help them develop leadership skills. "Bobby, can you please fill the buckets with water and put them on the grass? Gina will bring out the soap to add to the water, and we can all blow bubbles in the yard."

In this activity you will observe the dramatic play of several children in your care for at least a half-hour during free play (indoors or outdoors) and write a short description of the dramatic play that occurs: what children and make-believe characters were involved, the setting, and what activities took place. You will also record examples of what social skills children were developing or using during their play. Then, after reviewing your notes, you will develop a plan for what you can do to extend the children's play. This might include a way to involve a child who was excluded, props you can add, or words you can use to comment on the play. Finally, you will implement your plan and record what happens.

Read the example that follows. It is a summary of a complete half-hour observation. Then complete your own observations using the forms that follow.

Observation Summary: Encouraging Children's Play
(Example)

Location of play: *Dining room (a tent has been set up here)*

Dramatic play setting: *Camping out*   **Date:**   *February 11-14*

Children/Ages: *Tanya (4 years), George (6 years), Danny (34 months), Erin (16 months)*

Props used:

Tent (made out of a sheet draped over the table), two flashlights, backpack, thermos and cooler, plastic plates and utensils, two sleeping bags, tablecloth, books about outdoor plants and animals.

What happened:

Tanya and George were already playing when Danny came over. They told Danny they were going to play camping out. George said he would be the daddy and Tanya should be the mommy. Tanya said that was okay. Danny said he wanted to be the daddy. George told him he could be the daddy's best friend, and he could have a flashlight to use. Danny said okay.

Erin toddled over to the other children. She pulled herself up on the table. This made the sheet fall down on one side. (I waited to see how the others would handle the situation.) George and Tanya fixed the sheet. Then they gave Erin some plates and cups to play with. George put on the backpack and told Danny to pick up the thermos and cooler. Tanya told Erin to get a bag from the dress-up clothes rack. After Erin came back, Tanya asked her to help her fill it with the plates, utensils, and a tablecloth. George lined everyone up and they walked around the room and back to the tent. Erin toddled after them. She stopped in front of the shelf and pulled off a book.

When the other children got back to the tent, George said they should go to sleep. He and Danny put the sleeping bags in the tent. They all wanted to lie down right away. Tanya got in first, then Danny. There wasn't a sleeping bag for George. Tanya said she was hot so George could have hers. George told the children they had to go to sleep now.

Tanya came out of the tent. Danny came out too. The two children decided to set up a picnic. They spread the tablecloth out on the floor. Erin came over to the tablecloth.

Examples of social skills demonstrated:

There was a lot of give and take as they worked out who would play which role.

George acted as a negotiator, suggesting a role for Danny and offering a flashlight.

Tanya and George put the tent back together after Erin knocked the sheet off the table.

Tanya gave Erin some plates and utensils to play with.

Tanya had Erin get the bag and help her fill it.

Tanya gave her sleeping bag to George.

They all shared the props.

Tanya and Danny figured out another way to continue their play when they didn't want to do what George told them to do.

Ways to extend the play:

The children didn't use the books about the outdoors. I could say to them, "I saw a lot of interesting plants out in the woods. I wonder if there are pictures of those plants in these books?"

I could add some more props so the children could have a pretend fire to cook their food on. I will add some sticks and some pots and pans.

I can read a story about sleeping out of doors. "Three Days on a River in a Red Canoe" by Vera Williams would be good, or "Sleep Out" by Carol Currick.

What happened:

The children still aren't interested in the books. I will put the books on the shelf and use them when we go on a walk.

They used all the cooking props I added. All the children enjoyed them.

They continued to take turns in the tent.

I read the stories. The next day I saw Tanya and Danny pretending to go canoeing in the wagon.

Encouraging Children's Play

Location of play: _____

Dramatic play setting: _____ **Date:** _____

Children/ages: _____

Props used: _____

_____

_____

_____

_____

What happened:

_____

_____

_____

_____

_____

_____

_____

_____

_____

_____

Examples of social skills demonstrated:

_____

_____

_____

_____

_____

_____

_____

Review your observation notes and write down some ways in which you can extend the children's play. Implement your plans and record what happens.

Ways to extend the play:

_____

_____

_____

_____

_____

_____

_____

_____

_____

_____

What happened:

_____

_____

_____

_____

_____

_____

_____

_____

_____

_____

_____

_____

_____

_____

_____

_____

Discuss this activity with your trainer.

LEARNING ACTIVITIES

IV. Helping Children Learn Caring Behaviors

In this activity you will learn:

- to recognize children's caring behaviors; and

- to help children develop caring behaviors.

Caring behaviors develop throughout childhood.

Children develop caring behaviors over a long period of time. Some infants demonstrate caring behaviors very early in life. They get upset and cry when they hear another infant crying. Between the ages of 1 and 2, children begin to show real concern for others. When this concern is recognized and reinforced by parents and providers, children continue to develop caring behaviors. Between the ages of 2 and 6, children begin to develop skills in responding appropriately to the needs and feelings of others. By the time they enter the upper elementary grades, children are aware of and show concern about events affecting people outside their families and communities.

As they learn to get along with others, children are also learning caring behaviors. The most direct way in which children learn such behaviors is by watching the behaviors of adults and older children. During a typical day you might help Sean (2 years) find a lost sock, applaud Denise (4 years) when she finishes a difficult puzzle, congratulate Lisa (8 years) when she masters doing a handstand, and let each child know how much he or she is valued. In so doing, you are helping children learn to demonstrate positive feelings toward others. Your dependable and responsive interactions help children feel secure. In turn, this security allows a child to show concern for others and to be a cooperative member of the group.

Prosocial behaviors are valued by society.

Caring behaviors are sometimes called "prosocial" behaviors. They include social skills such as sharing and taking turns as well as behaviors such as the following:[2]

- **Showing empathy**

    Feeling and acting concerned when another person is upset or hurt.

    Sharing another person's happiness or excitement.

---

[2] Based on Janice J. Beaty, *Observing Development of the Young Child* (Columbus, OH: Charles E. Merrill, 1986), p. 111.

- **Showing generosity**

  Giving a toy or other possession to another person.
  Sharing a snack or toy with another person.

- **Helping**

  Helping another person do a job.
  Helping when another person needs assistance.

One can think of caring behaviors as examples of the "golden rule." People who behave toward others as they would like others to behave toward them are using caring behaviors. Providers model these kinds of behaviors in their relationships with children and with other adults. They also help children learn caring behaviors by letting them know that prosocial behaviors are valued by society.

Try these suggestions.

Some techniques to encourage prosocial behaviors in children follow:

- **Respond to a child's crying or request for help promptly.** Children learn how to treat others by imitating how they are treated. "Sofia (12 months), I heard you crying. Would you like me to hold your hand as you walk around the yard?"

- **Develop a loving and nurturing relationship with each child in your care.** Find time every day to spend some time alone with each child. When Ari (9 years) tells you in the morning that he is worried about his math test, be sure to remember to ask him about the test after school.

- **Encourage and acknowledge cooperation and thoughtfulness.** Barry (16 months) can hold out his arm so you can put it through a sleeve, Ben (34 months) can help Tim (20 months) peel his orange at lunch, and Julianna (9 years) can close the door after everyone comes in from outside.

- **Plan group activities that involve thoughtfulness and emphasize a sense of community.** "Teresa's mom called last night to tell me that Teresa has the chicken pox. We can make some get-well cards to let her know we miss her and hope she feels better."

- **Use each child's name often.** Call children by their given names when you talk with them. Practice pronouncing each name the way it is pronounced by the family. Hang pictures of children and families on the wall at child's eye level, and talk about who is who. Label the children's artwork and the shoeboxes where they keep their belongings. Sing songs with children's names in them, and use other techniques to encourage children to call each other by name.

- **Show respect for children as human beings.** Alert an infant before you pick him up: "Tommy, I'm going to pick you up now so I can change your diaper." Acknowledge what children say even when they can't have or do what they want: "I heard you ask for another cookie. You've had two cookies already, and that's all you can have today. If you are hungry, you can have an apple or some carrot sticks."

- **Give the children cooperative play ideas.** Provide activities that call for cooperation, such as moving a heavy chair, putting together a large jigsaw puzzle, folding a blanket, or creating a mural.

- **Give children opportunities to help you and other children.** Ask Fred (7 years) to bring you 4-month-old Lisa's blanket from across the room. Thank him for helping you and Lisa. Let children help you do "real work." They will enjoy helping you carry the easel outside or carrying the picnic bag to the park.

- **Help children express prosocial feelings**. "You can tell Carlos you were sad because he wasn't here yesterday."

- **Share your excitement and pleasure about things children do.** Take time to notice their creations and congratulate them on their successes. Stop to watch Sarah (9 months) pull herself up to standing, or Travis (29 months), who is learning how to pedal the tricycle.

- **Take pictures of the children on special occasions and throughout the year**. Put the pictures in small albums so children can handle them without your assistance. They will enjoy reliving fun times and talking about what they did together.

- **Make and read books with themes of helpfulness and friendship.** You might write and illustrate a book about the day Jeremy shared his cheese or when Kim helped Larry find his lost mitten. Ask open-ended questions about the stories. Let the children know that you value these kinds of behaviors.

- **Talk about exciting things that have happened to the children and providers.** When a child has had a happy experience, share that pleasure by giving out hugs or handshakes. "Tim, I know you are happy that you baked such a beautiful loaf of bread. Can I give you a hug?"

- **Help children learn how to talk about their feelings**. "When you are worried about something, you can talk to me about it. It's okay to have worries. I will listen carefully, and I won't make fun of you."

Prosocial behaviors are not learned quickly; providers need to be patient as children take their time in learning the skills of negotiation, sharing, and cooperation. It is natural for young children to put their own needs first. When these needs are met, they will gradually learn to think about the needs of others.

This learning activity has three parts. First you will observe the children in your care and record examples of how they use prosocial behaviors. Next you will note some examples of how you demonstrate and promote children's caring behaviors. Then you will make a book about some of the children's caring behaviors and read it with the children. Older children can help make the book. First read the examples that follow. Then use the blank forms that follow to record your examples.

Observation Summary: Caring Behaviors
(Example)

Child(ren)/age(s)	Caring Behavior
Bonita (3-1/2 years) *Susan (6 years)*	*Bonita fell down outside. Susan put her arm around her and helped her get up. Then Susan got me to come help. I said to Susan, "That was very nice of you to help Bonita. You are a thoughtful friend."*
Martin (9 months)	*Martin looked up when he heard laughing. He smiled and clapped his hands.*
Kent (4 years)	*Kent found a shiny rock outside and gave it to Tamila.*
Maddie (18 months)	*Maddie picked up a sponge and helped me wipe off the table.*
Dean (8 years)	*Dean saw Susan trying to get the wagon out of the shed. He went over to help her get it out.*

How You Demonstrate and Promote Caring Behaviors

(Example)

1. *Martin grabbed for his toes while I changed his diaper. I laughed with him and played "This Little Piggy."*

2. *I bumped my knee hard and said "Ouch!" Maddie came over as I was rubbing it. I said, "Can you help me rub it?" and she did.*

3. *I was folding the laundry and asked the children if they would like to help. Kent and Susan made a game out of matching the socks. Martin put the clothes on his head. We all laughed together.*

4. *Dean saw that Susan was having a hard time spreading peanut butter on her cracker. He offered to hold the jar for her. Susan smiled and nodded. Later on I said to Dean, "I think Susan really appreciated your help."*

5. *When Maddie's mom came at the end of the day, I asked her how her day was. Then I loaned her a book that she'd mentioned that she wanted to read.*

A Book About Caring Behaviors

(Example)

Write and illustrate a book about how the children use caring behaviors. You can use photographs, pictures from magazines, or your own illustrations. Some of the children may want to help you write and illustrate the book.

Describe your book below.

We wrote a book about the fun we had folding laundry together. Dean wrote down the words for us. Susan, Dean, and Kent drew pictures that we pasted in the book. Then we pasted the words and pictures on some cardboard that Kent's father had given us. We used some clear Contact paper to protect the cover. Then we punched holes in each page and laced it together with thick yarn.

Read the book to the children and describe their responses.

Martin and Maddie liked hearing their names. At the end of the story the older children asked to hear it again. I needed to change Martin's diaper so Susan said she would read the story. Dean said he would help her read his writing.

Observation Summary: Caring Behaviors

Child(ren)/age(s)	Caring Behavior

How You Demonstrate and Promote Caring Behaviors

A Book About Caring Behaviors

Write and illustrate a book about how the children in your care use caring behaviors. You can use photographs, pictures from magazines, or your own illustrations. Some of the children may want to help you write and illustrate the book.

Describe your book below.

_____
_____
_____
_____
_____
_____
_____
_____
_____
_____
_____

Read the book to the children and describe their responses.

_____
_____
_____
_____
_____
_____
_____
_____
_____
_____
_____
_____
_____

Discuss this activity with your trainer. Also, discuss caring behaviors with the children's parents.

V. Helping Children Relate Positively to Others

In this activity you will learn:

- to tell when a child needs your help to make friends; and

- to help individual children develop friendship-making skills.

Every young child needs a friend.

It is very important for providers to work with individual children to help them learn how to make friends. Every young child needs to have at least one friend to talk to, play with, disagree with, make up with, and care for. Some children seem to develop and use their social skills with ease. They are naturally outgoing and seem to know instinctively how to make friends and find their place in their group. They get a lot of pleasure from being with other children. Other children may take longer to get used to a group, but once they feel comfortable, they are able to join in and make friends.

Children who are not able to make friends and who continue to feel rejected are likely to have serious problems later in life. Such children often have low self-esteem and lack the social skills they need to develop friendships. They feel unloved. Because they aren't accepted by their peers, they have fewer chances to develop social skills.

Most children who have trouble making friends fall into one of three categories. (These are very broad categories and should not be used to label children.) They are shy or withdrawn, overly aggressive, or rejected by the group. If you have a child like this in your care, you can make a big difference in that child's life by helping him or her to become accepted.

Helping Shy Children Make Friends

Almost every group of children includes one or two children who are very shy. Providers may feel empathy for these children and want to help them become a part of the group. Before offering assistance, however, providers need to observe to see if the child is just moving at a slower pace than others. The child may need to have some successes with solitary play—for example, completing a difficult puzzle—before progressing to group play. A shy child may also need to sit back and observe other children at play to learn how to become part of the group. The child may begin by playing with one or two children. Then, after becoming more skilled, he or she will move on to playing with a larger group of children.

There are some shy children, however, who will need your intervention and help. You can offer this help in indirect ways without making it obvious to anyone else that the help is being offered. Saying things such as "be nice to Billy" or "can you let Mary play, too?" isn't helpful. These remarks tend to make the shy child feel self-conscious or embarrassed. The other children may go along with your suggestions for a time, but the shy child will not develop the social skills to cope when you are not there to intervene directly.

Try these suggestions.[3]

The following are suggestions for helping a shy child develop social skills.

- **Observe, observe, observe.** Watch what the child does and says, who the child talks to, and who the child watches. When the child is playing alone with blocks, is he or she building with concentrated attention or also watching the firefighters across the room? Observe to find out what the child likes to do, where his or her favorite places are, whether the child behaves differently outside, and what skills the child has.

- **Establish a connection with the child.** Use your observations to help you talk with the child. "I see you are watching John and Pam playing with the water." If the child responds positively, you can ask a question to extend the conversation. "Do you think John's cup will hold more water than Pam's? Perhaps you can do some water play tomorrow and figure out the answer." You might also comment on what the child is doing. "I see you are building with the table blocks." Such comments help the child feel more secure because he or she knows that the provider is paying attention.

- **Be playful with the child.** Encourage the child to express his or her ideas and feelings. "Jason, you seemed to really enjoy that story. What do you like to do on snowy days?"

- **Use what you know about the child's interests to create special situations.** For example, if you know that Holly really likes to cook, plan a cooking activity that involves several children working together. Include Holly when you conduct the activity, and ask her lots of open-ended questions to get her involved.

- **Help children find good friends.** Just as there might be a shy child in your care, there are probably several children who are very competent and sensitive socially. Try asking one of these children and the shy child to help you do a task. "Dean, could

[3] Adapted from Dennie Palmer Wolf, ed., *Connecting: Friendship in the Lives of Young Children and Their Teachers* (Redmond, WA: Exchange Press, 1986), pp. 58-62.

you please help Tommy and me carry the toys outside?" Or let both children know about an activity that you know both would be interested in. "Dean and Tommy, I know you both like woodworking. When you come home from school today you can get out the tools. I think there's enough room at the workbench for two children to build."

- **Help the shy child understand his or her feelings of shyness.** "It's okay to want to play alone when you don't know the other children too well. After a while you'll feel more comfortable and be ready to play with Carlos, Maddie, and the others."

Helping Aggressive Children Make Friends

In any group of children there may be one or two who are not able to control their behaviors. They use aggression as a means to express their unhappiness or to get their own way. These children do not know how to take turns, negotiate, or cooperate with others. They have not learned how to meet their own needs and those of the group. Because they are overly aggressive, other children do not want to include them in their play.

Providers also may have trouble relating to overly aggressive children. It is natural to want to avoid a child who frequently hurts other children or uses force to make others let him or her into the group. But because providers are professionals, they must learn to overcome their negative feelings about an aggressive child. It may help to remember that the children who hit or bully other children are troubled or in pain, emotionally. They feel unhappy or insecure, and they need their providers' help to learn positive ways of relating to other children. These children must feel safe and cared for before they can develop self-esteem and the social skills to make friends and play with other children.

Try these suggestions.

The following are some techniques that providers can use to help aggressive children:

- **Help the child understand the consequences of his or her actions.** "I think you want to play with Crystal and Susan. But when you knock their tower down, it makes them angry. It doesn't make them want to play with you."

- **Try to redirect a child's angry energy.** "Shawn, I know you are angry, but you may not hit Bonita. Use your hands to throw this ball at the wall."

- **Identify a challenging physical activity that the child really enjoys.** Set it up so several children can participate. "Denise, you're a great jumper. Use this chalk to mark how far you and Lloyd can jump. You can take turns jumping."

- **Spend time alone with the child but not immediately after the child has been aggressive.** "David, let's spend some time talking together. I'd like to hear some more about what you're doing for your science project."

- **Sit with the child and observe the other children at play.** Interpret what they are doing so the child can begin to understand how others use social skills. "Will just came over to the sandbox where Tamila and Renee are being mothers baking cakes. I think he wants to play with them. Will is making a cake to share with them. He's pretending to be a neighbor."

- **Help the child develop ways to achieve his or her goals without using aggression.** "I know you are very hungry and want to get your snack. Ask Shawn to move his things off the table so you can sit down and eat."

- **Use the child's positive characteristics to help him or her be accepted by the group.** "Chaundra collected some beautiful leaves on our walk. Let's put them on the table where everyone can see them."

Helping Rejected Children Make Friends

There are children in every group who are neither aggressive nor shy yet are still excluded from play. These children, who may be loud, clumsy, or bossy, do not know how to get involved with their peers. They may play with the blocks for a while, get up and move to the easel, try to join in with the children playing house, and then go back to the blocks. They seem to be unaware of the effects of their behavior. These children seem to want to play with others, but because they are not able to understand what the other children are playing, they don't know how to get involved. You may hear a lot of complaints about these children. "She's always butting in." "He talks too loud." "He knocked our buildings over."

Many of the techniques for helping shy or aggressive children are also effective for helping the rejected child. Often these children have some social skills but may not know how to use them. Observe these children to find out who in the group does accept them; then find ways to include them in projects with another child.

Try these suggestions.[4]

Providers can try these techniques for helping rejected children make friends.

- **Teach the child how to ask questions to find out what a group of children are playing.** "What are you playing?" "Who are you pretending to be?" "What are you building?"

- **Suggest that the child watch and listen to find out what the other children are playing before trying to play with them.** "Delores, if you sit here and watch Bonita and Tim play, I'll bet you can guess what they're doing. Which one do you think is the puppy?"

- **Encourage the child to discuss his or her feelings about being rejected.** "You look sad, Cynthia. Can you tell me what happened?" Telling what happened may help the child understand why he or she was rejected by the other children.

- **Coach the child on how to join and have fun doing what the other children are doing.** To a child who takes too long going down the slide (which annoys the other children), a provider could say, "Felipe, when it's your turn, slide down quickly. Then the others can have their turns. Very soon it will be your turn again. Everyone will have fun."

- **Help children state rules or the accepted behaviors of the group as a way to justify their attempts to be included.** "I'd like to play, too. There are only two people in the sandbox, so there's room for me to play there, too."

In this activity you will assist a child in your care who needs help learning to make friends. Observe this child for five minutes at several different times of the day. Review your notes and summarize your thoughts about the child. Use this new information and the suggestions in this learning activity to plan ways to help the child play with others. Implement your plan over the next two weeks and record what happens. Begin by reading the example on the next page.

---

[4] Based on Dwight L. Rogers and Dorene Doerre Ross, "Encouraging Positive Social Interaction Among Young Children," *Young Children* (Washington, DC: National Association for the Education of Young Children, March 1986), pp. 15-16.

Observation Summary:
Helping Individual Children Relate to Others
(Example)

Child: _Alex_   **Age:** _4 years 3 months_   **Date:** _March 10-11_

Observation Notes	Summary
Time: *5:35 PM* *Alex is with the other children, listening to my daughter Tracy read a story. He is sitting at the edge of the group. The door bell rings. The door opens and he turns to see who comes in. It's Toan's mom. My husband greets her. Alex follows Toan as he gets his coat and some things from his basket. Darnelle and Tracy say good-bye to Toan. Alex walks back to the group. He says, "I don't like this story."*	*Alex seems to want his dad to come. He is easily distracted. Perhaps he wants to go. He doesn't notice that the other children want to hear the story.*
Time: *7:20 AM* *Alex comes in with his father. He smiles. His father says, "Say hello, Alex." Alex says hello in a loud voice. Kara and Donny turn and look at him. I ask Alex what he would like to do. "Blocks," he says. Kara and Donny are playing too, building a tall tower. Alex builds beside them. Kara says, "Hey, we need all the blocks." Alex knocks his own building down. He gets up and goes to get a puzzle from the shelf.*	*If Alex knew how to join in with the block building group, he might have enjoyed it.*
Time: *10:45 AM* *Alex is helping serve snack. He carries a tray of cut-up fruit to the table. He puts the tray down, then stands behind the table. He smiles. When all the children have their fruit, Alex takes his. He sits down next to Maddie. She says, "I don't like bananas. Do you want mine?" Alex smiles and takes them. He says, "I like bananas but I don't like grapes." Maddie says, "Can I have them?" Alex agrees and lets her reach over and take them.*	*Alex seems to like Maddie. He let her have his grapes. He seemed to feel good about helping, too.*

Plan:

I will tell Alex that I know it's hard to wait for his parents at the end of the day. I will ask him if there is something he would like to do instead of listening to the story. I will explain that the other children do want to hear the story.

When I see Alex watching other children playing, I'll point out to him how the children are working and playing together—for example, "Kara just gave Donny that block because he needed one that size for his part of the road."

I'll try to set up some times when Alex and Maddie can play together or help me with something. They both like it when we paint outside. I'll ask them to help carry the easel outside one day next week.

Results (after two weeks):

Alex helps me clean up at the end of the day. It helps keep him busy so he doesn't watch the door as often.

Alex joined in with the water play today. He held the funnel while Tony poured.

Alex and Maddie painted outside. She is very talkative, so she kept the conversation going. Later in the week they rode tricycles together.

Observation Summary:
Helping Individual Children Relate to Others

Child: _____ Age: _____ Date: _____

Observation Notes	Summary
Time: _____	
Time: _____	

Observation Notes	Summary
Time: _____	
Time: _____	

Review your observation notes and summaries as well as the suggestions you've read. Develop a plan for helping this child. Implement your plan over the next two weeks, then record the results.

Plan:

_____

_____

_____

_____

_____

_____

_____

_____

_____

_____

Results (after two weeks):

_____

_____

_____

_____

_____

_____

_____

_____

_____

_____

_____

Talk to your trainer about how you helped this child.

SUMMARIZING YOUR PROGRESS

You have now completed all of the learning activities for this module. Whether you are an experienced FCC provider or a new one, this module probably has helped you develop new skills for promoting children's social development. Take a few minutes to review your responses to the pre-training assessment for this module. Write a summary of what you learned, and list the skills you developed or improved.

Discuss your response to this section with your trainer. If there are topics you would like to know more about, you will find recommended readings listed in the Introduction in Volume I.

Your final step in this module is to complete the knowledge and competency assessments. Let your trainer know when you are ready to schedule the assessments. After you have successfully completed these assessments, you will be ready to start a new module. Congratulations on your progress so far, and good luck with your next module.

ANSWER SHEETS

Promoting Children's Social Development

Helping Children Learn to Get Along with Others

1. **How did Ms. Waxler help the girls learn to get along with each other?**

   a. She gave them an indirect suggestion when she told them about a restaurant that had two waitresses.

   b. She stepped back to let them use their social skills to make their own decisions.

2. **How did Ms. Waxler help the girls feel good about solving their problem?**

   a. She praised them for solving their problem.

   b. She left them alone so they could continue playing.

Helping Children Understand and Express Their Feelings and Respect Those of Others

1. **How did Ms. Brown let the children know that she understood and respected their feelings?**

   a. She told the children what she thought they might be feeling.

   b. She told the children that she couldn't let them push each other.

2. **How did Ms. Brown help the children express their feelings?**

   a. She told the children to use their words.

   b. She stepped back so the children could work things out for themselves.

Providing an Environment and Experiences That Help Children Develop Social Skills

1. **How did Ms. Sequoia turn the daily routine of getting ready for lunch into an experience that helped the children develop social skills?**

   a. She asked for some helpers to get the table ready for lunch.

   b. She acknowledged Leroy's feelings about being "big" and Melissa's feelings about wanting to help.

   c. She told the children that the table looked "great."

2. **What social skills did the children learn as they got the table ready for lunch?**

   a. They learned to work together and help each other.

   b. They learned to feel good about themselves because Ms. Sequoia told them they were doing a good job and thanked them for their help.

GLOSSARY

Cooperative play
The type of play that typically begins in the preschool years. Children play together in a group that they organize and control. The group has a specific purpose, such as making something, playing a game, or acting out a real-life or fantasy situation.

Parallel play
Play that happens when 2- to 3-year-old children progress from solitary play to playing alone with other children nearby. Children use the same or similar kinds of toys or materials.

Peer
A friend or companion who is the same age or at the same developmental level.

Prosocial skills
Accepted behaviors, such as sharing or taking turns, which children learn and use to get along in society.

Social development
The gradual process through which children learn to get along with others and enjoy playing and living with others.

Solitary play
The first stage of play, when infants and young toddlers play alone, independent of other children. They use toys or materials that are the same as or different from those of other children in the group.

Module 10:
GUIDANCE

Guiding children's behavior involves:

- providing an environment that encourages self-discipline;

- using positive methods to guide individual children; and

- helping children understand and express their feelings in acceptable ways.

Children need adult guidance.

Children need adults to guide them—to help them learn what is acceptable and what is not, to help them learn to live cooperatively with others. How you as an adult offer this guidance depends on your goals for the children you care for. What kind of people do you want these children to become? Do you want them to behave out of fear or because they have learned what is acceptable and what is not?

There is a reason for all behavior. Children misbehave for many different reasons. They may be at a developmental stage where they need to test the limits of their own control. They may be forced into a schedule that conflicts with their natural rhythm. Their parents may have different rules and expectations than those at your FCC home, or there may be a school or family situation that is upsetting. Sometimes children behave inappropriately simply because they are bored, tired, curious, or frustrated.

There are reasons for children's behavior.

To help children learn self-discipline, FCC providers need to think about the reasons for children's behavior. For example, you may remove a child from the sandbox because she won't stop throwing sand. You also need to think about why the child was throwing sand. When you identify the need that the child was expressing, you can then try to meet that need. When you have to take something away (the opportunity to play in the sandbox), you must later replace it with what the child needs (perhaps some extra one-to-one attention).

Self-discipline is the ability to control one's own behavior. People who are self-disciplined make independent choices based on what they believe is right. They are able to balance their own needs with those of others. They can accept the results of their actions.

Positive guidance encourages self-discipline.

Adults who want children to learn to make their own decisions, to know the difference between right and wrong, to solve problems, and to correct their own mistakes have to provide positive guidance to help children develop self-discipline. This module is about guiding children's behavior in ways that assist them in developing self-discipline. FCC providers can help children gain self-discipline in many ways. Some actions, such as setting up safe places for running, can prevent certain behaviors. Others, such as redirecting children to climb on the climber rather than the table, are responses to children's behavior.

If you have developed a caring relationship with the children in your home, you are already doing a lot to help them achieve the goal of self-discipline. Children depend on you and want your approval. They look to you to help them learn what is acceptable and what is not. If you set limits that fit their developmental and individual needs, children will learn the limits more easily. If you are consistent in applying rules, children will try to follow them. If you set up an environment that supports self-control, children will find it easier to achieve this goal. And if you learn some techniques and words to use to guide children, you will help them develop self-discipline.

Listed below are examples of how FCC providers demonstrate their competence in guiding children's behavior.

Providing an Environment That Encourages Self-Discipline

Make sure there are no safety hazards. "Kristi, that was a good idea to store your toothpick sculpture in the top cabinet. It was too easy for the younger children to reach it on the low shelf."

Store toys and equipment on low, open shelves. "Sammy, please put the big blocks back on their shelf now. You can take them down again tomorrow."

Give children chances to make up rules. "Let's talk about some rules for taking care of our new guinea pig. After school today, we can ask Terry and Marcia to write them down on a big piece of cardboard. Then we'll hang up the rules where everyone can see them."

Prepare children for changes in advance. "In five minutes, it will be time to clean up and get ready for lunch. I'll set the timer so you'll know when the five minutes are over."

Arrange the materials and furniture to encourage appropriate behavior. "When Jan needs a quiet place to do homework, she sits at the table in the kitchen."

Plan child-initiated activities for most of the day. "Hi, Randy. After you tell me about your day at school, you can choose what you want to do this afternoon."

Treat children with politeness at all times so they will feel respected. "Terry, could you please help me by holding my bag for a minute? Thank you."

Using Positive Methods to Guide Individual Children

Prepare a written discipline policy to let parents know the positive guidance techniques to be used to help children develop self-discipline.

Allow children to learn from their experiences. "I'm sorry your shirt got wet, Andrew. Let's get a dry one to put on. What could you do differently next time so you'll stay dry during water play?"

Use logical consequences to help children be responsible for their actions. "Carla, there's a sponge by the sink you can use to clean up your spilled juice."

Redirect children to acceptable activities. "Susan's reading that book, Bobby. Pick another book to look at."

Securely hold a child who is screaming or thrashing. "Laura, I'm going to hold you close so you won't hurt yourself or anyone else. I will let you go when you are calm and ready."

Use simple, positive reminders to restate rules. "Please put your dirty dishes in the dishwasher, Jerry. Don't leave them on the table."

Know when ignoring inappropriate behavior is constructive. "Mr. Sanchez, some parents find that one of the best ways to get children to stop using curse words is to just ignore them. If you don't react to Eddie's words, he will soon stop using them to get your attention."

Assume the role of authority only when necessary—but do so firmly, so children learn to obey automatically at certain times. "Stay on the sidewalk, Chaundra. A car is coming."

Helping Children Understand and Express Their Feelings in Acceptable Ways

Make it easier to wait for a turn. "I know you feel angry because you think Marty has been riding the trike for too long. He said that after he goes around the yard one more time, you can have your turn."

Redirect an angry child to a soothing activity. "Jane, I can't let you hurt other people or things. I think you might have fun with the water play. We have some new turkey basters you can use."

Tell a child that you accept his or her feelings. "Tricia, I know you feel angry when Debby calls you names. Tell Debby you don't like it when she does that."

Use firm words and tones to help young children understand how someone else feels. "When you pull my hair it hurts me. If you want to play with hair, you can use the baby doll."

Model acceptable ways to express negative feelings. "Kevin, I've asked you three times to please use your inside voice. Your loud voice is giving me a headache."

Guiding Children's Behavior

In the following situations, FCC providers are guiding children's behavior in ways that help them develop self-discipline. As you read each situation, think about what the providers are doing and why. Then answer the questions that follow.

Providing an Environment that Encourages Self-Discipline

During nap time, Ms. Lee decides to call the local R&R agency for some advice. "I wish it were Friday," sighs Ms. Lee. "This has been a terrible week. It seems like the children are constantly fighting over the toys and just about destroying everything we have. I don't know what's the matter with them. And getting them to clean up is like pulling teeth." Ms. Richards, an R&R counselor, says, "I know what you mean. I've heard about that kind of fighting in other FCC homes. Suppose you set things up so sharing is less of a burden for the children. You could buy or borrow duplicates of the popular toys. Then you wouldn't have to spend so much of your time getting the children to share. And I think I have an idea that might help with the clean-up problem. You can make picture labels for the toys and materials, and you can tape them to the shelves and containers to show that everything has a specific place. Then clean-up will be more fun and challenging for the children." Ms. Lee agrees. "I'd like to try both of those ideas. Maybe I can control some of the behavior problems by changing the environment. That way I won't have to keep nagging the children."

1. **What behaviors did Ms. Lee find frustrating?**

   _____

   _____

   _____

2. **What suggestions did Ms. Richards have for dealing with the behavior problems?**

   _____

   _____

   _____

3. **How might these suggestions help?**

   _____

   _____

   _____

Using Positive Methods to Guide Individual Children

Ms. Kendall and the children are outside in the back yard. Travis, a very active 4-year-old, has collected some pine cones and is throwing them where the younger children are playing. Ms. Kendall pushes Laura in her stroller over to talk to him. She bends down, looks at him, and says, "Travis, you are learning to be a good thrower. But if you hit Josh or Sarah with a pine cone, they might be hurt or angry. They are too young to understand that you didn't mean to hit them. Where can you practice your throwing safely?" Travis looks around and answers, "Over near the garage." Ms. Kendall nods and says, "Yes, that's a good place. Josh and Sarah aren't playing there." Travis picks up his pine cones and walks over near the garage. Ms. Kendall watches for a few minutes, and then she and Laura go to play ball with the two toddlers.

1. **What did Ms. Kendall know about Travis?**

2. **How did Ms. Kendall let Travis know that she respected him?**

Helping Children Understand and Express Their Feelings in Acceptable Ways

Allie says, "I think I hear the school bus." "Me too," says Bradley. "The big kids are home." Allie and Bradley look at each other and smile. The two 4-year-olds hurry to the front door and wait for the "big kids" to arrive. Ten-year-old Donna and 8-year-old Carl come through the door. Carl goes in to the kitchen to put his school things away and to get his snack. Bradley tags along behind him, asking, "Will you play football with me? Please, please, please." As the two boys go in the kitchen, Allie asks Donna, "What did you do at school today?" "None of your business. Why are you always waiting for me? Don't you have anything else to do?" Donna pushes Allie out of her way just as Ms. Perez enters the front hall. Allie falls down and starts to cry. Ms. Perez gives her a hug, takes her in the living room, and helps her find something to play with. Then she goes back to talk to Donna. "Donna, usually you like Allie to greet you at the door. Today your words and your actions hurt her. When you're upset about something, you can come and talk to me about it. If I'm busy with one of the other children, I will talk with you as soon as I'm available." Donna looks at Ms. Perez and says in a sad voice, "I'm sorry I pushed Allie. My best friend wouldn't sit with me on the bus, and she really hurt my feelings. After I tell Allie I'm sorry, can we talk about it?" "I'll meet you in the kitchen," says Ms. Perez. "Let me say hello to Carl, then you and I can talk while you eat your snack."

1. **How did Ms. Perez help Donna learn to express her feelings in an acceptable way?**

_____

_____

_____

2. **When they meet in the kitchen, what do you think Ms. Perez could say to Donna?**

_____

_____

_____

Compare your answers with those on the answer sheet at the end of this module. If your answers are different, discuss them with your trainer. There can be more than one answer.

Your Own Self-Discipline

Your behavior is automatic.

You don't stop to think about everything you do; you just do it. When you put money in a parking meter, get up on time each morning, or thank a store clerk, you are probably acting without thinking about what you are doing. You have learned and accepted certain rules of behavior, and because you have self-discipline, you don't need to be reminded of them.

Self-discipline guides your behavior as an FCC provider.

- You let parents know in advance when you plan to take a vacation so they can find substitute care.

- You let a parent know you are angry with her by telling her what you feel.

- You volunteer to help a fellow provider who's having difficulty understanding the needs of a child.

List below a few examples of how self-discipline guides your behavior as a provider.

_____

_____

_____

_____

_____

Self-discipline also guides your behavior in other parts of your life.

- You remember to water the plants because you know they'll die if you don't.

- You clean the frying pan so it will be ready to use in the morning.

- You say no to a piece of cake because you are trying to lose weight.

List some examples of how self-discipline guides your behavior in other parts of your life.

_____

_____

_____

_____

Think of a time when you did not show self-discipline. What affected your loss of control?

_____

_____

_____

_____

_____

What does this tell you about what children need to gain self-discipline?

_____

_____

_____

_____

_____

Providers can model self-discipline.

Being in control of your own behavior usually results in enhanced self-esteem. Having good feelings about yourself will make you a more effective and skilled provider. Your self-discipline is a good model for the children. They will learn a lot from being cared for by a responsible and competent person.

When you have finished this overview section, you should complete the pre-training assessment. Refer to the glossary at the end of this module if you need definitions of the terms that are used.

PRE-TRAINING ASSESSMENT

Listed below are the skills that FCC providers use to guide children's behavior. Think about whether you do these things regularly, sometimes, or not enough. Place a check in one of the columns on the right for each skill listed. Then discuss your answers with your trainer.

Skill	I Do This Regularly	I Do This Sometimes	I Don't Do This Enough
Providing an Environment That Encourages Self-Discipline			
1. Providing a balanced daily schedule with time for both active and quiet play, indoors and outside.			
2. Providing a variety of materials and activities to meet children's needs and interests.			
3. Providing enough developmentally appropriate materials for the children, including duplicates of popular items.			
4. Involving children in setting limits and making rules.			
5. Making a place for everything with picture and word labels to show where things go.			
6. Keeping toys and other safe materials on low, open shelves so children can help themselves.			
7. Removing temptations and dangerous objects so children can safely play and explore.			
8. Providing a place for older children to store their toys and materials out of reach of the younger children.			

Skill	I Do This Regularly	I Do This Sometimes	I Don't Do This Enough
Using Positive Methods to Guide Individual Children			
9. Trying to understand why a child is misbehaving.			
10. Helping children use their problem-solving skills to resolve conflicts.			
11. Focusing on the child's behavior, not on the child.			
12. Stating directions and reminding children of rules in positive ways (e.g., "walk in the house").			
13. Reinforcing children's positive behavior with genuine praise.			
14. Giving children opportunities to make developmentally appropriate choices.			
Helping Children Understand and Express Their Feelings in Acceptable Ways			
15. Modeling appropriate ways to express negative feelings.			
16. Providing soothing activities (water play, playdough, or simple crafts) and redirecting children to them.			
17. Talking to school-age children about their day at school, their friends, their concerns, and so on.			
18. Reminding children to use words to tell others how they feel.			
19. Working with parents to help a child with a problem (such as hitting or sulking) express his or her feelings in acceptable ways.			

Review your responses, then list three to five skills you would like to improve or topics you would like to learn more about to help you guide children's behavior. When you finish this module, you will list examples of your new or improved knowledge and skills.

_____

_____

_____

_____

_____

_____

_____

_____

_____

_____

_____

Discuss the overview and pre-training assessment with your trainer. Then begin the learning activities for Module 10.

I. Using Positive Approaches to Guide Children's Behavior

In this activity you will learn:

- to recognize some typical behaviors of children from infancy through school age;

- to use your knowledge of child development to help children develop self-discipline; and

- to use positive approaches to guide children's behavior.

Discipline and punishment are very different.

Often the words discipline and punishment are used to mean the same thing, but they are actually very different. Discipline means guiding and directing children toward acceptable behavior. The most important goal of discipline is to help children gain inner controls. FCC providers discipline children to help them learn the consequences of their actions.

Punishment means controlling children's behavior through fear. Punishment makes children behave because they are afraid of what might happen to them if they don't. Punishment may stop children's negative behavior temporarily, but it doesn't help children develop self-discipline. Instead, it may reinforce their bad feelings about themselves.

Children need to make choices and decisions.

Children need choices and need to make decisions knowing what the logical consequences will be. FCC providers must clearly state in advance the choices and the consequences. For example, a provider might say, "Shawn, if you keep knocking David's blocks down, you will have to play with something else. Do you want to leave David's tower alone or play with something else?" This type of guidance helps a child develop self-discipline. It results in less anger and fewer power struggles than does punishment.

Understanding children's behavior is the first step in providing guidance and promoting self-discipline. By learning more about what children can and can't do at each stage of development from infancy through school age, you are more likely to have appropriate expectations for them.

215

Guiding Infants' Behavior

Young infants like and need to be held a lot during the day. This warm, physical attention allows them to feel cared for and secure, which helps them develop a sense of trust in the world. When infants cry, respond to them immediately. This won't spoil them at all. Instead, your quick and dependable responses will help them learn to trust their world.

Until they are at least 6 to 8 months old, infants cannot control their own behavior. Adults need to step in so that infants don't get hurt. For example, you should remove a mobile from a crib as soon as an infant is strong enough to pull it down, and you should distract an infant who is about to poke another child in the eye.

Between 10 and 12 months of age, infants begin to realize that adults don't approve of some of the things they do. Your tone of voice or firm "no" can help older infants in your care learn what the limits are. Your home should be arranged so that these active children can explore safely. Remember that the goal is not to produce "good babies" but rather to produce active, curious, and safe explorers.

Try these suggestions.

These suggestions can help you guide infant's behavior.

- Keep infants away from potential problems. If an infant is climbing up on the coffee table, move him or her over to the pillows stacked on the floor.

- Remove temptations or dangerous objects. For example, close the bathroom door and keep pencils and other sharp objects on a high shelf.

- Distract an infant by offering a different toy if the one the child wants is unsafe or being used by someone else.

- Separate infants who are hurting each other. If they are pulling each other's hair, sit down between them and show them how to be gentle.

- Use your tone of voice and facial expressions to express your feelings rather than a lot of words.

- If nobody will be hurt, give infants a chance to work things out themselves. One infant may not even notice or care when another picks up the toy he or she has been playing with.

- Use "no" sparingly. This word will be more effective if you save it for dangerous situations.

- Organize daily routines so that infants do not have to wait long to have their needs met.

The chart that follows shows several typical behaviors of infants and age-appropriate positive guidance approaches. In the blank spaces at the bottom, add an example of the behavior of an infant in your care and the positive guidance you offered to help the child develop self-discipline.

Typical Behavior	Positive Guidance
Betty (4 months) cries off and on all day.	Hold her, rock her, see if she is hungry or in pain. Try to comfort her so she learns she can trust you to help her.
Lou (9 months) pulls himself to standing and reaches for the pencil you left on the table.	Remove the pencil. Put it out of reach so Lou won't be tempted again. Offer Lou something safe to hold instead.
Ed (10 months) throws a block across the room for the third time. He looks at you and smiles.	Tell him "no." Be sure your face and voice look and sound serious. Give him something soft like a beanbag and a container. Say, "You can throw this in the laundry basket."

Guiding Toddlers' Behavior

Toddlers can try your patience. They want to be independent and do things themselves. This need for independence must be balanced with the need to learn necessary limits. Although toddlers often forget what you tell them from one minute to the next, they are beginning to learn what is acceptable behavior and what is not. They also are able to make some decisions for themselves. Give them clear, simple, choices so they can feel a sense of control over their lives.

Toddlers can be very possessive and are not yet ready to share. You can encourage sharing, but remember that it will be a long time before toddlers generously share their toys. To avoid unnecessary conflicts, make sure you have duplicates of their favorite toys.

By this stage of development, toddlers are starting to use words to express their feelings. They can listen and usually understand what you say to them. The words you use and your tone of voice are powerful tools in guiding a toddler's behavior. A calm but firm tone conveys that you care and that you mean what you say. Angry and loud words may startle toddlers so they don't hear what you are saying.

217

Try these suggestions.

These suggestions can help you guide toddlers' behavior.

- Use positive suggestions to get toddlers to do what you would like them to do. "Let's put the toys back on their shelves," is more successful than a direct command such as "clean up those toys."

- Play games so toddlers can say "no." For example, you can ask questions such as these: "Do shoes go on your ears? Do shoes go on your hands? Do shoes go on your nose?" The children will have great fun shouting, "No! No! No!"

- Let toddlers know you recognize their feelings by making statements such as this: "I know you miss your mommy. When she comes to pick you up, you can give her a big hug."

- Let toddlers know that you understand that they feel angry, but you will not let them hurt people or things. "I know you feel angry because Eric bumped into your block tower, but I can't let you hurt Eric."

The chart that follows shows several typical behaviors of toddlers and age-appropriate positive guidance approaches. In the blank spaces at the bottom, add an example of the behavior of a toddler in your care, and the positive guidance you offered to help the child develop self-discipline.

Typical Behavior	Positive Guidance
You ask Karen (25 months) to help you pick up the toys. When you hand her a block to put on the shelf, she throws it down and says, "No!"	Allow Karen to say "no." Respond calmly: "Okay. Maybe you'll want to help in a few minutes." In a few minutes ask her again; but this time, try making clean-up a game: "Let's see if we can put all the blocks on the shelf."
It is naptime. Joey (22 months) runs around the room, dragging his blanket behind him. He doesn't want to lie down on his mat.	Give him some notice to help him get ready for his nap. Put on a tape and say, "It will be naptime as soon as this song is over." Then rub his back, sing a song, or have him tell you what he wants to do after his nap.
Eric (22 months) has just fallen asleep. Your telephone rings and wakes him up. He starts crying.	Help Eric understand what he is feeling. Hold him or perhaps rub his back again. Explain, "That noise woke you up. It surprised you. You weren't ready to wake up yet." Try to help him fall asleep again.

Guiding Preschool Children's Behavior

Most preschool children have a beginning understanding of the difference between right and wrong and the effect of their actions. Because of this, they are developmentally capable of learning self-discipline. They can use words to express their feelings and to work out problems. Of course, they don't always do this. Although preschool children are less likely to have all-out tantrums than toddlers, they sometimes lose control and express their feelings by hitting, kicking, or screaming. Conflicts and disagreements are to be expected. Preschool children need understanding adults to help them use their words, not their hands or feet, to express their anger or frustration.

Most preschool children are not yet able to understand the long-term consequences of their behavior. Providers can help children learn the immediate, natural consequences of their actions. For example, if a child breaks a toy, you can help the child understand that he or she cannot play with the toy until it is fixed.

Preschool children feel more comfortable when they can follow established routines. Order and consistency in the day help these children develop a sense of security and self-control. When a child can say, "I know what we do after snack, we go outside!" he feels in control of the day.

Try these suggestions.

These suggestions can help you guide preschool children's behavior.

- Reinforce positive behavior during a private moment. "Peter, it was nice of you to give Arnold the helicopter to play with."

- Recognize when children are restless and suggest something more active. "I have an idea for Tanya and Reggie. Let's put some music on and show the younger children how to dance."

- Involve children in making rules so they can make decisions. Discuss why the rules are important. "We need to keep the scissors out of the reach of the babies. What would be a good safety rule for using and storing the scissors?"

- Set up a system (for example, a sign-up sheet or a timer) for taking turns with popular toys or activities. If children can see when they will have a turn, they will find it easier to wait. "Kevin, the sign says it will be your turn to use the firefighter's hat after Yancey is finished with it."

- Invite children to help you so they can feel important for the good things they do. "Mark, will you please help me change Jonathan? He likes it a lot when you make smiley faces for him."

- Hold an out-of-control child until he or she gains control again. Stay with the child until he or she has calmed down and can listen to your words. "Shane, I can see you are upset. I'm going to hold you until you calm down. Then we can talk about what happened."

The chart that follows shows several typical behaviors of preschool children and age-appropriate positive guidance approaches. In the blank spaces at the bottom, add an example of the behavior of a preschool child in your care, and the positive guidance you offered to help the child develop self-discipline.

Typical Behavior	Positive Guidance
Lorrie (3 years) and Dana (32 months) are fighting over a funnel during water play. Lorrie is using the funnel.	Help the children think of a way to both have fun with water play. Give Dana something else to play with while she is waiting for Lorrie to finish using the funnel. Write yourself a note to buy or make another funnel.
Dennis (5 years) and Carlos (4 years) bump into one another by accident.	Make sure nobody is hurt. Encourage the children to laugh about their collision: "You guys made such a loud noise, I thought the house was falling down."
Susan (4-1/2 years), who used to forget, hangs up her coat three days in a row.	Reinforce the behavior using genuine praise: "I really like the way you hung up your coat."

Guiding School-Age Children's Behavior

School-age children know the differences between appropriate and inappropriate behavior. However, they are still children, and they will act irresponsibly simply because of their young age. At about age 8 or 9, they gain a true understanding of right and wrong. They are interested in rules and are very concerned that problems be handled fairly. Younger children are able to solve some of their own problems, but the school-age years are perhaps the time when children are most interested in solving their problems with minimum adult intervention.

School-age children are more able than younger children to tell an adult what is bothering them, and they will offer solutions. For example, 8-year-old Tracy may say, "Tom cheats at Monopoly! I don't think he knows the rules at all." With a little prompting from an adult, Tracy might suggest going over the rules again so that everyone is sure that Tom knows how to play. As an FCC provider, your job is to be a good listener and to help children come up with solutions to their own problems.

Try these suggestions.

These suggestions can help you guide school-age children's behavior.

- Plan your daily schedule so that you have time to pay attention to the school-age children when they arrive after school. Spend a few minutes hearing about their day—the good experiences and the frustrating ones. To help children remember that they had some good experiences along with the frustrating ones, try asking: "Tell me about two things you learned today." or "Tell me two things that happened today that made you feel special."

- Provide a quiet place, away from the other children, where school-age children can do their homework if they choose. It can be very distracting and frustrating to be interrupted by younger children when you are trying to work on a difficult task. "Renee and Tyrone are working on their homework now. We'll turn down the music so our noise doesn't bother them."

- Ask children about their interests and what kinds of materials and activities they would like to use in your home. If you respond to their needs and interests, they are more likely to become actively involved and less likely to get into "trouble." "Your dad says that you like airplanes. Maybe we can find some books on airplanes at the library."

- Allow children to select their own materials and activities from what you have available. Respond to their requests for assistance, but give them the freedom to plan and carry out their own projects. "It looks like you have everything you need to continue your collage. I'll be in the living room reading a story if you need me."

- Give school-age children a safe place to store their belongings and their projects. This storage area should be out of the reach of the younger children. "The board games are on the top shelf in the hall closet. Be sure to put them back when you are finished."

- Encourage school-age children to be involved with the younger children by playing with them, reading to them, teaching them how to do things, and so on. This helps the school-age children feel a part of the family child care group and not just "part-timers." "Lan has been helping Katy learn how to tie her shoes. Katy is really eager to learn, and Lan is a very patient teacher."

The chart that follows shows several typical behaviors of school-age children and age-appropriate positive guidance approaches. In the blank spaces at the bottom, add an example of the behavior of a school-age child in your care, and the positive guidance you offered to help the child develop self-discipline.

Typical Behavior	Positive Guidance
Josh (8-1/2) goes outside without cleaning up after snack.	Leave the dishes on the table. When Josh comes inside, remind him that the rule is to clean up before going out. Then ask him to clean up before doing anything else.
Marcus (8 years) and Jerry (7-1/2 years) are fighting over a board game. Jerry tips the game over onto the floor.	Help Jerry to calm down, then assist him in picking up the game pieces. Ask the boys what happened, and help them develop their own solution. They might need to take a break, or they might need to read the rules again.
Sharon (9-1/2 years) goes into your bedroom without permission and puts on some of your perfume.	Remind Sharon of the rules in your home. "My bedroom is off-limits to all the children. Nobody is allowed to go in there without my permission." Ask her if she needs help finding something to do. If so, spend a few minutes with her until she comes up with something to do.

Guiding the Behavior of Your Own Children

For many providers, one of the nice things about running a family child care home is that you are able to be at home with your own children. Having your own children involved in your profession can also be challenging. Some children find it difficult to adjust to sharing their home, their toys, and, most importantly, their parent with other children. They may not be able to say in words how they feel about the other children "taking over" their home. They may try to tell you with their behavior: crying more than usual, clinging to you throughout the day, refusing to share their toys, pushing other children away, or insisting on sitting on your lap. All of these behaviors are normal ways for a child to say, "You are my mommy and I want to be sure I am still the most important to you."

Try these suggestions.

Do not be surprised if at first your children like the idea of having other children around and then seem to change their minds and want everyone to go home. This is normal. A reassuring word from you, an extra story at bedtime, or some time alone together will help your children feel more secure.

- Be sure that your children have a space of their own in the house that can be off limits to FCC children.

- Try to have separate toys for the "visiting" children so that your children don't have to share their toys with the others.

- Ask your children to help choose toys for the FCC program.

- Set aside some time during the day to spend time with just your children.

FCC providers can use a variety of approaches to guide children's behavior. No one approach works for every child or every situation. The approach used should relate to the child and to the problem.

Discuss with your trainer the different approaches you use to guide the children in your care.

LEARNING ACTIVITIES

II. Arranging Your Home to Promote Self-Discipline

In this activity you will learn:

- to observe children's behavior for clues to problems in the environment; and
- to arrange your home and display materials in ways that help children develop self-discipline.

The environment may work against you.

There are times when no matter how hard you try, everything seems to go wrong. Two children are crying, the floor is covered with toys, and the kitchen counter is so cluttered that you can't find a clean spoon. Susannah is wet and you can't find her extra set of clothes, and Jerry's mother is looking for his hat, which she says they left yesterday.

In addition, the children seem restless. The older children are complaining that the younger ones are in their way. The younger ones are running a lot in the house, fighting over toys, and wandering around unable to choose things to do. All the children seem easily distracted and have trouble sticking with tasks. They are using materials roughly and are very uncooperative at clean-up time.

There are many possible reasons for these behaviors. Most young children act in these ways sometimes, and even the most organized and competent provider has bad days from time to time. But if you feel overwhelmed or see the children misbehaving day after day, it's a good idea to check the way you have arranged your home. How you arrange the furniture and select and display materials can be working against you. The environment can encourage the very behaviors you want to discourage. When children feel that their environment is overcrowded, hard to maneuver in, or physically uncomfortable, they get frustrated and often act out.

An effective environment supports growth and development.

An effective environment for family child care facilitates children's growth and development and provides a warm, cozy atmosphere where children feel safe and secure. The rooms in the home have spaces for children's play, for storing play materials in easy reach of the children, for storing children's personal items, for displaying children's work, and for communicating with parents. Areas that are out of bounds to the children are blocked off. Objects that active children might break are stored in closets or on high shelves. All in all, your home should be a place that welcomes children and lets them know that your home is a safe and interesting place to be.

Children feel respected in this kind of environment because there are special places where they can keep their belongings safe. They know where to play, so they are less likely to wander. Children know which things are clearly theirs and which are off-limits, so they learn to respect the rights of others. And when children have a wide variety of interesting and age-appropriate toys and materials to play with, they are more likely to become involved in purposeful activities throughout the day.

Try these suggestions.

One way to encourage positive behavior is to create specific areas in your home for different activities.

- **Identify which areas of your home are "off limits"** to the children. For example, a tool shed or storage area can be locked, and rooms that you don't want to use for your program can be blocked off by a closed (and locked) door, a gate, or a large piece of furniture. Store breakable items in these off-limit areas.

- **Designate areas for different kinds of activities**. You might have a protected place for block play, an easy-to-clean area for messy activities such as art or water play, and an area for active play such as musical games and dramatic play.

- **Establish comfortable places for quiet activities** such as looking at books, drawing with crayons, and listening to stories.

- **Set aside a place for older children** to keep their games and special materials such as craft supplies, scissors, markers, and glue. A bedroom could be a quiet and private place for school-age children to play or do their homework.

- **Allow for traffic flow** so that children are not constantly bumping into crawling infants or interrupting each other's play.

When the environment is working, children are busy and happily engaged in play, fights are few, and the day proceeds well. In contrast, when the environment is not well-planned, children may be confused and generally unhappy. Of course, there are many possible reasons for children's misbehavior, but it's a good idea to consider how the physical environment might be contributing to the problems.

In this activity you will consider how the arrangement of your home affects children's behavior. You will look at some common behavior problems and how the environment can be the cause— or the solution. On the next page are several examples. After reading them, you'll plan ways to change the environment so that your home arrangement can help you address common behavior problems.

Arranging Your Home to Promote Self-Discipline
(Example)

Children's Behavior	Possible Problems in the Environment	How You Might Change the Environment
Children run around the house in circles, squealing excitedly.	*There is too much space or perhaps all the rooms connect. The home isn't divided into smaller areas.*	*Use shelves and furniture to divide the space better. Restructure the layout of the home so that there's no circular pathway. Make one room out of bounds, use a piece of furniture to block a pass-through, or use furniture to define a play area.*
Infants and older children constantly bump into each other or interfere with each other's activities.	*There is no safe place for infants to crawl. The toddler children don't have an area large enough for moving about. There might not be clear paths for moving around the play areas in the room.*	*Use gates, soft pillows, or other temporary barriers to create safe crawling spaces. Create pathways around the play areas.*
Children act as if they are in "school," and there is little interaction with the provider or each other.	*The home has been structured into a mini-school.*	*Leave places for children to work on activities, but put back the elements of a home that make family child care special (e.g., sofas, pillows, plants).*
Children run "wild" when outside.	*The outdoor area has not been organized.*	*Organize the outdoor area into activity areas that promote learning (e.g., a sand box, an old tree trunk for woodworking, a garden, and so on).*

Arranging Your Home to Promote Self-Discipline

Children's Behavior	Possible Problems in the Environment	How You Might Change the Environment
Wandering around, unable to choose something to do.		
Easily distracted; having trouble staying with and completing tasks.		
Using materials roughly and resisting clean-up.		
Asking for assistance each time they want to play with something.		
Running around outside without using toys or equipment or becoming involved with activities.		

Check your answers with the answer sheet at the end of this module. There can be more than one answer.

Think about the children in your group. Do you see any of the same problem behaviors? If so, which ones?

_____

_____

_____

_____

_____

Look at the arrangement of your home. Are there any changes you could make to improve the arrangement? Use the space below to note the changes you wish to make.

_____

_____

_____

_____

_____

Before you try out your ideas, discuss them with your trainer.

III. Using Words to Provide Positive Guidance

In this activity you will learn:

- to use words to guide children's behavior; and
- to use words to remind children of rules and limits.

Your words and tone of voice are powerful.

Children listen to and understand what you say to them. Your words and your tone of voice are powerful guidance tools. Angry, insensitive words can make children feel sad, ashamed, or angry. Using words in positive ways, however, can promote children's self-discipline. Your caring words help children understand their own feelings and those of others.

Adults often talk to children with a loud "discipline voice." It is better to talk to children in a natural though firm tone of voice all the time. When children hear a quiet, firm tone, they feel safe and cared for. Try to get close enough to a child to speak at a normal level. When an adult shouts, children may be so startled that they don't really hear the words. Getting close to a child by crouching or kneeling allows you to have a private discussion. Look into the child's eyes, touch an arm or shoulder, give him or her your full attention, and make sure you have the child's attention.

If you're not sure how your voice sounds when you're talking to children, try tape-recording a part of the day. Play it back and ask yourself, "Would I like to listen to this person all day?"

The words you use are important.

The words you use also are very important. Sometimes an adult who is angry with a child lets out a flood of words. This may make the adult feel better, but the child probably does not hear the message. Try to use simple statements, spoken once, so the child can focus on the real issue. Use clear statements that include brief descriptions.

- **Describe what happened:** "Theresa, you tore Joey's pictures two times this morning."

- **Tell the child what behavior is not acceptable:** "I can't let you tear other children's work."

- **Tell the child what behavior is acceptable:** "Leave Joey's paper alone. It's his work."

- **Suggest a consequence for the behavior:** "Joey feels bad that you tore his picture. Let's get some tape and fix it. Then you can tear some magazines for a collage, or you can read a story with me."

229

This example includes offering the child two choices, both of which are acceptable to the provider. Be careful to offer choices only when you mean them. When you ask a child. "Would you like to clean up now?" it sounds as if the child has a choice. The child could easily say "no." Probably you really mean "it's time to pick up now."

You can use words to give directions in a positive way. Instead of saying "no running" or "don't leave your coat on the floor," you can say "walk" or "hang your coat on the hook." Children respond well to positive directions.

Your words can show respect for children's feelings and help children feel good about themselves. Avoid comparing one child to another. Instead of saying "Susan is nice and quiet at story time— can you be quiet like Susan?" you could say, "Please be quiet now so we can begin the story." Phrases such as "six-year-olds don't suck their thumbs" should also be avoided. They make children feel bad, and they don't change behaviors.

The chart below provides more examples of words you can use to provide positive guidance.

Situation	What You Might Say
Jack (8 months) reaches for Paula's (18 months) spoon as she sits in the highchair next to him.	"Here, Jack, I have another spoon for you to use. You don't have to take Paula's, you may have your own."
Bob (13 months) and Franklin (2 years) both want to sit in your lap.	"There's room for both of you to sit on my lap and look at a book. You can both share my lap, and we can all share this big chair."
Dean (9 years) wants to play a board game, but none of his friends want to join him.	"Dean, it's hard when your friends say they don't want to play with you. They still like you. This time they want to do something else. Maybe they will want to play the game tomorrow. Would you like to work on your wood carving now? I'll help you get your tools down from the shelf."
Jim (5-1/2 years) watches from the doorway while the younger children use playdough at the kitchen table.	"Jim, why don't you come and join us? We have plenty of dough and some special cookie cutters that are good for kindergartners to use."
Lloyd (3-1/2 years) and Chaundra (5 years) both want to play in the same corner.	"There is space for both of you to play in the corner. You can share the space. Each of you has the trucks you want to use. Let's talk about who can drive near the gas station and who can go by the school. Maybe later you'll decide to change places."

Using words to guide children's behavior takes some practice. It may be a while before new ways of talking to children feel natural to you. You will be rewarded when the children you care for let you know how much better they feel because of your understanding and caring.

In this learning activity, you will practice using words to guide children's behavior and help them learn self-discipline. First read the examples on the next page. Then write down words that you can use in typical family child care situations.

Words You Use to Provide Positive Guidance
(Example)

When a child bites another child:

"You may not bite people. I won't let you bite Dan or anyone else. Here is the teething ring that you brought from home. It will make your mouth feel better."

When a child sits alone, looking sad:

"Would you like to talk about how you're feeling? I will listen while you tell me what you're thinking about. Then maybe together we can help you feel better."

When a child hurts another child out of frustration:

"Simon, it's okay to want to be my helper at snack time, but I can't let you hit Carol. She can put the fruit on the plate. I'll give you another job."

When a child watches the others playing but doesn't know how to join in:

"George, if you want to be included in the game, you can ask the other children if you can play. They already have a doctor, but we can find out who else they need."

When a child takes playdough from another child:

"You may have some of your own playdough. You don't need to take Tamila's playdough from her. Ask Tamila to share her playdough or ask me for some."

When a child paints on another child's picture:

"You may paint a picture of your own. I can't let you paint on Lamont's paper. You can have your own piece of paper, and Lamont can have another piece too. Or you can ask Lamont if he wants to paint a picture with you."

When a child screams because there aren't enough of one kind of toy:

"It's okay to want to have your own shovel like the other children. But screaming doesn't help you get a shovel. You need to use your words. Ask if anyone is ready to give you their shovel. Or let's see what else you can use to dig with."

When a child is upset because a friend won't play:

"You want to play with Kenny. You feel a little sad when he says no. He just feels like playing alone right now. I'll play ball with you or you can ask someone else to play with you."

Words You Use to Provide Positive Guidance

When a child calls another child *stupid*:

_____

_____

_____

_____

_____

_____

When a child refuses to clean up:

_____

_____

_____

_____

_____

_____

When a child watches other children playing but doesn't know how to join in:

_____

_____

_____

_____

_____

_____

When a child bites another child:

_____

_____

_____

_____

_____

_____

When a child talks very loudly:

_____

_____

_____

_____

_____

_____

When a child tears another child's painting:

_____

_____

_____

_____

_____

_____

When a child sits alone, looking sad:

_____

_____

_____

_____

_____

_____

When (add your own example here):

_____

_____

_____

_____

_____

_____

Now share your words with your trainer. You could also write these words on a chart and hang it in your home to help you get used to using them.

LEARNING ACTIVITIES

IV. Setting Rules and Limits

In this activity you will learn:

- to set clear, simple rules and limits and communicate them to children; and
- to enforce rules consistently.

Children need a few simple rules.

Rules and limits help both children and adults understand what behaviors are acceptable. Children need simple rules that are stated clearly and positively. For example, "walk in the house so you don't hurt yourself" rather than "don't run in the house" tells children what they can do and why. Children feel safer when they know that adults have set limits. These feelings of security tend to make children feel freer to explore and experiment.

Young children often act on impulses. FCC providers can help children understand the consequences of their actions: "Screaming won't make Vanessa give you the book, Tim. When she has finished reading it, you can have a turn." Providers also help children learn that limiting what they are doing now may mean they can do something else later. "If we stop playing a little early and clean up now, we can go for a walk before your parents come to pick you up."

It's important to have just enough rules to keep your FCC home functioning smoothly. When there are too many rules, children can't remember what to do. Too few rules might mean that the children aren't safe and that the environment is disorderly.

Rules should reflect ages and stages.

Rules should reflect what children are like at each stage of development. Because you care for children of a wide range of ages and stages of development, you may have different rules for different ages. For example, there are some materials and equipment that should be available to the school-age children but not to the others. It would be unfair to ask the school-age children to use only materials that are safe for the younger children. Instead, you can establish rules about who can use these materials, where, and how they are to be safely stored at the end of the day. Conversely, you might expect Lars (4 years old) to keep the puzzle pieces on the table, but you would not expect the same behavior from Todd (14 months).

Children can help create rules.

Children respect rules when they understand the reasons behind them. They also are more likely to follow rules if they help create them. Talk to children about the consequences of actions. "What might happen if we squirt water on the floor?" Children could come

235

up with answers and also think of a rule: "Keep the water in the water table. When the water spills, the floor gets slippery. Someone might fall and get hurt."

Some rules and limits are set by the way the home is arranged. Rooms that are off-limits can be labeled (with a STOP sign perhaps) to remind children that the rooms aren't for their use. (How the environment affects children's behavior is discussed in Learning Activity II.)

Many times during the day you'll remind children of the rules and limits. Children are more likely to internalize rules when your reminders are positive and delivered in a brief, firm manner. Some examples follow below.

Instead of This	Say or Do This
"Will you stop screaming!" or "Sit over there and shut up!"	"Use quiet voices inside; you can talk loudly outside."
"Haven't I told you not to hit other children?"	"If you feel like hitting, use the punching bag."
"If you don't put that shovel down right now, I'm going to take it away."	"Use the shovel to dig with; if you want to throw something, you can throw the ball."
"Get down off that table this minute!"	"Keep your feet on the floor. Climb only on the climber."
"If you can't use those properly, I'm going to take them away from you."	"Scissors are not toys. Use them carefully."
"Did you dump the puzzle pieces on the floor again? I told you not to do that."	"Keep the puzzle on the table so the pieces don't get lost."
"Get out of the way! The others can't see!"	"Sit down on the rug so the others can see."
"If you don't shut your foul mouth, I'm going to tell your father. He'll make sure you stop using that bad language."	"Please don't use those words here. I don't want to hear them, and I don't want the other children to learn to say them."
"You're dripping paint all over the floor."	"Wipe your brush on the jar so it won't drip."

Review and revise rules as children grow.

As children grow and mature, they can handle more freedom, more activities, and more responsibility. In response, you'll need to review and revise the rules in your home. Providers need to be careful observers to see when individual children or the whole group can handle greater freedom. There is a fine line between keeping children safe and keeping them from having chances to grow and be independent. The limits set for a 2-year-old in September may need to be adjusted in a few months' time.

In this activity you will use positive phrases to list the rules you have in your home. Then you'll answer some questions about one of those rules. First read the example below, then complete the blank form that follows.

Rules for the _Conley_ FCC Home
(Example)

Staying healthy and safe:

Serve yourself as much food as you think you are able to eat.

Climb on the pillows or the climber, not on the table.

Wash your hands before and after eating snacks or lunch.

Stay in the back yard during outdoor play.

Respecting the rights of others:

Be gentle with other people; don't hurt them.

Ask for permission before using other people's things.

When someone is using a toy you'd like to play with, ask him or her to let you know when he or she is finished.

When you want to be alone, you can go to the quiet corner in the living room.

Not hurting others:

Use your words to tell others how you feel.

If you feel like hitting, you may hit the punching bag.

Blocks are for building, not for throwing.

Caring for our equipment and materials:

Everyone helps at clean-up time.

Books are important; they are for reading, not tearing. Turn the pages carefully.

Keep the puzzle pieces on the table.

Select a rule from your list. Answer the questions below.

Rule: *Everyone helps at clean-up time.*

Why do you have this rule?

My home is set up so that children can get toys themselves and put them back when they are finished. They feel good about doing things for themselves, and they learn self-discipline.

How do you fit this rule to each child's development, strengths, and needs?

Most of the children are able to clean up by themselves. For the children who need help, I break down the tasks into smaller ones.

How do you follow through and support your words with actions?

If a child doesn't respond to a reminder, I walk over to the child. Then I kneel or crouch and repeat the reminder: "Peter, pick-up time." If reminders don't work, I might lift a child off the climber, take a brush out of a hand, help put the puzzle pieces back, and so on.

Give an example of a simple, clear statement that states the rule positively.

"It's clean-up time. Let's put the toys away so we can go outside."

What might you say to respect and acknowledge a child's feelings?

"Juana, you seem worried about your diorama. Would you like to store it on the top shelf of the closet? We can get it down again tomorrow for you to finish."

How do you act with authority and show confidence?

When we need to get ready for another activity (lunch, nap, or going outside), I always give children a ten-minute reminder, then a five-minute one. I never apologize when I announce that it's clean-up time. When a child is slow to stop playing, I walk over and re-state that it is clean-up time. I don't ask the child to clean up. I just say, "It's clean-up time."

Rules for the _____ FCC Home

Write down some of the rules you have established for your home.

Staying healthy and safe:

_____
_____
_____
_____
_____

Respecting the rights of others:

_____
_____
_____
_____
_____

Not hurting yourself or others:

_____
_____
_____
_____
_____

Caring for our equipment and materials:

_____
_____
_____
_____
_____

Select a rule from your list. Answer the questions below.

Rule: _____

Why do you have this rule?

_____

_____

_____

How do you fit this rule to each child's development, strengths, and needs?

_____

_____

_____

How do you follow through and support your words with actions?

_____

_____

_____

Give an example of a simple, clear statement that states the rule positively.

_____

_____

_____

What might you say to respect and acknowledge a child's feelings?

_____

_____

_____

How do you act with authority and show confidence?

_____

_____

_____

Discuss this activity with your trainer.

LEARNING ACTIVITIES

V. Responding to Challenging Behaviors

In this activity you will learn:

- to look for the reasons behind a child's challenging behavior; and
- to develop a plan for responding to challenging behavior.

Some normal behaviors might be annoying.

Some children's behaviors that may drive you crazy are really signs that they are developing normally. For example:[2]

- Lucy (3 months) starts to cry and Seth (6 months) joins in. Lucy just woke up and is hungry. Seth was startled by Lucy's cries, so he joined in.

- Dion (16 months) spends the day filling containers and dumping them out. He enjoys using his physical skills; learning about size, shape, and volume; and exploring cause and effect.

- Carla (2 years) yells, "No. Mine!" when another child wants to share a toy. She needs to feel a sense of ownership before she will be ready to share.

- Barbara (2-1/2 years) takes half an hour to wash her hands. She is exploring and experimenting with the properties of soap and water.

- Gerry (3 years) spills his milk at lunch every day. He wants to do things for himself and doesn't notice when he elbows his cup.

- Kim (3-1/2 years) shouts "Spiderwoman!" and swishes her cape around all day. This beginning stage of dramatic play helps her feel powerful and in control of her fears.

- Chuck (4 years) is very interested in watching Sarah (4-1/2 years) get undressed. He is very curious about the differences between boys and girls.

- Trevor (4-1/2 years) always wants to win and be the "biggest" and the "best." He is developing a sense of self and needs activities without winners and losers.

- Katherine (5 years) bosses the younger children around. "No, not like that. Do it this way." She feels good about her growing skills and more competent than the younger children.

---

[2] Based on California Child Care Resource and Referral Network, *Making a Difference* (San Francisco, CA: California Child Care Resource and Referral Network, 1986), pp. 14-15. A poster depicting these "annoying behaviors" is also available.

- Hilary (9-1/2 years) rebels against authority after a long school day. "I'm not going to the park with you and the little kids. My mom says I can stay here by myself." (You and her mother agree that Hilary is too young to stay alone.) Hilary needs to know that you acknowledge her age and abilities.

Children express feelings through behavior.

Often, young children cannot say how they feel. Even after they begin talking, they may still find it hard to express their feelings with words. Sometimes they don't know why they are feeling angry or frustrated. When children kick, cry, bite, or have temper tantrums, providers need to think about what the behavior means. You can then respond in ways that help children control their behavior. Children's behaviors may be telling you many different things.

- "I feel lonely. That's why I'm crying."

- "I am angry. That's why I hit Shawn."

- "I am afraid. That's why I won't let go of your hand."

- "I want to be good at something. That's why I keep ripping up my pictures."

- "I need some limits. That's why I'm running around the room."

- "I can't do what you asked me to do. That's why I threw my sneaker at the wall."

Accept children's negative feelings.

It's important for providers to accept children's negative feelings. We all have days when we feel bad or don't want to do certain tasks. Providers can help children learn to recognize when they aren't feeling good. You also can provide ways for children to express their negative feelings without hurting themselves, other people, or the things in your home. When you see that children are feeling frustrated, you can redirect them to make something with playdough, play with sand or rice in a basin, or begin finger painting. These are soothing activities that help many children feel better. When children feel very angry, throwing beanbags or hammering may help release their feelings.

Some inappropriate behaviors are accidental or careless more than deliberate. A child may accidentally spill paint and then laugh when asked to clean up, for example. Such behaviors should be responded to firmly but quietly; they don't need to be dwelt upon, as they aren't part of a pattern of challenging or limit-testing behaviors.

Challenging behaviors occur again and again.

Challenging behaviors, such as biting or temper tantrums, are likely to occur again and again. This often means that something in the child's life is upsetting. The child doesn't know how to express her feelings with words, so she acts out.

In such cases, all the adults who care for the child need to discuss the possible causes of the problem. Perhaps a situation at home or at school is causing the child to be upset or frustrated. Or the environment in your home may be causing the child's behavior. The schedule, activities, or the way the home is arranged may not meet this child's needs.

You can reassure the child's parents that there are times when some children behave this way, but the behavior cannot be allowed in your FCC program. You can then agree on a plan for consistent responses to the behavior. It is very important to let the child know that he is still loved and cared for even if he has a problem behavior.

Children feel scared when they lose control.

When children hurt others **by hitting, scratching, kicking, and so on**, respond by getting down at the child's level and clearly stating the rule forbidding this behavior: "Alexandra, I cannot let you hurt people. You can use your words to say what you want. If you feel angry you can punch the pillows or do some hammering." You may need to hold the child until she calms down. Children feel scared when they lose control and your firm arms can help the child feel that someone is in control. It may take a few minutes, but the child will quiet down and you will be able to discuss what happened: "Do you want to talk about what made you feel so angry? I could see that you were having a hard time." Reassure the child that you understand and want to listen to her feelings. It is best to let the child recover before discussing alternative ways to handle anger and frustration. You might want to do this during a quiet, one-to-one moment later in the day, or even the following day: "Yesterday, when you felt bad you hit Carl. Next time you feel bad, what could you do instead?" This discussion can serve as a rehearsal so that the next time the child begins to lose self-control, there will be an alternative to lashing out at someone else. "That sounds like a good plan. You could use the punching pillow to help you feel better." Later, when the child has finished punching the pillow, be sure to offer support: "I noticed that you were punching the pillow to help you feel better. Do you want to talk about it?"

Reactions to biting are emotionally charged.

One of the most emotionally-charged challenging behaviors is **biting**. Parents and providers have very strong reactions to biting and may overreact, rather than trying to solve the problem. The parents of a child who has been bitten are likely to be horrified, and afraid that their child is not safe in your home. The parents of the child who did the biting may be embarrassed, ashamed, defensive, and unsure of how to handle the situation. Providers need to understand what may cause a child to bite, and work with parents to stop this unacceptable behavior.

The reasons why children bite are related to their stage of development.

One of the ways infants learn about the world is to put everything in their mouths. Infants who bite may be exploring, rather than being aggressive. They are trying out their teeth on a nice soft object (an arm, leg, or cheek), which is unfortunately attached to another child. The victim's screams may be enough to stop the biting. If not, step in and make it clear by your words and tone of voice that biting is not okay. Comfort the child who was bitten and put some ice on the sore spot. The infant can help you comfort the hurt child so he or she will begin to understand the connection between the biting and the child's distress.

When toddlers bite, they too are usually unaware that their biting is hurting someone. They may be frustrated about something and seeking a physical release. Or they may be looking for some attention. You will need to step in quickly when a toddler bites another child. Again, comfort the child who was bitten. Ask the toddler who did the biting to help you get some ice for the sore spot, and involve this child in helping the victim feel better. Calmly tell the toddler that biting is not allowed, because it hurts. Help both children find an activity to become involved with. When toddlers bite repeatedly, something may be bothering the child to cause this reaction. Talk with the child's parents to find out what might be causing the biting.

When an older child (preschool children or school age) bites, there is likely to be something happening in the child's life to cause the problem. As with the younger children you need to state the rule clearly, comfort the victim, involve the child who did the biting in comforting the bitten child (if the bitten child will permit this), and help both children find something else to do. In addition, you will need to talk with the child and the parents to find out what might be behind the behavior. When a child is learning to control the urge to bite, it may be helpful to give the child something acceptable to bite (for example, a clean washcloth) without hurting anyone.

Children may have temper tantrums when words aren't sufficient.

Some children have **temper tantrums**, times when they lose control of themselves and scream, kick, cry, and otherwise express their total frustration. These are times when their words are not enough to express their feelings. Temper tantrums are most typical of toddlers and preschool children, however, some school-age children may have tantrums because they are frustrated, or because they want to get attention. During tantrums, a provider may need to protect the child, and other people and things in the environment, by firmly holding the child's arms and legs until the child calms down. When the tantrum is over, the child will recover more quickly if no harm came to people or objects. Once calm is restored, you can talk about what happened and what the child could do differently in the future. It is important to let the children know that you accept their feelings and will be a good listener.

Many tantrums can be prevented by providing an appropriate program. Tired and frustrated children are more likely to have tantrums than those who are well-rested, fed nutritious meals and snacks before they get too hungry, and provided with age-appropriate materials and activities. Also, when you observe children you will see when they are getting tired or frustrated and you can direct them to soothing activities such as water or sand play or listening to soft music.

In this learning activity, you will think of a child in your home whose behavior is challenging. You will describe the behavior and your response. Next you will talk with the other adults who care for the child about the child's behavior. Together, you will develop a plan for responding to the behavior. Review the example below, then complete the blank form that follows.

Responding to Challenging Behaviors
(Example)

Child: _Renee_   **Age:** _3 years, 3 months_

What behavior is challenging?

Renee hits other children.

How often does this occur?   **How long has it been going on?**

Two or three times a week.   _Two weeks._

When does it happen?

When Renee wants to use a toy that someone else is playing with. Sometimes when she's outside in the yard and wants to swing or slide, and other children get there first.

How do you respond now?

I comfort the child who was hit and get the child ice, if necessary. Then I take Renee aside and tell her she cannot hit people. Then she has to sit on the grass for two or three minutes.

How does the child respond?

She cries and screams. Then she sometimes pulls up the grass or sucks her thumb.

Did something happen at home to upset the child?

Renee has a new baby brother who shares her room. She doesn't seem very interested in him. Renee doesn't hit at home.

Did something happen at your FCC home to upset the child?

I can't think of anything that has changed.

Conclusion:

Renee may feel jealous of her new brother. I need to look at the ways I'm responding now to see how I could improve. I need to help Renee use her words to express her feelings about the new baby.

Plans for responding to this behavior at the child's home and at the FCC home:

Renee's parents will help her express her feelings about her baby brother. They will try to set up a special place at home that is just for Renee.

In my home, I also will provide ways for Renee to talk about her brother. I will read "A Baby Sister for Francis" by Russell Hoban. I can ask the other children who have baby brothers or sisters at home to tell us what it's like.

When Renee hits, I will still comfort the hurt child. Then I will respond to Renee. I will bend down, hold her firmly, look in her eyes and say, "It hurts people when you hit them. I won't let anyone hit you. I won't let you hit anyone." Then I will try to get her involved in a calming activity, such as playing with playdough, water, or sand. I know Renee hits when she wants a turn on the swing or wants something another child has. I will not let her have the turn or the toy if she hits.

Responding to Challenging Behaviors

Child: _____   **Age:** _____

What behavior is challenging?

_____

_____

_____

How often does this occur?   **How long has it been going on?**

_____   _____

_____   _____

_____   _____

_____

When does it happen?

_____

_____

_____

How do you respond now?

_____

_____

_____

How does the child respond?

_____

_____

_____

Did something happen at home to upset the child?

_____

_____

_____

Did something happen at the FCC home to upset the child?

_____
_____
_____
_____

Conclusion:

_____
_____
_____
_____

Plans for responding to this behavior at the child's home and at the FCC program:

_____
_____
_____
_____
_____
_____
_____
_____

What happened when you tried out your plans? Has the challenging behavior changed or gone away?

_____
_____
_____
_____
_____
_____
_____

Discuss this activity with your trainer.

SUMMARIZING YOUR PROGRESS

You have now completed all of the learning activities for this module. Whether you are an experienced FCC provider or a new one, this module has probably helped you develop new skills for guiding children's behavior. Take a few minutes to review your responses to the pre-training assessment for this module. Write a summary of what you learned and list the skills you developed or improved.

Take some time now to review your discipline policy in light of what you have learned in this module. Revise or adapt your policy to incorporate your knowledge and skills and provide copies for the parents of the children in your care.

Discuss your responses to this section with your trainer. If there are topics you would like to know more about, you will find more recommended readings listed in the Introduction in Volume I.

Your final step in this module is to complete the knowledge and competency assessments. Let your trainer know when you are ready to schedule the assessments. After you have successfully completed these assessments, you will be ready to start a new module. Congratulations on your progress so far, and good luck with your next module.

A N S W E R   S H E E T S

Guiding Children's Behavior

Providing an Environment That Encourages Self-Discipline

1. **What behavior did Ms. Lee find frustrating?**

   a. The children are constantly fighting over toys.

   b. They are rough with the toys and are destroying them.

   c. They resist cleaning up.

2. **What suggestions did Ms. Richards have for dealing with the behavior problems?**

   a. Borrow or buy some toys so there would be duplicates of popular ones.

   b. Make picture and word labels and tape them to the shelves to show that there is a place for everything.

3. **How might these suggestions help?**

   a. Children won't have to share as often and sharing is difficult for young children.

   b. An orderly environment with labels for all materials teaches children that the toys and materials are important and should be cared for.

   c. Clean-up will be a matching game, and children may find it more interesting and challenging.

   d. Ms. Lee won't have to give the children negative messages about their behavior.

Using Positive Methods to Guide Individual Children

1. **What did Ms. Kendall know about Travis?**

   a. Travis could help find his own solutions to problems.

   b. Travis liked to throw things.

   c. Travis responded well when his behavior was redirected.

   d. Travis was very active.

2. **How did Ms. Kendall let Travis know that she respected him?**

   a. She walked over to him and bent down to talk to him.

   b. She told him he was learning to be a good thrower.

   c. She asked him to think of a safe place where he could throw pine cones without hurting anyone.

Helping Children Understand and Express Their Feelings in Acceptable Ways

1. **How did Ms. Perez help Donna learn to express her feelings in an acceptable way?**

   a. She explained that Donna's words and actions hurt Allie.

   b. She let her know that she was available whenever Donna needed to talk about a problem.

   c. She agreed to meet Donna in the kitchen to discuss what happened on the bus.

2. **When they meet in the kitchen, what do you think Ms. Perez could say to Donna?**

   a. First she could ask Donna what happened and listen as Donna tells her.

   b. She could acknowledge Donna's hurt feelings.

   c. She could help Donna think about how to talk to her friend about her feelings.

   d. She could remind Donna that it isn't all right to hurt other children with words or actions.

   e. She could let Donna know that she has confidence in her ability to work out her problem with her friend.

Arranging Your Home to Promote Self-Discipline

Children's Behavior	Possible Problems in the Environment	How You Might Change the Environment
Wandering around, unable to choose something to do.	Perhaps the home is too cluttered, choices are not clear, or there aren't enough age-appropriate materials to choose from. Nothing appeals to the children, so they are bored.	Get rid of the clutter. Make your home simpler. Put away things you've finished using. Make new games, puzzles, and prop boxes. Put out some new art materials.
Easily distracted; having trouble staying with and completing tasks.	Areas are too open, so children can see everything going on in the home.	Use shelves to define areas so children are not distracted by other activities.
Using materials roughly and resisting clean-up.	Materials on the shelves are messy. There is no order to the display of materials, so children don't know where to put things.	Make a place for everything. Use picture and word labels to show where materials go.
Asking for assistance each time they want to play with something.	Children cannot reach the toys they want to use, or perhaps they are stored so haphazardly that the children cannot find what they need.	Create storage areas using a bookcase or a closet with open shelving. Use milk cartons, dishpans, fishnet bags, and so on to store toys and materials.
Running around outside without using toys or equipment or becoming involved with activities.	Children may need some help to get involved in outdoor activities.	Organize the outdoor area into interest areas. Include a sandbox with sifting and digging tools, a wading pool filled with water and basters, a place to use riding toys, a gardening spot, an old tree trunk for carpentry, and a picnic table for eating or painting.

GLOSSARY

Challenging behaviors	Behavior such as biting or temper tantrums that is often difficult to handle.
Consequence	The natural or logical result of a behavior.
Discipline	The actions that adults take to guide and direct children toward acceptable behavior.
Limits and rules	Guidelines set by FCC providers and children as to what is acceptable behavior.
Positive guidance	Methods that FCC providers use to help children learn to behave in acceptable ways, and develop self-discipline.
Punishment	Control of children's behavior by use of force and fear.
Self-discipline	The ability to control one's own behavior.

Module 11:
FAMILIES

OVERVIEW

Working with families involves:

- communicating with parents often to share information about their child's experiences and development;

- offering a variety of ways for parents to participate in their child's life at the FCC home; and

- working together with families to meet children's needs.

Parents and providers work as a team.

Recent studies on parent involvement in child care have shown that the most effective child development programs are those which actively promote and encourage parent participation. By parents, we include any nurturing adult who might be taking on the role of parent—be it a grandparent, an aunt, or a close family friend. Whoever takes on this parenting role is the person we are addressing in this module. When parents and FCC providers work as a team, they can share information and discuss ways to provide children with consistent care. Good working relationships with families enable providers to really get to know the children in their care and thus be more responsive to each child's needs.

Parents are the most important people in children's lives. Parents and children are developing a relationship that will continue long after they leave your care. One of your roles is to enhance that relationship. FCC providers can acknowledge parents' roles as the first and primary educators of their children by reinforcing family ties and by doing whatever they can to increase parents' pleasure in their children. By strengthening the connection between child and parent, you are supporting the child's development in the years to come.

Parents can teach you a lot about their children—what they like to do, what they don't enjoy, things they do well, skills they are developing. FCC providers can share similar information with parents on a regular basis. In this way, parents can be connected to their children's lives at the FCC home and feel good about the quality of care their children are receiving.

Working with families can be a very rewarding part of your job. Most parents are concerned about their children and want to do what's best for them. Let them know that you share their concerns and that you want to provide high-quality child care. Make sure they know that you enjoy caring for their child and that you share their excitement when their child helps make breakfast, makes up a song, or masters her multiplication tables.

Providers work with families in a number of ways.

FCC providers work with families in a variety of ways. Daily conversations with parents are opportunities to get to know each other and to exchange information about a child's activities. FCC providers also encourage parents to become involved with their child's life at the FCC home. Parents should always be welcome at your FCC home. For parents who cannot visit during the day, you can offer a variety of other ways for them to participate. Often parents have questions about their child's development. They may ask you about child development or how to respond to their child's behavior. Though sometimes you will respond by drawing on your own knowledge and experience, remember that it's part of your role to help parents discover what works for them and their child. You can help parents feel confident and competent by asking them what they try at home and encouraging them to talk with other parents.

Listed below are examples of how FCC providers demonstrate their competence in working with families.

Communicating with Parents Often to Share Information About Their Child's Experiences and Development

Encourage parents to drop in at any time during your hours of operation. "Mrs. Jackson, we're looking forward to your visit at lunch today."

Share some good news with parents every day. "Connie's been trying hard to roll over. When I put her on her back, she kicks and squirms and almost makes it over to her tummy."

Use information about children's interests that was provided by parents. "Look, Teresa, this puppy has spots just like the ones on your puppy, Trixie."

Give parents information about their child's routines and activities. "Mary and Diego worked on their castle today. They play very well together."

Suggest ways parents can extend learning at home. "Mark really enjoys it when we have water play. When he takes a bath, you could give him some plastic cups and bottles so he can practice pouring."

Learn something about each parent as a way to build trust. "I thought of you last night, Dr. Parker, when I watched the television special on Seattle. Do you still have family living there?"

Offering a Variety of Ways for Parents to Be Involved in Their Child's Life at the FCC Home

Give parents opportunities to make decisions about their child's activities. "Now that Deena's in third grade, she's been asking to go to the playground with the other school-age children. How do you feel about that?"

Ask parents to help you include their culture in your activities. "Would you let us see the photographs you took on your trip home? The children would really like to see Young Lee with her grandmother and her cousins. She told us she got all dressed up and ate with chopsticks."

Share information on topics in which parents have expressed interest. "Several parents asked for ideas on helping children understand and express their feelings when a relative dies. When I mentioned it to my trainer, she told me about a workshop coming up at a local hospital next month. I'll share that information with the parents."

Sponsor a weekend fix-up day when parents and FCC providers work together to spruce up or make new equipment. "Mrs. Hanes, the children are having a great time jumping on the old tires you set up."

Find innovative ways for working parents to help when they can't come to the FCC home during the day. "Thanks so much for bringing our FCC photo album up to date, Mrs. Peterson. I never have time to arrange the new pictures."

Working Together with Families to Meet Children's Needs

Support families under stress. "It's often hard to adjust when there's a new baby at home. I'll help Sherrie as much as I can while she's with me."

Work with parents to figure out strategies for dealing with a child's behavior. "I've noticed that Nancy sleeps less and less at naptime. How long has she been sleeping during naptime at home?"

Help parents understand how much their children are learning through everyday activities. "When Jessica builds with the blocks, she is learning a lot about math concepts. Young children learn best when they can play with real objects. When she's older, she'll be able to apply this to adding and subtracting. Next time you buy Jessica a new toy, you might consider buying her some blocks."

Use familiar terms instead of jargon when you talk to parents. "Even though Sammy seems sure of himself, like most school-age children, he also worries a lot about things such as whether he's as smart as his classmates or whether his friends really like him."

Interpret children's behavior to their parents. "Loren is happy that her grandma's coming to visit. Today when she and Darnell played house, they told their babies that grandma was coming over."

Working with Families

In the following situations, FCC providers are working with families. As you read each one, think about what the providers are doing and why. Then answer the questions that follow.

Communicating with Parents Often to Exchange Information About Their Child's Experiences and Development

Yesterday was an exciting day for Janet. For the first time, she climbed to the top of the ladder and went down the slide by herself. Ms. Cruz watched her go down the slide and gave her a big hug when she reached the bottom. Over the last few weeks, Ms. Cruz and Janet's parents, the Carters, have been sharing information about Janet's progress. First she watched the other children use the slide, then she climbed up the ladder holding Ms. Cruz's hand, and recently she climbed up and down the ladder by herself. Ms. Cruz knew that Janet's family was very pleased that she was learning to conquer her fears. She decided not to say anything about Janet's accomplishment so they could see it for themselves. Today Janet and her mother arrive a little early. "Guess what," Mr. Carter says. "Janet went down the slide by herself." Ms. Cruz smiles and says, "You must be very excited. Janet is really going to explore the world in different ways now that she has learned to take a risk. We'll be very careful to make sure she can explore safely."

1. **Why did Ms. Cruz decide not to share the news of Janet's accomplishment?**

   _____

   _____

   _____

   _____

   _____

2. **What kinds of information will Ms. Cruz and the Carters need to share now that Janet is learning to take risks?**

   _____

   _____

   _____

   _____

   _____

Offering a Variety of Ways for Parents to Be Involved in Their Child's Life at the FCC Home

One day at pick-up time, Mr. Bradley asks Ms. Franklin how he can be involved in her FCC program: "I know Jerry only comes here after school, and I'm not sure what I can do, but I want to be more involved in his life at your home." Ms. Franklin expresses pleasure and asks Mr. Bradley several questions about his work and other interests. Then she says, "Often children really enjoy learning about something an adult is interested in. Your excitement makes them excited too. I could tell from your tone of voice when you mentioned hiking and being outdoors that you really enjoy it. That's something the children like to do, too. We are going on a field trip to the state park next month; perhaps you could join us." Mr. Bradley thinks for a minute, then says, "Well, if you can give me plenty of notice, I think I could get the time off. I might need some tips on how to help five children of different ages enjoy the outdoors, but I'd like to try it." A few weeks later, Mr. Bradley and Jerry arrive with backpacks and a pair of binoculars. "I read that article on including children of all ages in activities, and I'm ready to help!" He and Ms. Franklin help the children get ready for the trip. He is surprised at all the things Ms. Franklin must plan for. "I didn't realize how careful you are. I wouldn't have known to bring an emergency kit complete with parents' phone numbers." At the end of a very busy day, Mr. Bradley turns to Ms. Franklin and says, "Thank you for your help. I'll be glad to come back again. This was a lot of fun, and it was great to see Jerry with his friends."

1. **How did Ms. Franklin help Mr. Bradley think of something he could do with Jerry and the other children at the FCC home?**

_____

_____

_____

_____

2. **How did Ms. Franklin help Mr. Bradley feel more comfortable about working with a multi-age group?**

_____

_____

_____

_____

_____

Working Together with Families to Meet Children's Needs

"I just don't know what to do," says Ms. Thomas when she drops off her daughter, 3-year-old Marita, one morning. "Marita's been coming here for almost a month now, and she still cries and clings to me when I leave. I have to go to work; I can't stay with her all the time. Do you have any suggestions?" Ms. Kent says, "Marita usually stops crying a few minutes after you leave. It takes some children awhile to get used to being separated from their parents. I'll keep working with her to help her feel secure. What can I do to help you? Would you like to call me sometime to talk about separation? I could tell you more about what Marita does during the day." Ms. Thomas says, "That would be great. Let's talk tomorrow evening." Ms. Kent says, "I'll be looking forward to your call. Remember, this is a partnership. We'll work together to help Marita deal with separation." Ms. Kent holds the crying Marita and tells Ms. Thomas, "Feel free to call me and check on her after you get to work." As Ms. Thomas leaves for work looking a lot less worried, she waves and calls to Marita, "Goodbye! See you after naptime!" Marita calms down, and she and Ms. Kent pick out a story to read together.

1. **What did Ms. Kent do to help Ms. Thomas understand Marita's behavior?**

_____

_____

_____

_____

_____

2. **How did Ms. Kent help Marita and her mother cope with separation?**

_____

_____

_____

_____

_____

Compare your answers with those on the answer sheet at the end of this module. If your answers are different, discuss them with your trainer. There can be more than one answer.

Your Own Family Experiences

What is a family?

You bring many firsthand experiences to your role working with families. Most of us grew up in a family. Some of us are now raising families of our own or have grown children. Our own experiences influence how we view families, what we think a family should look like, and how parents should raise their children.

Think for a moment about what the word "family" means to you. Do you think of a mother and father and one or more children living together? Do you think of different kinds of family relationships?

The families of the children you work with may resemble your own, or they may be very different. Children may be growing up with a single mother or father or with stepparents. Some children are being raised by grandparents or by a teenage mother living at home with her own parents. Some families face stress caused by unemployment, serious illness, or frequent moves.

Parenting can be a difficult job.

The traditional view of a family as a mother and father and several children does not always apply today. In fact, only 7 percent of families in the United States consist of a mother who works in the home, a father who works outside the home, and their two children. Additionally, the stresses families experience today can make parenting a very difficult job.

It is not uncommon for FCC providers to blame parents when their children are having problems. This is especially true when FCC providers and parents have very different values and approaches to raising their children. It may help to remember that all parents want the best for their children and are probably trying as hard as they can to be good parents.

Spend a few minutes thinking of how your own views and life experiences may affect the way you work with families. Consider the following questions:

1. **Who did you consider to be part of the family you grew up in?**

_____

_____

_____

2. **How are families today different from the family you grew up in?**

_____

_____

_____

_____

263

3. What pressures do parents have today that your parents didn't experience?

_____

_____

_____

_____

_____

4. What pressures are the same?

_____

_____

_____

_____

_____

5. How do you think your views and experiences affect your work with families?

_____

_____

_____

_____

_____

_____

_____

_____

_____

_____

_____

When you have finished this overview section, you should complete the pre-training assessment. There is no glossary in this module.

P R E - T R A I N I N G   A S S E S S M E N T

Listed below are the skills that FCC providers use in their work with families. Think about whether you do these things regularly, sometimes, or not enough. Place a check in one of the columns on the right for each skill listed. Then discuss your answers with your trainer.

Skill	I Do This Regularly	I Do This Sometimes	I Don't Do This Enough
Communicating With Parents Often To Share Information About Their Child's Experiences and Development 1. Learning each parent's name and something about him or her to build trust.			
2. Providing parents with daily information about their child's routines and activities.			
3. Encouraging parents to visit the FCC home at any time during hours of operation.			
4. Suggesting a variety of ways to extend the child's learning at home.			
5. Holding regularly scheduled conferences to share information about each child's progress and to make plans for the future.			
Providing a Variety of Ways for Parents to Be Involved in Their Child's Life at the FCC Home 6. Involving parents in making decisions about their child's care.			
7. Sharing information on topics in which parents have expressed interest.			

Skill	I Do This Regularly	I Do This Sometimes	I Don't Do This Enough
8. Providing ways for parents to participate when they can't come to the FCC home during hours of operation.			
Working Together with Families to Meet Children's Needs 9. Helping parents understand the stages of child development so they can respond appropriately to their child's behavior.			
10. Working with parents to develop strategies for dealing with children's behavior and responding to their needs.			
11. Helping parents understand the reasons for their child's behavior.			
12. Providing support to families under stress.			
13. Helping parents recognize signs that a child is ready to learn something new.			
14. Helping parents understand how much their child is learning through everyday activities.			

Review your responses, then list three to five skills you would like to improve or topics you would like to learn more about to help you work with families. When you finish this module, you will list examples of your new or improved knowledge and skills.

_____

_____

_____

_____

_____

_____

_____

Discuss the overview and pre-training assessment with your trainer. Then begin the learning activities for Module 11.

I. Developing a Partnership with Parents

In this activity you will learn:

- to recognize and address the need that parents and FCC providers have to share information about children; and

- to develop and maintain a partnership with parents.

Strong partnerships benefit everyone.

The quality of your FCC program depends on the strong partnerships developed between you and the parents of the children in your care. Each partnership must be based on respect, trust, and the understanding that the child's development will be enhanced when all the adults who care for the child work together.

Developing a partnership may take a lot of work. Sometimes providers and parents have different views on child rearing. They may even have different ideas about a child's strengths, interests, and needs. Parents and FCC providers may not always understand each other's point of view and may disagree about how to solve a problem. What they almost always have in common, though, is genuine concern for the well-being of the child.

Strong partnerships benefit everyone involved. Parents feel reassured about their parenting skills and what is happening during child care. FCC providers also feel confident about their role, and they learn more about how to provide care that is based on their own and the parents' understanding of the child's needs, interests, and strengths. Children feel more secure knowing that both their parents and their FCC providers will keep them safe and help them learn.

The Initial Meeting

Your relationship with a child's parents begins when a family first comes to meet you and see your FCC home. Although the parents probably don't know you, they are thinking about leaving their child with you for most of the day, five days a week. It is natural for them to want to learn as much as they can about you, your program, the members of your own family, and the other children in your care. You will want to get to know the parents and to learn as much as you can about the child for whom you may be providing care—the child's personality, skills, health, special interests, family members, and so on.

269

Tell the parents something about yourself and why you chose to be a family child care provider. Give them a tour of the areas of your home that are used for family child care and the equipment and materials that are available for the children to use. If you keep a photo album of the FCC program, you can share this with the parents as you describe a typical day's activities. Be sure to describe how you use routines as important opportunities for learning.

Begin to get to know the parents, too. Ask about their interests, what kind of work they do, and how they feel about bringing their child to family child care. Reassure parents that you accept them as the most important persons in their child's life. Let them know how you will work with them to share information about their child and to make decisions about their child's care.

Parents will respect your business-like approach.

In this initial meeting you will want to present yourself as a warm and loving person who also has excellent business skills. You might think that parents won't care about your business skills, however, they are likely to respect your efficiency. Most parents want to leave their children with a professional provider whose organizational skills enable her to give the children plenty of attention.

Additional topics you might discuss during this visit include:

- your qualifications, experience, and training;

- members of your own family—children, spouse, others;

- how you would work with the parents to help their child get used to you and the other children;

- positive guidance strategies you use to help children develop self-discipline;

- neighborhood outings and get-togethers with other providers;

- age-specific issues such as toilet learning or providing a place and time for children to do their homework; and

- policies and procedures regarding your fees, hours of operation, late pick-ups, back-up providers, vacations (yours and theirs), responding to emergencies, sick children, and so on.

It's a good idea to close the meeting by agreeing on a time to get back in touch. Provide the parents with written copies of your daily schedule, policies, and so on. Suggest that they spend some time thinking about whether your FCC home is a good placement for their child. (You also will need time to think about whether you want to provide care for this child.) If you and the parents decide that your program is right for the child, agree on a time to meet again to

review and sign the contract for care and to plan for the child's first day. (See Module 12: Program Management for more information on business practices.)

Establishing the Partnership

When a child first comes to your FCC home, you and the parents will continue getting to know each other through brief conversations at drop-off and pick-up times. Show that you are interested in the parents by always greeting each by name. Share interesting, positive information about their child's day. Let them know by your attitude and tone of voice that their child is well cared for: "Susanna had fun today. She played with Carrie in the sand box, she painted, and she sat in my lap at story time." These kinds of daily communications will build trust and acceptance, which will lead to a strong partnership.

If parents don't respond to your efforts to establish a partnership, try to put yourself in their place. Try to understand their feelings about leaving their child with you. Often parents are concerned about not spending as much time with their children as they would like. It's helpful to think about your own feelings about the parents and how you may be conveying these through your tone of voice, facial expressions, or the kinds of information you share.

Although you do many things for children that parents also do (such as providing guidance or serving lunch), a provider's role is not the same as that of the parents. Always remember that parents need your support, but they don't need you to take over their role.

Maintaining a Strong Relationship

Once a trusting relationship has been established, you can strengthen the partnership through continued communication and appreciation for each partner's role in caring for the child. The partnership also grows when both parents and provider can see how the child benefits from their teamwork. "Janine doesn't cry any more when you leave. I think your idea of making her a book of family pictures to keep here really worked."

Try these suggestions.

Some suggestions for maintaining a strong partnership follow:

- **Respond to parents' concerns or questions even though they may seem trivial.** Such concerns are important to the parents and therefore should be acknowledged. "Yes, some 2-year-olds can zip their jackets, but many, like Gregory, aren't ready yet. I will provide more opportunities for him to use his finger skills, such as practicing on a zipper board."

- **Try parents' suggestions,** unless you think they will hurt the child, even when they differ from what you would do. "We'll be sure to let Jason do his homework in the kitchen if you think it's easier for him to concentrate in there."

- **Help parents focus on their child's accomplishments** rather than comparing their child to others the same age. "Denise always has a smile ready. She brings the sunshine into our home even on rainy days."

- **Treat parents with courtesy and respect no matter what is said or done.** "I think I understand what you are saying, but I would like some time to think about whether I want to change my policy about how much of a discount to give for two children from the same family."

- **Help children and parents feel good about belonging to the same family.** "Professor Courtland, Erica is so excited when she knows you're coming for lunch. She really likes it when the other kids talk about your visits."

- **Wait until you are asked before offering advice.** When you are asked, make sure you are clear about facts versus opinions. "According to most child development experts, children Billy's age are too young for formal reading lessons."

- **Acknowledge events and transitions in the child's and parents' lives.** "Congratulations on your promotion! Your wife told me the whole family had a party to celebrate."

- **Try to be flexible enough to respond to families' real needs.** One of the many advantages of family child care is that you often have the "luxury" of being flexible. You should avoid being taken advantage of, but if a father really needs to pick up his child half an hour late because he has to work late, you can reduce this family's stress by being flexible. (Depending on your policies, you might want to charge an additional fee for this service.)

- **Tell parents about the good things that happen each day.** It's not necessary to report every time their child has a fight or loses his or her temper. Share problems when you need to work together to help the child. "When Danielle gets angry, she hits the other children. I'd like to get together with you to discuss ways to help her."

- **Be sensitive to normal guilt feelings parents may have when they leave their children with you.** Be careful not to make assumptions about parents or judge them because their lifestyle is different from yours.

- **Help parents and children get through pick-up times as smoothly as possible.** Sometimes children use pick-up times to "get their parent's goat" by acting out, refusing to put on their coats, and so on. If the parents agree with your approach, take the lead in these situations. The child is still in your home, so your firm request will most likely be followed. The parents can assume the leadership role once they get to the car.

- **Keep in touch when the child is absent or ill.** "Hello, Mrs. Carson, how is Paula's ear infection today? We all miss her and hope she'll feel better soon."

- **Maintain confidentiality when parents share private information with you.** "I'm glad you told me about this. It will help me work with Brendan. You don't need to worry about me telling someone else. I understand that this was said in confidence."

Keeping Parents Informed About the Program

One of your most important responsibilities is to keep parents up-to-date on activities at your FCC home. Parents feel like real partners when they know specific things that are happening. For example, they like to know there's a new sandbox in your backyard, that you are participating in training, that you and the children will make vegetable soup for lunch today, and that this month's FCC workshop for parents is on promoting self-esteem. Some of this information is communicated during pick-up and drop-off times. These times, however, are usually too brief to keep all the parents informed about everything that you and the children have been doing.

Try these suggestions.

Here are some other suggestions for keeping parents informed.

- Establish a **message center** where each family has a box, folder, or message pocket (shoe bags work well for this). These can be used to provide parents with general news and information about their child.

- Provide each family with a **journal** that stays at your home and can be used by both you and the parents to share information about a child. Notices or flyers can be tucked in the journal so parents will see them.

- Set up a **parent bulletin board** in an area such as the front hall that all parents pass by. Post articles, a calendar of events, reminders of upcoming meetings, the week's menus, and other items of general interest.

- Write a **family newsletter** to cover the activities and news of your FCC home. If you care for school-age children, they might be interested in writing it. The children may help decide what to include, and you might suggest that they write about snacks and meals, upcoming events, and special accomplishments. ("Maggie has learned to crawl." "Terrence won the checkers championship.")

In this learning activity, for three days you will keep track of the ways you and the parents of the children in your care maintain effective partnerships. If the parents don't mind, you can tape record drop-off and pick-up times. If parents seem uncomfortable being taped, then take notes to capture the conversations between you and the parents. At the end of three days, play back the tape or review your notes to hear how you and the parents supported each other and maintained strong partnerships. You can use the blank form to organize the examples from your notes or tape. Begin by reading the example on the next page.

Maintaining Strong Partnerships
(Example)

You responded to a parent's concern or question.

Kim's stepfather asked me if I would make sure that she has a good snack because she has basketball practice this evening. I said I would be sure that Kim has an extra-healthy snack this afternoon.

You agreed to try a parent's suggestion.

Drew's father said that they are trying at home to cut down on the amount of time that Drew walks around sucking his thumb and carrying his blanket. He asked me to try keeping the blanket in the closet so Drew would have to ask for it if he wants it. We agreed that I would put it in the closet but would let Drew have it if he asked for it. We don't want to make too big a deal about it.

You told a parent about something good that happened to his or her child.

I told the Carters that Laura had really enjoyed making cornbread today. She especially liked cracking the eggs.

You treated a parent with courtesy and respect.

I explained to Mrs. Reese that even if Sandy does feel better in the morning, she shouldn't come back to the FCC program until her fever has been gone for a full day.

You and a parent solved a problem together.

Mr. Hill and I worked out a new system for sharing information. He's always in a hurry and doesn't have time to write in the journal. Instead, he will write me a note before eating breakfast and put it in Kathy's bag with her diapers and bottles.

You suggested ways for parents to extend their child's learning at home.

I told the Reeses how much Sandy enjoys tearing up old magazines and pasting the pieces on construction paper. I suggested that they save their old magazines so Sandy can do this at home.

A parent said something that made you feel appreciated.

Drew's mother told me that she really liked the way I take time to say goodbye to each child and tell them I hope they have a great evening at home with their parents.

Maintaining Strong Partnerships

You responded to a parent's concern or question.

_____

_____

_____

_____

_____

You agreed to try a parent's suggestion.

_____

_____

_____

_____

_____

You told a parent about something good that happened to his or her child.

_____

_____

_____

_____

_____

You treated a parent with courtesy and respect.

_____

_____

_____

_____

_____

You and a parent solved a problem together.

_____
_____
_____
_____
_____

You suggested ways for parents to extend their child's learning at home.

_____
_____
_____
_____
_____

A parent said something that made you feel appreciated.

_____
_____
_____
_____
_____
_____

Discuss this activity with your trainer.

LEARNING ACTIVITIES

II. Working Together to Support Children

In this activity you will learn:

- to recognize the different kinds of information about individual children that parents and providers can share; and

- to exchange information with parents so you both can help children grow and develop.

Parents and providers bring to their partnership different sets of knowledge about children. Typically a parent's focus is on an individual child, whereas a provider has a broader view based on knowledge of child development and experiences working with many children in a small group setting. When parents and providers combine their knowledge and information, they can create a total picture of the child. The information that parents and providers share each morning and afternoon about a child's behavior and activities helps them plan to best meet the needs of the child. In addition, sharing information about the child's growth and development helps parents feel good about their decision to have you care for their child. Here are some examples of the kinds of information each half of the partnership can provide.

What Parents Know

Parents have information about the following areas in a child's life:

- **Health and growth history.** "After Ben's check-up at the pediatrician, I'll let you know how the treatment for his 'toeing in' is progressing. I know you'll want to hear about his condition so we can work together to coordinate his treatment."

- **Relationships with other family members.** "Carla really enjoys being with her cousin. Every morning they eat together and talk about their plans for the day."

- **Ways the child likes to be held or comforted.** "When Yancey is tired, he likes to have his back rubbed. It helps him settle down."

- **Which foods the child enjoys.** "Tom started eating carrots today. He really enjoyed them."

- **What the child did last night, over the weekend, or on vacation.** "We had a great vacation at the beach. Roxanne tried surfing for the first time, and she was pretty good!"

- **Which foods the child can or cannot eat.** "Donna's doctor has provided a statement that she is allergic to all kinds of berries. He has suggested some alternate foods that she can eat."

- **How the child reacts to changes in routines.** "Sonia gets very upset if I ask her to dress before breakfast. She likes to eat first, then put her clothes on."

- **What the child likes to do at home.** "Timmy always wants to stay in the bathtub and play. He hates to get out."

- **What the child is afraid of.** "Travis is afraid of clowns. We're not sure why, but he always cries when he sees one."

- **Who the child plays with at home.** "Kurt likes to hang around with Ricky, our 12-year-old (going on 17) neighbor. He and Ricky like to listen to music and talk about rock stars."

- **The family's lifestyle.** "We like to get outdoors as much as possible. Peter likes to go hiking with us in the mountains."

- **How the child "used to be" as well as how the child is now.** "When he was 3, Nick liked books about trains and trucks. Now that he's 10, he's more interested in reading magazines about sports car racing."

- **What happened last night or over the weekend.** "Karen woke up three times last night. I think she's going to be a little tired this morning."

What FCC Providers Know

An FCC provider has information about the following areas in a child's life:

- **Favorite play materials.** "After you leave in the morning, Tanya goes right to the blocks. She really likes to make tall buildings."

- **Which toys are too frustrating.** "Cory isn't ready to do the farm puzzle yet. He's learned to pick out the ones that don't have as many pieces."

- **What challenges the child enjoys.** "Shauna is spending a lot of time taking apart that old clock radio. She really wants to see how everything fits together."

- **How the child plays with others.** "When we go to the playground, Janna likes to watch before she joins in with the other children."

- **How the child reacts to changes in the environment.** "Whenever I put out new props for dramatic play, Ellen is the first child to use them."

- **How the child tells others what he or she is feeling.** "When Gina is angry with another child, she says, 'I don't like you. You're not my friend.'"

- **What the child talks about during the day.** "Today Carlos talked about going to see his cousin, Louis. He's very excited about it."

- **What the child does when his or her parents leave.** "Today I heard Jerry telling Sandy, 'Don't cry, your mom will come back soon!' I think that's his way of assuring himself that you will always come back."

- **What the child did today.** "Mark helped cook lunch today. We had chicken and cheese burritos."

In this learning activity you will focus on sharing information with the parents of a child in your care. Select a child and family with whom you feel comfortable but would like to know better. Let them know you have selected them. For two weeks, record your daily communications with the parents—any information you each shared. At the same time, look for any changes in how you are able to meet this child's needs. Read the shortened example that follows; then begin the activity.

Daily Communication Record
(Example)

Child: _Donna_   **Age:** _3-1/2 years_

Parents: _Dr. Karen Anderson and Mr. Frank Lopez_

How long child has been in your care: _4 months_

Observation period: _June 6-20_

Day One

A.M.   *Greeted Dr. Anderson and told her about this activity. She was pleased to hear that I am working on this module. She told me Donna is excited about playing dress-up.*

P.M.   *Mr. Lopez came to pick up Donna. I told him that Donna played dress-up with her friend Sheila. They put on lots of jewelry. He said she likes to wear her grandma's jewelry.*

Day Two

A.M.   *Mr. Lopez brought Donna. Dr. Anderson had told him I was doing this learning activity. He wished me luck. I told him we were going to set up water play outside today and that Donna really liked to use the turkey baster to fill up cups and bottles. He asked if she could do that at home. I told him she could do it at the sink, in a dishpan, or in the bathtub. He seemed pleased with my ideas.*

P.M.   *Dr. Anderson picked up Donna. I told her Donna helped us carry out the water play toys today and that Donna ate a big lunch and made fruit smoothies this afternoon. She was surprised because Donna doesn't eat much fruit at home. I said that often the children eat more when they help make it. She told me Donna would be late on Friday because she's going to the dentist for the first time. I asked if Donna has expressed any concern about going to the dentist. She said, "Yes, a little." I asked if Donna knows what to expect. She said, "No, I don't think so." I said she could borrow our book, "Going to the Dentist." She and Donna could read and discuss the book. It would give Donna an idea of what to expect. Dr. Anderson thanked me and took the book with her.*

First Weekly Summary
(Complete after five days)

Information you shared:

That I'm doing this learning activity.

Donna played dress-up with Sheila.

Donna likes to use the baster.

Ways Donna could play with a turkey baster at home.

Donna helped carry the water play toys.

Donna likes fruit smoothies.

Information parents shared:

Donna is excited about dressing up.

Donna likes to wear her grandma's jewelry.

Donna doesn't eat much fruit at home.

Donna is going to the dentist, and she's a little scared.

How has the partnership helped you meet this child's needs?

Donna seems to like seeing her parents laugh and talk with me.

I know more about what Donna likes to do.

I can suggest things for her parents to do with her at home.

I suggested a book to help her parents prepare her for going to the dentist.

Daily Communication Record
(Example)

Child: _____ **Age:** _____

Parents: _____

How long child has been in your care: _____

Observation period: _____

Day One

A.M. _____

_____

_____

_____

P.M. _____

_____

_____

_____

Day Two

A.M. _____

_____

_____

_____

P.M. _____

_____

_____

_____

Day Three

A.M. _____

_____

_____

_____

_____

P.M. _____

_____

_____

_____

_____

Day Four

A.M. _____

_____

_____

_____

_____

P.M. _____

_____

_____

_____

_____

Day Five

A.M. _____

_____

_____

_____

_____

P.M. _____

_____

_____

_____

_____

First Weekly Summary
(Complete after five days)

Information you shared:

_____
_____
_____
_____
_____
_____
_____
_____
_____
_____
_____
_____
_____
_____

Information parents shared:

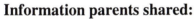

_____
_____
_____
_____
_____
_____
_____
_____
_____
_____
_____
_____
_____
_____

Day Six

A.M. _____

_____

_____

_____

_____

P.M. _____

_____

_____

_____

Day Seven

A.M. _____

_____

_____

_____

P.M. _____

_____

_____

_____

Day Eight

A.M. _____

_____

_____

_____

P.M. _____

_____

_____

_____

Day Nine

A.M. _____

_____

_____

_____

P.M. _____

_____

_____

_____

Day Ten

A.M. _____

_____

_____

_____

P.M. _____

_____

_____

_____

Second Weekly Summary
(Complete at the end of another five days)

Information you shared:

_____
_____
_____
_____
_____
_____

Information parents shared:

_____
_____
_____
_____
_____
_____

Review all your notes and complete the following:

How has the partnership between you and the parents helped meet this child's needs?

(Give at least five examples)

_____
_____
_____
_____
_____
_____

Discuss this activity with the child's parents and agree on ways to keep in touch on a regular basis. Also discuss it with your trainer.

III. Offering Ways for Parents to Be Involved

In this activity you will learn:

- to use techniques for parent involvement; and

- to plan and implement a parent involvement strategy.

Most parents are interested in becoming involved in their child's life at your FCC home, but they may not know about all the different ways they can contribute to the program. Sometimes parents can arrange their work schedules so they can occasionally eat lunch with the children or come on a walking trip around the neighborhood. These daytime visits benefit both parent and child; however, many parents are not able to participate in this way. You need to suggest a variety of options for parent involvement that match parents' interests, skills, and schedules. Part of your orientation for new parents could include completing a brief questionnaire about how they can play an active role in their child's development.

In addition to matching parents' interests with several options for involvement, you also need to let parents know how much their participation benefits your FCC program. Parents who come to visit during the day may enjoy themselves so much that they don't need much encouragement to offer to do it again. The parent who sews new curtains for the children's puppet theater, however, may never see the theater in action. In such a case, be sure to send a note home thanking the parent. You could describe how the children are using the theater or enclose a picture of the theater in action.

Try these suggestions.

Here are some suggestions for offering parents ways to become involved in your program.

- Organize a **family dinner** when parents can eat dinner with their children and your family at the FCC home. The children can help you prepare some simple food, or each family can bring their specialty to a potluck feast.

- Provide opportunities for parents to **work together on projects** over a period of time, such as building a new sandbox or turning over soil for a garden. When a project is completed, hold a celebration party.

- Set up a **job jar** containing index cards listing FCC program-related jobs you never get around to doing that a parent could do at home. Parents can select a job from the jar, then see you for additional instructions. Jobs could include repairing broken toys, mending dress-up clothes, or making Lotto boards or other materials for the program.

- **Open the FCC program for an evening or on the weekend** when the children come to your home as though it were a regular day. Parents come too and play with the children, lead activities, serve snacks, or sit back and observe how their child plays with others.

- Set up a **parent center** where you display books, magazines, brochures, and other resources of interest to parents.

- Ask a parent to organize a **photo album** about the FCC home. You can provide the pictures and the book; the parent can put it together. Include a cover page thanking the parent who organized the album. Lend the photo album to parents so they can look at it at home with their children.

- Use parents as **book reviewers**. Parents may read children's books or books on child development or parenting that they'd like to recommend. Provide a book review form that they can complete, listing the title, author, publisher, and price. For children's books, leave space on the form for parents to record what ages the book is appropriate for, what the book is about, and why they and their child liked it. You can hang these reviews on your bulletin board and use them to select books for your FCC home.

In this learning activity you will try out a parent involvement strategy. Select from those mentioned earlier, or make up one of your own. First read the example; then complete the chart that follows it to describe the strategy you chose and how it helped parents become involved.

Parent Involvement Strategy
(Example)

Strategy:

Parent volunteers will make audiotapes of themselves reading stories. I have a tape player, but most of the story tapes you can buy are too expensive or the stories are not of interest to the children.

Plans:

I will mention this project to parents at pick-up and drop-off times. I will supply blank tapes, and they can borrow my tape recorder and microphone if they don't have their own. The books can come from my collection or the library, or they can be favorites children have at home. I'll try to make sure we tape a variety of books. The tapes will be used in the quiet corner where children like to go to be alone for awhile.

Results:

Two parents volunteered to make tapes. Each parent made four tapes, so now we have a good supply for the quiet corner. The children really enjoy hearing their parent's voices on tape. Both parents said they would be happy to make more tapes whenever we need them.

Follow-up:

I will make this an ongoing parent involvement project. I asked Mrs. Porter, one of the parents who made tapes, to help me keep track of which books we tape. I think the children would like it if all the parents took a turn making story tapes. This could be a good project for parents who are not able to visit during the day.

Now select a parent involvement strategy you would like to implement. Write your plans on the form that follows this page. After implementing your strategy, write the results and some plans for follow-up.

Parent Involvement Strategy

Strategy:

_____
_____
_____
_____
_____
_____

Plans:

_____
_____
_____
_____
_____
_____

Results:

_____
_____
_____
_____
_____
_____

Follow-up:

_____
_____
_____
_____
_____
_____

Discuss this activity with your trainer. You might also discuss the activity with another provider.

IV. Planning and Participating in Parent-Provider Conferences

In this activity you will learn:

- to prepare for a parent-provider conference by reviewing information about a child's development; and

- to participate in a parent-provider conference.

Once or twice a year, it is important for you to meet with each child's parents to review how the child is progressing in all areas of development and to set goals for the child's continued growth and learning. Conferences are times when you can discuss topics that may not come up in everyday conversations. Parent-provider conferences are opportunities to focus on one child and family without any distractions or interruptions. A conference can be an opportunity to explain your goals for children and to reaffirm your partnership with the parents. Although much information about the child is shared daily, conferences are times when you and the parents can discuss the child in-depth, look back over time, and strengthen your commitment to this partnership.

Parents will also have goals for the conference. Often parents want to be reassured that you like their child, that you are competent, and that you think they are doing a good job caring for their child. They may have a specific concern they would like to discuss or a suggestion for how they would like you to work with their child. They may also have a concern about your FCC program or a complaint about something you did or didn't do.

Planning for Conferences

Explain to parents during your initial meeting how often conferences take place, their purpose, and what is discussed. When it's time to schedule a conference, ask parents what is the best time for them to meet with you. This should be a time when you are not caring for children. Ask them to think of any questions they might have and topics they want to cover. Tell them you hope to learn more about the child's life at home so you can better support the child's growth.

To make the best use of the time set aside for the conference, it's important to do some planning. You will need to think about what points you want to cover. Review your observation notes and any other written materials that provide objective information about the child. You can also collect samples of the child's artwork or other creations. Organize your notes to make sure you have covered all areas of development—physical, cognitive, language, social, and emotional. If you have any concerns about the child's health, these should be documented.

Parents often want to know what the child is like in a group situation. They want to know as much as possible about what their child does all day, who he plays with, what makes him happy or sad, and what he enjoys doing. Try to collect "stories" to share that will help parents picture and understand how their child spends his day.

Sometimes providers feel a little uneasy before a conference. It may help to role-play with your trainer, a friend, or your spouse. You can practice sharing your observations and answering the kinds of questions the parents are likely to ask. You may want to get your trainer to attend your first conference to help you overcome any initial discomfort.

Participating in the Conference

At the start of the conference, try to establish a relaxed and comfortable tone. Anticipate at least five minutes of social conversation before beginning your more serious discussions. Begin by telling the parents how the conference will proceed: "I'm so glad you could both come today. Let's begin with your question about what Karen does all day. I have several observations to share with you. Then I'd like to hear more about what Karen does at home."

During the conference, be sure there are many opportunities for parents to provide input and ask questions. Be very careful to avoid sounding like "the expert." Offer advice only when asked and only when you know the answer to a parent's questions. Leave diagnosis of a child's condition to medical and other professionals.

After discussing all areas of the child's development, the next step is to set some goals and develop strategies to promote the child's development. These strategies will be implemented at home and at the FCC program. These goals and strategies will serve as the framework for discussions at the next conference.

Try these suggestions.

Here are some other suggestions for conducting successful conferences.

- Begin and end the conference with a positive statement about your relationship with the child. "I really enjoy Timothy's sense of humor. He's at an age where children love to tell silly jokes."

- When parents seem reluctant to talk about their concerns, ask them an open-ended question. "Is there anything else about Rebecca or what we do here in my FCC program that you'd like to discuss?"

- Summarize your discussion at the end of the conference, emphasizing what actions you each have agreed to take. "I will spend more time looking at books with Laura now that I know she likes to do that at home. And you'll bring in her special books from home, so we can read them before naptime. That will make her feel more secure."

- When parents ask you for advice about handling a specific situation, respond in ways that help them discover what will work best for their child. You might share a suggestion based on your experience or one that you observed other parents trying. Sometimes, just by listening, you can help parents see that they already have an answer. "I think that would probably work very well for Nicky. If you let him choose between several acceptable items—for example, his red sweater, the blue one, or a sweatshirt—it will probably put an end to your fights about what he should wear to school."

In this learning activity you will plan, implement, and evaluate a conference with the parents of one of the children in your care. Begin by reading the shortened example. Then develop your own plan, including information from your own observations. Conduct the conference; then answer the evaluation questions.

Planning a Parent-Provider Conference

Child: *Justine*　　　　　　　　　　　　**Parent(s):** *Mr. and Mrs. Ferraro*

Age: *8-1/2 years*　　　　　　　　　　　**Age at last conference:** *8 years*

Date of conference: *March 23*　　　　　**Date of last conference:** *September 20*

What does this child like to do?

Justine likes to read to the younger children. She enjoys talking to me about her school work. She likes our cooking activities.

What makes this child happy?

Justine loves to sing. Listening to music cheers her up when she's down.

What makes this child sad?

Daniel doesn't come on Wednesdays. She always seems to feel a little sad when he's gone.

With whom does this child play, and in what ways?

She enjoys playing with Daniel. He's about the same age as she is, and they enjoy playing board games together. She also likes playing with Toni, who is 8 months old. She likes to read to Toni and play peek-a-boo.

Anecdotes to share:

About a month ago, it was very gloomy outside and all the children seemed restless. I asked Justine if she thought it would be fun to get dressed up and have a parade. She thought it was a great idea and got all the others organized. She helped them put on dress-up clothes with scarves and beads and even painted their faces with our special face paints. I took pictures for our FCC photo album.

Concerns/goals:

I would like to see her more interested and involved in physical activities. I don't think she's getting enough exercise. Also, she gets quite frustrated when she tries to do things she's never done before, such as playing a new board game.

Conference Evaluation

After the conference, think about what happened and answer these questions:

How did you start the conference?

I welcomed the Ferraros to my home and let them know how much I enjoy caring for Justine.

How did you encourage parent input?

I asked them to tell me what they would like to know about Justine's activities before and after school. I encouraged them to offer their ideas and suggestions throughout the conference.

How did you work together to set a goal or solve a problem?

They also were interested in helping Justine get more involved in physical activities. They agreed that we should encourage her to get some more exercise. We developed some strategies for encouraging her to be more active. I will observe to learn what kinds of physical activities she does enjoy and plan to do them more often. We also agreed to encourage her interest in cooking by taking it to the next level.

What will you and the parents do to help this child grow and develop over the next six months?

I will encourage Justine to spend more time participating in activities that develop her large motor skills, and I will think of new activities that she might enjoy. Her parents will talk to Justine about taking swimming or gymnastics lessons.

Mrs. Ferraro will share some family recipes for snacks that Justine and the other children can make. Justine is ready to handle recipes that require more complicated cooking techniques.

How did you summarize and end the conference?

I reviewed our discussion, restated the goals we agreed on, and described what each of us had agreed to do for Justine.

I gave them copies of the photographs I took on the day we had the parade. I'd been saving them as a surprise. I encouraged them to let Justine know what we discussed and share with her what we each agreed to do to help her become more involved in physical activities and to increase her cooking skills.

What would you do differently next time?

I would allow more time for the conference. I felt a little rushed because I needed to drive my daughter to her swimming lesson.

Planning a Parent-Provider Conference

Child: _____ **Parent:** _____

Age: _____ **Age at last conference:** _____

Date of conference: _____ **Date of last conference:** _____

What does this child like to do?

_____

_____

_____

What makes this child happy?

_____

_____

_____

What makes this child sad?

_____

_____

_____

With whom does this child play, and in what ways?

_____

_____

_____

Anecdotes to share:

_____

_____

_____

Concerns/goals:

_____

_____

_____

Now hold your conference with the child's parents. Ask for their ideas on suggested goals, and add them to the list above if you both agree.

Conference Evaluation

After the conference, think about what happened and answer these questions:

How did you start the conference?

_____

_____

_____

_____

_____

How did you encourage parent input?

_____

_____

_____

_____

_____

How did you work together to set a goal or solve a problem?

_____

_____

_____

_____

_____

What will you and the parents do to help this child grow and develop over the next six months?

_____

_____

_____

_____

_____

How did you summarize and end the conference?

_____

_____

_____

_____

What would you do differently next time?

_____

_____

_____

_____

_____

Discuss this learning activity with your trainer.

V. Resolving Differences

In this activity you will learn:

- to listen to parents' concerns and try to understand their viewpoints; and

- to work with parents to resolve differences and solve problems.

Disagreements may occur.

No matter how hard you work at maintaining partnerships with the parents of the children in your care, there will be times when you or the parents will be upset or angry about something related to the child's care. Some of these disagreements will be easy to resolve. For example, if a parent is angry because his daughter's mittens have disappeared three times this week, you can apologize and promise to work out a better system for storing the child's belongings. Other situations will be more complex; parents and provider will need to spend some time listening and communicating with one another to understand and respect each other's viewpoints. For example, if a parent expects you to spank her child when she wets her pants, you might schedule an evening meeting to discuss the situation and the positive approach you use to help toddlers learn to use the toilet.

Often a parent's anger results from a misunderstanding or miscommunication about your policies or use of developmentally appropriate child care practices. You might need to remind parents of policies (which you may have already provided in writing), or you might need to explain how the care you provide is based on knowledge of child development. It is an important part of your job always to treat parents with respect. When resolving differences with upset or angry parents, first acknowledge their feelings and concerns. Then try to understand why they are angry or upset. Finally, work with them to develop solutions that are in the best interests of the child and the parents. Your goal is to solve the problem without damaging the partnership you have worked hard to establish and maintain.

Try these suggestions.

Here are some suggestions to help you resolve differences in ways that will strengthen your partnerships with parents.

- Remember that some conflicts are to be expected. They are part of life when two (or more) individuals work together to foster the growth and development of the same child.

- Talk with someone else about the situation to help you get an objective picture of what is happening. A Resource and Referral (R&R) counselor, another provider or your spouse might be able to provide a different perspective.

- Be willing to apologize when an apology is in order. When you make mistakes acknowledge them, and let parents know what you will do to avoid repeating them.

- Keep the child's best interests in the forefront as you address differences with parents. Children need to trust both their parents and their provider.

- Try to look at the situation through parents' eyes. Listen to them with an open mind so you can truly understand their concerns.

You have a responsibility to provide care based on your knowledge of child development and what is appropriate practice in facilitating children's growth and development. Even when you and a child's parents work as a team, there will be times when parents ask you to do something contrary to your professional judgment. When this happens, explain your position and try hard to understand the parent's viewpoint. As an early childhood professional, you may need to stand firm in your belief regarding what is right for the child. It may help to remember that the developmentally appropriate practices presented in this training program and others are based on years of research that have identified the most effective ways for adults to support children's growth and development.

In this learning activity you will think about how you resolve differences with parents of the children you care for. Begin by reading the three examples on the next page that describe how one FCC provider handled some difficult situations. Then read the situations described on the next page and describe how you would respond. Remember, your goal is to resolve differences while keeping the lines of communication open between you and the parents.

How Would You Respond in These Difficult Situations?

1. Dinner at Grandma's

Today Reverend Greene arrives one hour early to pick up Gregory (27 months). Gregory has been playing outside and is quite dirty. Reverend Greene says in a controlled but obviously angry voice, "I told him this morning that we were going to his Grandma's house for dinner. I thought he'd tell you to have him ready." You overcome the urge to say "but you are an hour early" and focus on solving the problem—getting Gregory clean. What will you do?

First, I will calmly explain that I must continue caring for the other children, but Reverend Greene is welcome to use the bathroom to get Gregory clean. I will suggest that Gregory change into his emergency clothes for the visit with Grandma. Later I will call Reverend Greene to explain that I can honor special requests such as having a child ready early if I know about them in advance. I will also explain that Gregory is not old enough to relay messages to me. I will remind him that if either one of us is too busy to talk during drop-off time, there is room on the sign-in sheet to write each other notes.

2. An Earlier Bedtime

This afternoon when Mrs. Henderson picks up Lauren (4 years), you tell her that Lauren has been tired and a little cranky the past few days. You suggest that she might need an earlier bedtime. Mrs. Henderson responds in a strained voice, "We like to spend time with Lauren in the evenings. After all, we don't see her all day." You sense that Mrs. Henderson feels that you are questioning her good judgment and criticizing her parenting skills. What will you do?

I will apologize to Mrs. Henderson for making a suggestion before getting more information about the situation. Next, I will tell her that I recognize how important it is for parents to spend time with their child each day. Then I will let her know that when Lauren is tired, she misses out on a lot of the fun we have during the day. Finally, I will suggest that we talk over the phone later in the evening to see if we can work out a solution.

3. Always Late

You've been taking care of Carlotta (6 years) for several months. Frequently during this time her parents have been late paying you, and several times a week they are late picking her up. Most of the time this is not a problem; however, several times you missed your exercise class because they were late. You really like taking care of Carlotta, but you are upset by her parents' behavior. It's gotten to the point where you are no longer friendly when you see them and don't take the time you should to share information about the child. What will you do?

I need to put on my business person hat to deal with this problem. I will ask Carlotta's parents to meet with me in the evening or on the weekend to discuss this situation. During the meeting I will reassure them that I enjoy caring for Carlotta and want to continue doing so. I will explain that our contract states that payment is due every Friday and that Carlotta will be picked up no later than 6:00 p.m. I will offer to renegotiate the contract; for example, I could charge an additional fee for extending the hours of care, if the current arrangement does not meet their needs.

How Would You Respond in These Difficult Situations?

1. Neighborhood Picnic

Today was a very busy day. In the morning you and the children prepared a picnic lunch; then you walked to the park to meet another FCC provider and her children. The two groups of children played well together and really enjoyed each other's company. Unfortunately, with all the excitement, you forgot that Darlene's stepfather was picking her up early today to take her to the dentist. When you get back to your house, you find Mr. Kaminski waiting in his car. What will you do?

_____

_____

_____

_____

_____

_____

_____

_____

2. Carrot Muffins

Yesterday was Kenny's birthday. His mother brought a big box of carrot muffins to share with the other children. You celebrated Kenny's birthday in the afternoon when the younger children were rested from their naps and the older ones were home from school. Polly (8 years) has a weight problem, and her mother has asked you to provide only low-calorie, nutritious snacks. You let Polly have one muffin along with the other children. You meant to ask her mother if Polly's diet could be amended for this special occasion, but as usual the morning was pretty hectic, and you forgot. Today when Polly and her mother arrive, Mrs. Giovanni expresses her concern. "I thought we agreed that you would help Polly stick to her diet. She told me you had carrot muffins for snack yesterday. What's going on here?" What will you do?

_____

_____

_____

_____

_____

_____

_____

_____

3. Caitlin Doesn't Take Naps!

The Randalls have enrolled their daughter Caitlin (28 months) in your FCC program. You met several times to discuss your program—a typical day, your approach to discipline, fees and other policies—and you have all signed the parent-provider agreement. They seem very comfortable with you and are pleased that you have room for Caitlin. On Caitlin's first day, they arrive a little early to provide some time for Caitlin to get used to her new setting and to discuss any final details concerning her care. Ms. Randall says, "By the way, one thing we forgot to tell you is that Caitlin doesn't take naps. She has lots of energy and never seems to want to rest. We just let her decide when she's tired." This is certainly something you should have discussed earlier! All of the children in your care take naps or rest quietly. What will you do?

_____

_____

_____

_____

_____

_____

_____

_____

_____

_____

_____

Discuss your responses with your trainer.

LEARNING ACTIVITIES

VI. Reaching Out to Families

In this activity you will learn:

- to recognize signs that families are under stress; and

- to provide support to families under stress.

Parents of young children—especially first-time parents—often suffer from too much stress in their lives. Perhaps they don't get enough sleep, feel guilty for having to put their child in child care, are under pressure at work, or don't know how to deal with their child's troublesome (but probably normal) behaviors. Because they view providers as people who are caring and knowledgeable about children, most parents will feel comfortable seeking your advice about child rearing and other problems. As an FCC provider you are in an excellent position to provide help to parents who, for a variety of reasons, are experiencing stress.

You can reach out to parents by providing support, encouragement, and information. You can:

- recognize when parents are under stress;

- help parents locate resources; and

- give parents information and guidance on child growth and development.

Recognizing When Parents Are Under Stress

When a family is under stress, the parents may seem disorganized, frequently forgetting important items such as diapers or bottles of formula. A parent might seem frustrated when a child is slow to get ready to go home, or the parent might state that he or she doesn't know how to handle the child's independent behavior. Parents under stress might be unwilling to accept help, or they might be more interested in talking about their own problems than their child's.

When you see signs of stress, it is important that you do not add to them. You can wait for another day to discuss their child's problem behavior or tell them about your upcoming vacation. On the other hand, you will want to share information about their child's day that will help them get through a difficult evening. For example, letting a parent know that a teething infant has been cranky all day allows you

to discuss ways to help ease the infant's pain. Because the parent knows why the infant is crying, he or she is less likely to be frustrated or angered by the crying and more likely to provide the comfort the child needs. When parents feel less stress, they are more likely to interact positively with their children and less likely to become angry and lash out at them.

Here are some causes of stress:

- serious illness or death of a family member;

- an unplanned or unwanted pregnancy;

- separation and divorce;

- failure to receive a promotion;

- unemployment; and

- geographic and social isolation.

Make an effort to really get to know the parents of the children in your care. Invite parents into your home when they bring their children in the morning and pick them up at the end of the day. Place a suggestion box in a prominent place and draw attention to it. Invite parents to visit often and make them welcome. Remember that you and the parents are part of a team working for the child's good.

When you think parents may need professional help, offer resources which may help. Your job is to help parents get the support they need, not to provide it yourself.

Helping Parents Locate Resources

Parents often need information on where in the community they can get help for themselves, their child, or the family. Your local R&R, hospitals, or colleges may provide you with information about parent education opportunities. Here are some things you can do to help.

- Call parents' attention to resources, newspaper or magazine articles, workshops, and television or radio shows on stages of child development, positive guidance, and family life. Chances are if you find an article or show of interest, it will also be interesting to parents.

- Post notices of special programs offered by community groups.

- Display books on topics of interest to parents—stepparenting, juggling home and work responsibilities, child development, communication, health and nutrition—and invite parents to borrow these resources.

- Tell them about services provided by the support organizations in your community.

- Provide names, phone numbers, locations, and hours of operation when you suggest a program or event.

- Offer reluctant parents help in contacting other resources.

Giving Parents Information and Guidance on Child Growth and Development

Some parents know very little about child development. Because they have inappropriate expectations for their children's behavior, they may think their child is being difficult or disrespectful, and they might lash out at their children rather than helping the child learn appropriate behavior. Here are some things you can do to help.

- Tell parents about workshops on topics relevant to their child's stage of development—soothing colicky babies, adjusting to a new sibling, toilet learning, helping children with homework, and fostering independence, to name a few.

- Include information on growth and development in your newsletters or on your parent bulletin board. When possible, give examples based on the children in your care. "Now that Teresa can pull herself up, it won't be long until she's walking!"

- Encourage parents to attend parent education workshops.

- Lend books or videotapes.

- Meet with parents to discuss particular problems.

- Introduce parents whose children are of similar ages and suggest they share experiences and strategies that work.

Also, during drop-off and pick-up times and during longer visits during the day, without any extra effort or planning you can model for parents various developmentally appropriate ways to meet children's needs. For example, several parents might see the following interactions between a provider and the children in her care:

Ms. Danforth encourages Gina (28 months) to help put away the blocks. Next she talks and laughs with Evan (6 months) as she diapers him. Then she asks Bart (4 years) a question about his painting—"How did you make these long, squiggly lines?" A few minutes later she asks Patty (9 years) her opinion about a community recycling program.

These parents might comment:

- "I can't get her to put her toys away at home."

- "He squirms around so much at home that I just want to get the diaper changed as quickly as possible."

- "All his paintings look the same to me."

- "I never thought to talk to her about 'adult' topics."

The provider can then use these comments to open conversations about why she promoted the toddler's self-help skills, took advantage of the diapering routine as an opportunity to communicate with the infant, supported the preschool child's creativity by asking about his painting, or encouraged the school-age child to think and express her opinions. When you demonstrate positive ways of working with children, you do a lot to help parents improve their interactions with their children.

In this activity you will keep records of times when you reached out to parents in response to their requests or because you noticed that they needed your support. Over the next few weeks, make a note of these requests. Write down the problem or need you or the parent identified, how you responded, and what the outcome was. Begin by reading the examples that follow.

Reaching Out to Families
(Example)

Child: *Larry*   **Age:** *8 years*   **Date:** *October 23*

Problem or Need:

Larry is having difficulty adjusting to a new school. He wants to move back to where his family used to live. He threatens to run away from home. At family child care he hits and pinches the other children when they get in his way.

What parents asked for or what I saw was needed:

Ideas on how to help Larry adjust to his new home, school, and child care situation.

My response:

We talked about the problem. I suggested they spend extra time with Larry alone. I also gave them information about youth sports teams (Larry is a basketball fanatic), and I recommended contacting the counselor at the elementary school. I've heard from my friends that she is very good.

The outcome:

Larry's parents say that the suggestions seem to be working. Larry is not as upset, and he really likes spending extra time with his mom and dad. They signed him up for basketball, which will start next week. They contacted the school counselor, and she has begun meeting with Larry.

Reaching Out to Families

(Example)

Child: *Germaine*   **Age:** *21 months*   **Date:** *October 23*

Problem or Need:

Germaine has been having a hard time getting to sleep at night. She gets up several times, asks for a drink, begs for another story, and so on. Her parents are exhausted!

What parents asked for or what I saw was needed:

Help in getting Germaine to fall asleep within a reasonable amount of time.

My response:

We talked about the problem. I described the rituals we go through at naptime. They will try some of those, and they will put her to sleep a half-hour later than usual. Also, they will read her a story while she is in bed. They had been reading it before they put her in bed.

The outcome:

It took a few days, but Germaine finally settled into a new pattern. Her parents said that she likes lying in her bed and listening to a story and that it seems to help her settle down. Also, the later bedtime means that she is sleepier when she goes to bed, so she is falling asleep more easily.

Reaching Out to Families

Child: ———————————— **Age:** ——————— **Date:** ———————

Problem or Need:

_____

_____

_____

_____

What parents asked for or what I saw was needed:

_____

_____

_____

_____

My response:

_____

_____

_____

_____

The outcome:

_____

_____

_____

_____

Discuss your responses with your trainer.

Reaching Out to Families

Child: _____ **Age:** _____ **Date:** _____

Problem or Need:

_____

_____

_____

_____

What parents asked for or what I saw was needed:

_____

_____

_____

_____

My response:

_____

_____

_____

_____

The outcome:

_____

_____

_____

_____

Discuss your responses with your trainer.

Reaching Out to Families

Child: _____ **Age:** _____ **Date:** _____

Problem or Need:

_____

_____

_____

_____

What parents asked for or what I saw was needed:

_____

_____

_____

_____

My response:

_____

_____

_____

_____

The outcome:

_____

_____

_____

_____

Discuss your responses with your trainer.

SUMMARIZING YOUR PROGRESS

You have now completed all of the learning activities for this module. Whether you are an experienced FCC provider or a new one, this module has probably helped you develop new skills in working with families. Take a few minutes to review your responses to the pre-training assessment for this module. Write a summary of what you learned, and list the skills you developed or improved.

Discuss your responses to this section with your trainer. If there are topics you would like to know more about, you will find recommended readings listed in the Introduction in Volume I.

Your final step in this module is to complete the knowledge and competency assessments. Let your trainer know when you are ready to schedule the assessments. After you have successfully completed these assessments, you will be ready to start a new module. Congratulations on your progress so far, and good luck with your next module.

A N S W E R   S H E E T S

Working with Families

Communicating with Parents Often to Share Information About Their Child's Experiences and Development

1. Why did Ms. Cruz decide not to share the news about Janet's accomplishments?

   a. She knew that Janet's parents were very excited and wanted to be there when Janet first went down the slide alone.

   b. She knew Janet would go to the park with her parents, and they would enjoy the surprise.

2. What kinds of information will Ms. Cruz and the Carters need to share now that Janet is learning to take risks?

   a. Other tasks that Janet is trying to master.

   b. What they can do to help her to take safe risks.

Providing a Variety of Ways for Parents to Be Involved in Their Child's Life at the FCC Home

1. How did Ms. Franklin help Mr. Bradley think of something he could do with Jerry and the other children at the FCC home?

   a. She asked him about his work and interests.

   b. She told him she'd noticed that he was excited about doing things outdoors.

2. How did Ms. Franklin help Mr. Bradley feel more comfortable about working with a multi-age group?

   a. She told him that all the children liked being outdoors.

   b. She gave him an article to read.

Working Together with Families to Meet Children's Needs

1. **What did Ms. Kent do to help Ms. Thomas understand Marita's behavior?**

   a. She explained that Marita's behavior was typical of 3-year-olds.

   b. She explained that Marita was getting used to being separated from her parents.

2. **How did Ms. Kent help Marita and her mother cope with separation?**

   a. She scheduled a phone conversation with Ms. Thomas to tell her more about separation and what Marita did during the day.

   b. She told Ms. Thomas to feel free to call to check on Marita.

   c. She held Marita while she calmed down, then read her a story.

Module 12:
PROGRAM
MANAGEMENT

O V E R V I E W

> **Managing a family child care program involves:**
>
> - observing and recording information about each child's growth and development;
> - planning an individualized program to meet children's needs; and
> - running a family child care business.

FCC providers have many roles.

Family child care providers play many roles. The most obvious role is to provide for children's health, safety, and developmental needs. But caring for children involves much more. It includes building children's self-esteem and responding to their explorations of the world around them. It involves supporting families and helping parents deal with working outside the home. And it also includes being a manager and taking steps to ensure the smooth operation of the program.

Picture yourself standing in the middle of a room wearing a shirt smeared with applesauce. You are rubbing the back of a crying infant while trying to convince a toddler to begin putting blocks back in the can rather than scattering them around the rug. In situations like this, it may be difficult to think of yourself as a manager. On a daily basis the challenging realities of providing care for children tend to take over, therefore, it's important to take time to think about your management role. Planning, conducting, and evaluating your program are the managerial tasks that will assist you in becoming more effective in promoting children's development, guiding their learning, setting up the environment, and handling other responsibilities.

Each day, providers make countless decisions, ranging from how best to respond to a child's question to who to hire to prepare a tax return. (During a one-hour period, jot down all the choices you make. You'll be amazed!) To make decisions that add up to a good program, you must know all the children in your group so you can meet their individual needs. By systematically observing children and recording what they do and say, you can gather the information you need to plan for each child. That planning leads to implementing a high-quality program and evaluating it for any necessary changes.

As a manager, you must also be aware of the national, state and local laws and regulations that govern family child care programs, and keep up-to-date on any changes that occur in those regulations.

Listed below are examples of how providers demonstrate their competence in managing a family child care program.

Observing and Recording Information About Each Child's Growth and Development

Watch and listen to a child at play and write down what he or she does and says. "Mr. Lopez, let me tell you what I noticed when I observed Maria riding her bicycle up and down the sidewalk. She might be ready to have the training wheels removed."

Use systematic observation to record information that is objective and accurate and avoids labeling. "Carmen used both hands to pick up the cereal on the highchair tray."

Work with parents to identify each child's strengths, needs, and interests. "Could you tell me what activities Henry enjoys, Mrs. Lee, so that I can plan ways to extend his interests?"

Use all opportunities to gather information about children. "You've climbed to the third rung on the jungle gym, Leroy. I don't think you've done that before!"

Planning an Individualized Program to Meet Children's Needs

Share ideas with other providers or attend workshops that provide new ideas. "I'd like to plan some outdoor winter activities. Do you have any resources or suggestions?"

Use information gathered from observing children to plan for each child. "Sam and Travis have been quickly putting together all our puzzles lately. I will need to provide some new activities to help them increase their eye-hand coordination skills."

Include parents in planning for their children's growth and development. "Pam has been trying lots of new foods. Let me tell you about the foods she especially likes in case you want to serve them at home, too."

Be aware of special needs of children with disabilities. "Since Francine is deaf, I need to be sure she stands where she can feel the vibration of the music from the stereo speakers when we do our exercises to music."

Give substitute providers adequate information on the planned activities and needs of individual children. "I keep this weekly plan posted on the closet door. It shows the special activities planned for the week and the names of the children I want to encourage to participate."

Running a Family Child Care Business

Follow sound business practices. "Since I am doing child care in my home, I should purchase liability insurance. I will call the family child care association to see if they have a group policy, and I will check my insurance policy."

Develop policies and procedures. "My contract with parents clearly states that payment for child care services must be received on Monday of each week care is to be provided."

Complete management tasks according to a schedule. "Every Friday during naptime I will record my receipts for expenses for the week."

Develop a system for maintaining records. "Now that I've patched up Paul's skinned knee, I need to fill out the accident report and put it in the hall so I can share it with his parents."

Managing a Family Child Care Program

In the following situations, FCC providers are being effective managers. As you read each one, think about what the providers are doing and why. Then answer the questions that follow.

Observing and Recording Information About Each Child's Growth and Development

As Matt rips lettuce leaves in half, Ms. Gross crouches near the table. Index cards and a pen are in her pocket. "You're ready to finish making your sandwich, Matt. What do you want to put on the bread?" "Tunafish!" Matt answers. He picks up the knife and holds it with his fist, straight down. Then he dips it into one of the bowls on the table. He holds the bread in his left hand and spreads tuna fish partly on the leaf and partly in his palm. "Why don't you lay the bread on the plate to do that?" Ms. Gross asks. "Okay," says Matt. Ms. Gross helps Matt hold the bread down on the plate. Matt finishes spreading the tunafish, puts another piece of bread on top, and takes a bite. Ms. Gross jots down on a note card that Matt chose tunafish, how he dipped the knife into the bowl, how he attempted to spread the tunafish, how he responded to a suggestion, and how he completed the task.

1. **How did Ms. Gross use a daily routine to gather objective and accurate information about Matt?**

    _____

    _____

    _____

2. **What are three things Ms. Gross learned about Matt?**

    _____

    _____

    _____

Planning an Individualized Program to Meet Children's Needs

After a week of beautiful spring weather, Ms. Sponsel decides it's time to focus on what the children are doing during outdoor play time. She asks the parents to let her know what they see their children doing at home—in their backyard or on weekend trips to the park or playground. To collect more ideas for outdoor play, she also asks two other providers in her neighborhood to observe their own groups playing outdoors. She offers to share the results of all her research.

Ms. Sponsel thinks about her objectives for children as she watches them play outside each day. She carries some index cards with her so she can jot down what she sees them doing—Billy and Hannah chasing bubbles, Kisha climbing up and down the ladder to the slide, Gracie lying on a blanket trying to roll over. Over the weekend, Ms. Sponsel reviews all the ideas she has collected and plans to introduce some new materials and activities during the coming week. She also makes a list of things she needs to collect for future outdoor activities.

1. **How did Ms. Sponsel include parents in the planning process?**

_____

_____

_____

2. **How did Ms. Sponsel use observation information for planning?**

_____

_____

_____

Running a Family Child Care Business

As Ms. Velardi and her husband plan their vacation, she makes a list of things she must do to insure the children in her FCC home are cared for in her absence. She lists questions she needs to research in the FCC regulations such as, "Are their any other legal requirements for a substitute besides age and medical report?" "Does the substitute care have to take place in my home, or can the substitute care for the children at her home?" Next she makes a list of tasks: 1. Review the FCC Rules & Regulations and call my licensing worker if necessary. 2. Contact my regular substitutes to see who will be available. If no one is available, contact my resource and referral agency for names and interview someone right away. 3. Notify parents right away about dates I'll be gone and who will substitute for me. 4. Arrange a time for the children and parents to meet the substitute before I go on vacation.

1. **What does Ms. Velardi do to ensure she is in compliance with regulations governing FCC?**

_____

_____

_____

2. How does Ms. Velardi minimize the disruption in care for the children and their families?

_____

_____

_____

Compare your answers with those on the answer sheet at the end of the module. If your answers are different, discuss them with your trainer. There can be more than one answer.

Managing Your Own Life

Managing your home and business lives is very challenging.

FCC providers manage child care programs within their homes. They also have the added challenge of managing their home life in the same setting as their workplace.

The skills you use in each role—as provider and family member—are complementary. Many of the things you do in your personal life contribute to your performance as a manager. You may be responsible for paying bills, buying food and clothing, deciding on major purchases such as a car or furniture, or planning a vacation or weekend outing. The same skills you use in managing at home can help you manage your FCC program. When you make a grocery list, for example, you consider what foods each member of your family likes, how many people will be eating each meal, and what ingredients you need for each recipe. You can do this because you observe each member of your family, include them in planning balanced meals, and follow recipes—the "policies and procedures" for food preparation.

The more orderly and efficient you are in managing your home, the easier your life is. Good management gives you more time to spend on things other than chores. Think about times when careful management makes it easier to get chores done efficiently:

- You plan which errands need to be run and do them all at once rather than making several trips.

- You make sure you have all the tools and materials you need before starting a project such as painting the kitchen cupboards or baking a cake.

- You keep records of all bills and file receipts promptly.

- You keep emergency phone numbers posted beside the telephone.

- You talk with your family about what to do in case of fire and develop an evacuation plan.

- You plan outings or vacations that are of interest to everyone.

- You borrow a folding table and extra chairs from a neighbor when you are having a crowd over for a holiday meal.

Organizing your time and your environment to work *for* you rather than *against* you helps you manage more effectively. Use the chart on the following page to identify ways to manage your life more effectively.

Frustrating Situations in My Daily Life	What I Could Do To Improve the Situation
I spend time practically every day searching for my keys.	*I will put a hook on the inside wall by the door where I will hang my keys every day when I get home.*
My own children complain that the house is too crowded.	*With their help, I will set aside a special place for only my children to use.*

When you have finished this overview section, you should complete the pre-training assessment. Refer to the glossary at the end of this module if you need definitions of the terms that are used.

Listed below are the skills used by FCC providers who are effective managers. Think about whether you do these things regularly, sometimes, or not enough. Place a check in one of the columns on the right for each skill listed. Then discuss your answers with your trainer.

Skill	I Do This Regularly	I Do This Sometimes	I Don't Do This Enough
Observing and Recording Information About Each Child's Growth and Development 1. Watching and listening to each child and writing down what he or she does and says.			
2. Recording children's behavior in an objective, accurate way and avoiding the use of labels.			
3. Asking parents for information about things their children do at home and including that information with observations.			
4. Observing each child during different periods of the day: arrival, indoor and outdoor play, meal, naps, and departure.			
5. Recording many instances of a child's play before drawing conclusions about that child's abilities, interests, and needs.			

Skill	I Do This Regularly	I Do This Sometimes	I Don't Do This Enough
Planning an Individualized Program to Meet Children's Needs			
6. Planning developmentally and culturally appropriate activities for the group.			
7. Using observation information to plan for each child in the group.			
8. Including information from parents when planning activities for children.			
9. Planning for changes in the environment, special activities, and specific experiences for specific children.			
10. Including evaluations of the experiences provided for children as part of planning for future activities.			
11. Working with the local child care association, R&R agency, and other providers to offer input on program issues.			
12. Knowing social services, health, and education resources and using them as needed.			
13. Learning about addressing the needs of children with disabilities.			

Skill	I Do This Regularly	I Do This Sometimes	I Don't Do This Enough
Running a Family Child Care Business			
14. Knowing and understanding responsibilities as outlined in regulations governing FCC.			
15. Interviewing and completing a contract and enrollment form for each family prior to accepting a child in care.			
16. Completing management tasks according to a schedule.			
17. Following an organized system of recordkeeping.			
18. Filing state and federal taxes on time.			

Review your responses, then list three to five skills you would like to improve or topics you would like to learn more about to help you manage your FCC program. When you finish this module, you will list examples of your new or improved knowledge and skills.

_____ _____

_____

_____

_____

_____

_____

_____

_____

_____

_____

Discuss the overview and pre-training assessment with your trainer. Then begin the learning activities for Module 12.

I. Using a Systematic Approach to Observing and Recording

In this activity you will learn:

- to identify reasons for conducting observations; and

- to develop a system for regularly observing and recording children's behavior.

Why It Is Important to Observe Children

At some point in their lives, most adults spend time observing children. They watch them play and thrill at hearing their first words, first phrases, and first sentences. They watch them grow and marvel at their first steps, first hops, and first words. Observing children is an ongoing process for people with children in their lives.

Observations of children made by providers may be different from those made by parents because each observes children for different reasons. The observations of an FCC provider are used to provide high-quality care for all children. High-quality care is based on knowledge of each child and the use of accurate information to meet each child's needs. When providers know how each child is growing and developing and plan a program based on this knowledge, the care they provide is more likely to be developmentally appropriate.

Providers observe children for a variety of reasons.

- **To determine each child's interests, strengths, and needs**. "Bobby likes to organize the things he collects on our neighborhood walks. He sorts his collections in egg cartons."

- **To plan a program based on the interests, strengths, and needs of each child.** "Thank you for letting me know about Helen's interest in dinosaurs. Jessie shares the same interest, so I'm going to use a dinosaur theme in several activities next week."

- **To measure each child's progress**. "I've recorded Sarah's new skills in gross motor development."

- **To resolve particular problems** a child might have. "I've been keeping notes, and I think Jim seems to hit other children when he doesn't know how to ask for a turn."

- **To report children's progress** to parents, colleagues, and specialists. "I'd like to set up a meeting with you, Mrs. White, to talk about Jared's progress."

333

- **To evaluate the effects of the environment** and the activities of the family child care home. "This weekend I'm going to review my observation and planning notes so I can think about how successful my activities are."

How to Observe

To undertake these and other tasks, providers must observe children carefully and systematically. This involves watching, listening to, and writing down what children do and say as it happens, according to a particular method. The information written down is called a recording. To determine each child's interests, strengths, and needs, more than one observation and recording are required. Providers must observe individual children daily as they play indoors and outdoors, eat, prepare to sleep and wake up, arrive in the morning, and leave at the end of the day.

A series of brief (5- to 10-minute) observations can provide the information needed to assess a child's level of development. These observations should take place over a period of time. You can make recordings during your daily routines and activities with children. As you get in the habit of making frequent observations and recordings, you will sharpen your observation skills and have important information to share with parents at the end of the day.

Some providers feel that making observations and recording them will take away from their time with children. They try to jot down at the end of the day the things that happened. It's impossible, however, to remember accurately everything that happened: what each child did and said, new skills each child attempted, and so on. It is best to record observations throughout the day as you interact with children or as soon as possible after the observation. Here are two examples of providers completing recordings:

- Ms. Lopez is helping Dwayne learn to cut with a knife. She talks with Dwayne as he tries a variety of ways to hold his knife and praises him when he is able to cut his food with the knife. After lunch Ms. Lopez helps the group settle down for their naps. Then she gets her pad and records how Dwayne tried to use a knife.

- Ms. Brady holds one end of a jump rope, and 8-year-old Marcia holds the other. Several children take turns jumping. After a few minutes she asks Rocky to take her place. She pulls a few index cards from her jacket pocket and records the names of the "jumpers" and a few notes on each child's skill in the activity.

Tips for observing children.

Developing a system can help you integrate observing and recording into your day. Here are some suggestions for observing children systematically.[1]

- **Write what you see**, not what you think is happening.

- **Jot notes frequently**. Carry a pad or index cards and pencil.

- **Write in short phrases** rather than complete sentences, to save time.

- **Try to abbreviate** and shorten what a child said—don't try to write all the words, but get the gist of what is said. (However, if you're observing language development, it is important to get as much detail as possible. Try using a tape recorder and listening to the taped conversation at a later time.)

- **Describe** *how* a child is doing or saying something.

- **Develop a system of abbreviations or initials** for materials and equipment; for instance, for colors of paint, use red-r, blue-b, black-bl, and so on.

- **Use arrows** to indicate movement.

- **Underline words** to indicate a particular intensity (for instance, "said loudly").

- **Work out a schedule** to regularly observe all the children in your care.

- **Have a reason for observing**—for example, to assess fine motor skills or to find out how a child plays outdoors.

- **Share your observations** with your trainer in a confidential and professional manner.

- **Use your observations** when you make recommendations to parents about their children's interests, needs, and progress in your program.

To be complete, recordings must include several facts:

- the observer's name;

- the child's name;

- the date of the observation;

- the setting (where the activity is taking place, the time of day, and who is involved—for example, "Debby and Ron sit on the floor in the living room after lunch, looking at books"); and

- the behavior (what the child you are observing does and says).

---

[1] Adapted from materials developed by the Head Start Resource and Training Center (College Park, MD: University of Maryland, 1975).

Throughout the year, recordings should be made in all areas of each child's development. It is helpful if you can organize your observations in categories such as the following:

- fine and gross motor development;
- cognitive development;
- language development;
- creativity;
- self-discipline;
- self-help skills;
- self-esteem; and
- social development.

Observation is an ongoing process.

A single observation cannot provide a complete picture of a child. Children, like adults, don't behave in the same ways all the time. Illness, reactions to events at home or at the FCC home, and other things affect what a child does and says. Children's abilities, interests, and needs change over time; therefore, observation is an ongoing process. When providers have collected several recordings on a child, they can make comments such as the following:

- "Tara has a special interest in books about animals."

- "Sarah can build a tower with the large cardboard blocks."

- "Leo can match primary and secondary colors. He can name red and black."

To draw conclusions such as those just given, providers must be sure that their recordings are both objective and accurate. Objective and accurate recordings include only the full facts about what is seen and heard. They do not include labels or judgments. Compare the following excerpts from an observation of a child at the water play table.

Example 1
(Objective and Accurate)

Behavior: *Tony moved the water back and forth with the funnel. The water splashed inside and outside the basin. Some fell on other children's shoes. Tony looked at their shoes and began to giggle.*

Example 1 is an objective recording. It includes only the facts of what Tony did ("moved the water back and forth"), what happened ("the water splashed inside and outside the basin"), and his reaction ("Tony began to giggle"). Accurate recordings include *all* the facts about what a child does and says in the order they happen. Information is not omitted or recorded out of order. Read the following two examples about the same observation.

Example 2
(Not Objective)

Behavior: *Tony was bad today. He angrily splashed the water on the floor and on other children at the water basin. Then he laughed at them.*

Example 2 is not an objective recording. A label ("bad") is used and judgments are made ("he angrily splashed the water," "he laughed at them"). Given what the provider saw, he or she could not know what Tony was laughing at or whether he acted in anger. A recording that he was "bad" does not tell anything useful about his behavior, since "bad" is a word that means different things to different people.

Example 3
(Not Accurate)

Behavior: *Tony stood at the water basin looking to see if a provider was watching him. He giggled and began to splash water on other children.*

In Example 3 a fact is added that has not been observed ("looking to see if a provider was watching him"). A fact is omitted ("Tony moved the water back and forth with the funnel"). And a fact is written out of order ("He giggled and began to splash water...").

Making an objective and accurate recording such as Example 1 takes practice. This skill can be developed during regular child care activities. When you play with a child in the sandbox, you gain valuable information. Take a moment to record that information. Opportunities for taking brief notes are present throughout the day. With practice, you can complete recordings as you play with, care for, and eat with young children. Some examples follow.

Examples

Child: _Nicholas_   **Age:** _4 mos_   **Date:** _Oct 6_

Setting: _On the patio with other children running and playing in the yard, late afternoon._

Behavior: _Nicholas is on his belly on a blanket. John (10 years) walks onto the patio singing a song, "I'm coming for Nicholas, I'm coming for Nicholas..." He comes up behind Nicholas, who doesn't respond to the sound of John's singing. John walks around in front of Nicholas and crouches down. When Nicholas sees John, he squeals and waves his arms and legs. He smiles at Nicholas._

- -

Child: _Natalia_   **Age:** _3 yrs, 3 mos_   **Date:** _Feb 4_

Setting: _Near the front door, at morning arrival time; the other children and I are in the living room with puzzles._

Behavior: _Natalia enters, holding her father's hand. He pulls her parka off over her head. Natalia smiles at her father as he pats her hair down. Father nods at me as Natalia sits on the floor and silently lifts her foot up. He kneels down and takes her boots off. Then he lifts her up into his arms, gives her a hug, and says, "I'll see you later." He sets her down and leaves. Natalia stands in the hall looking into the living room. Her expression is calm. I say, "Good morning, Natalia." She gives me a small smile. After about 15 seconds she moves to the couch and sits down._

- -

Child: _Anthony_   **Age:** _8 yrs_   **Date:** _Aug 30_

Setting: _Pick-up time, kitchen table, three children at the table drawing with markers._

Behavior: _Anthony's mother lets herself in the front door and yells hello as she comes into the kitchen. When Anthony sees her, he says an excited hello and jumps up to see her. Anthony gives his mother a strong, long hug and then says "I've been working really hard on this picture. Do you like it?" She says, "I sure do. I especially like the different colors you used. Let's take it home to show Dad." The two of them begin to gather up his pictures._

- -

Child: _Mike_   **Age:** _4 yrs, 2 mos_   **Date:** _Aug 30_

Setting: _Outdoors, Mike in the fort with Julie and Chris._

Behavior: _Mike climbs ladder into fort, hand over hand, and stands on platform._

"I'm fort leader. Everybody, let's go." He slides down ramp. Julie and Chris follow. "Up the ladder again," he yells. All climb up ladder. "Let's stay here now and be lookouts for dinosaurs." All sit.

After making several recordings about a child engaged in a variety of activities, you will learn a lot about that child. For example, when you review these recordings you might learn about the child's:

- ability to choose an activity;

- interest in "messy" play;

- eye-hand coordination;

- temperament;

- ability to manipulate an object; and

- understanding of limits.

You can then use this information as you plan new ways to address the child's needs and interests.

Checking Out Your Observations

In addition to recording in an objective and accurate way, providers must be sure that they are seeing and hearing what others are seeing and hearing. People often perceive the same situation differently. Eyewitness accounts of an accident demonstrate how several people, seeing the same event, have different stories to tell. This may happen to providers as well.

One provider may see Todd (9 months) dumping a can of blocks on the rug and Linda (20 months) feeding her baby doll dirt before Julie snatches it away and tries to drown it. Another provider, watching the same children, may observe Todd messing up the room, Linda smearing mud on a doll, and Julie taking it away to give it a bath. Knowledge of what a child has done in the past, your feelings about a certain type of behavior, tone of voice, and many other factors influence what you observe and record.

It is useful to compare your recordings about a child with the observations of another adult, ideally your trainer or another provider. If the two observations are similar, an accurate record of a child's growth and development is being maintained. If they are very different, the information collected may not be useful. Two adults with different perceptions of a child's behavior should observe the child together over a short period of time. After each observation they can compare their recordings and discuss what they have seen. This method helps ensure accurate recordings. If the recordings still differ greatly, your trainer can assist in resolving the differences.

In this learning activity you will practice observing and recording. Select a child to observe daily, for a two-week period. Observe the child for 5 to 10 minutes, once per day. Ask your trainer to observe the same child at the same time as you are observing at least once. Compare your recordings after each co-observation and at the end of the two-week period.

To record your observations, you can use the form provided (make several copies), a small note pad, or index cards. Your recordings should include at least the information asked for on the observation form.

Observation Form

Child: _____ **Age:** _____ **Date:** _____

Setting: _____

Behavior: _____

_____

_____

_____

_____

_____

_____

_____

_____

_____

_____

_____

Discuss your recordings with your trainer. If they are objective and accurate, begin the next learning activity. If your recordings are not objective and accurate, select another child to observe and repeat this learning activity.

LEARNING ACTIVITIES

II. Individualizing the Program

> **In this activity you will learn:**
>
> - to use observation information to better understand each child's interests, strengths, and needs; and
>
> - to plan appropriate activities for each child in your group.

Individualizing helps children feel competent.

Individualizing a program means setting up an environment and offering daily activities that reflect and respond to children as individuals. It means knowing, for example, that Ursula (4 years) likes to put together puzzles with many pieces, 4-month-old Brandon takes a long nap after lunch, and Theresa (7 years) likes to have her snack before she talks about her day at school. Providers who individualize their program know what individual children are working on and provide activities such as stringing beads or helping prepare lunch to encourage children to develop their skills. They help children of all ages feel competent by including them as partners in daily routines according to their abilities.

As you live each day with children, you learn a lot about who they are. You see their style of exploring and interacting with the world, what skills they are developing, and what they like to do and learn about. Systematically observing and recording can help you confirm your impressions and fill in your pictures of each child. You can also learn about children by talking with their parents. As discussed in Module 11, parents know their children best of all. By developing a partnership with parents, you will have their help in getting to know their child.

Individualizing involves setting up the environment and interacting with children in ways that help them grow and develop. You provide experiences to match each child's interests. You also provide toys and activities that allow children to practice their newly acquired skills. And you offer them challenges to move to the next step. The preschool child who can eat with a spoon and fork may be ready to use a knife to butter her bread or slice fruit for snack; and the child who can play a word creation game with great skill may be ready for a more challenging way to expand his vocabulary. You give each of these children opportunities to try new things.

You and the children are unique.

Although your program may look like other FCC programs because you do many of the same things, such as taking neighborhood walks, playing outdoors, preparing and eating meals together, and making playdough, your program is unique because you and the children are. You can show respect for the individuals in your home by hanging pictures of the children's families on the wall, organizing naptime so you are able to help Jake fall asleep by rocking him, and listening to the jazz tape that Dennis and his father brought to share.

In this activity you will have the opportunity to practice your observation skills again. You'll observe two children over a two-week period. First decide how you will record your observations. You can use a notepad, index cards, or copies of the observation form in Learning Activity I. Your recordings should include at least the information asked for on the observation form. Observe each child for a 5- to 10-minute period at least once each day. After you have collected all your observations, re-read them to see what you have learned about these children.

Two "Individualization Summary Forms" are provided in this activity: one for observing infants and toddlers and one that is more appropriate for preschool and school-age children.

On the next page you will find examples for each version of the Individualization Summary Form. It shows how one provider summarized what she learned from her observations of four children. (Although you will observe only two children in this activity, we suggest you duplicate the Individualization Summary Forms and use them to collect information about all the children in your care.)

Individualization Summary Form: Infants and Toddlers
(Example)

	Child: _Carlos_ **Age:** _11 months_	**Child:** _Valikia_ **Age:** _2 years_
How would you describe this child's temperament?	*Carlos is rather quiet in a new situation. Once he feels comfortable, he smiles and is more active.*	*Valikia is easily upset by the slightest change.*
Is there anything new happening at home or at FCC that might be affecting him or her?	*Not that I know of.*	*Valikia's grandparents are visiting for the week.*
What skills is this child working on?	*Carlos cruises by holding onto the furniture. His parents and I think he is on the edge of taking his first step.*	*Valikia is learning to put on her coat using the "flip-flop" method.*
What new experiences can you provide to build on these skills?	*I can walk with Carlos holding his arms. I can offer Carlos a chair to push across the floor.*	*We can write a book about Valikia putting on her own coat.*
How can your environment reflect this child's interests and skills?	*The other children and I can keep the floor clear of small objects so Carlos won't trip. I can check to be sure table corners are padded in case he slips and falls.*	*We can ask Valikia's mother to bring in a picture of her grandparents.*
Choose a daily routine (nap, dressing, snack, toileting). Describe how you include this child in ways that respond to his or her needs.	*I allow a little extra time to help Carlos fall asleep at naptime, and I don't get upset if he can't sleep. It's often hard for an "almost walker" to fall asleep.*	*I allow Valikia plenty of time to put on her own coat when we go outside.*

Individualization Summary Form: Preschool and School-Age Children
(Example)

	Child: _Gary_ Age: _4-1/2 years_	Child: _Sandra_ Age: _8 years_
How does this child usually play (alone, with one or two friends, in a group)?	_Likes to look at books by himself. Plays with two or three children outdoors. Likes circle-time songs and dances with small groups._	_With two others or in large group—Sue, Stan, and Nakia most often._
What kinds of play does this child like (favorite toys and activities, quiet or active play)?	_Spends some free play time reading books. Most often builds with table toys and large hollow blocks._	_A lot of time spent with small dolls and furniture. Also likes tag outside and climbs well on equipment at playground._
What kinds of play does this child start, join in, or invite others to join in?	_Likes to be by himself with books. Often starts games outside or builds with table toys. Waits to be invited into the circle but enjoys songs a lot._	_Usually invites one friend to play with dolls. Will join in outdoor play. Sometimes initiates._
What skills has this child acquired?	_Can turn pages of book without tearing. Can name some words. Can lift heavy objects and build towers. Can balance small and large objects._	_Can play cooperatively in small or large groups. Uses imagination to make up stories about what the dolls are doing._
What new experiences can you provide for this child to build on these skills?	_Read with him and point to words as I read them. Put small cube blocks out on shelf._	_Provide new props for doll play. Invite her to organize a group game._

Individualization Summary Form: Infants and Toddlers

	Child: _____ Age: _____	Child: _____ Age: _____
How would you describe this child's temperament?		
Is there anything new happening at home or at FCC that might be affecting him or her?		
What skills is this child working on?		
What new experiences can you provide to build on these skills?		
How can your environment reflect this child's interests and skills?		
Choose a daily routine (nap, dressing, snack, toileting). Describe how you include this child in ways that respond to his or her needs.		

Individualization Summary Form: Preschool and School-Age Children

	Child: _____ Age: _____	Child: _____ Age: _____
How does this child usually play (alone, with one or two friends, in a group)?		
What kinds of play does this child like (favorite toys and activities, quiet or active play)?		
What kinds of play does this child start, join in, or invite others to join in?		
What skills has this child acquired?		
What new experiences can you provide for this child to build on these skills?		

Discuss with your trainer your observation recordings and your plans for the children you observed. If you found it difficult to complete your recordings, talk with your trainer about why that was so, and try to find ways to make it possible to record observations on a regular basis.

Provide new experiences for the children you observed in this learning activity. Observe them again for several days to assess any changes in their interests or strengths. Plan to observe all the children in your group on a regular basis to provide an individualized program.

LEARNING ACTIVITIES

III. Planning the Program

In this activity you will learn:

- to recognize planning as an effective management tool; and
- to develop weekly plans.

Planning helps you be well-prepared for each day.

Planning forces you to think about what you want to do and how you will do it. It means taking time to think through what activities you will offer each week, what materials you will need, and which children you want to focus on.

Providers who plan for each week are better prepared. They have the materials they need ready and can focus on the children rather than searching for a wooden spoon or another paint brush. Therefore, their daily program runs more smoothly. The children are involved and engaged in activities suited to their needs and interests.

Planning provides you with a sense of order that can be elusive in a family child care setting. Having plans gives you the flexibility to meet children's individual needs. Even when you end up changing your plans—a common occurrence—you have an overall picture that allows you to make effective decisions.

When a walk to the park stops just outside the front door where two toddlers discover their reflections in the windows and begin dancing, you can make a decision about how best to respond. You may decide to let them dance as long as they wish. Or, if the dancing turns into a tumbling match or baby Leon starts fussing, you may insist on gathering everyone together and continuing on your way.

Planning also gives providers the satisfaction of evaluating their own growth. Having a clear idea of your goals for children gives you the freedom to experiment with activities and materials. Knowing what you want to accomplish allows you to judge for yourself how you are doing and make necessary adjustments in how you are managing the program. Two types of planning are useful in family child care programs: long-range and weekly.

Long-Range Planning

Long-range planning involves thinking ahead, perhaps a month or more, about your goals for the program and the children in your care. You may have set up files where you store ideas for activities and sources of supplies and equipment. For example, if you observe several children pretending to go to the store, you might want to put together a grocery store prop box for the children. You will need some time to collect the items for the prop box, such as a cash register, play money, and shopping bags. You will need to begin collecting empty food containers and cans for the store. Let parents know what you are planning and enlist their help in collecting what you need. By planning ahead, you will be ready with the materials and props you need.

Long-range planning also is necessary if you want to arrange a special event such as going on a walk to meet the older children at school or celebrating a holiday. Thinking ahead and planning ahead ensure that special events will really happen.

Weekly Planning

Weekly plans are more detailed than long-range plans. You may use your own planning format or one provided by the FCC program. What works well for one provider may not work for another. A good place to start is to ask yourself this: "What do I need to plan that will help me be a better manager?"

Many providers find it useful to plan in the following categories.

- **Theme**—Themes based on children's interests and significant events in their lives or environments are more likely to be successful. The theme guides planning of materials and activities. For example, if the theme is "going to the doctor," you might add new props for dramatic play; take out of the library some books on doctors and going to the hospital; and arrange for one of the children's parents—a nurse or doctor—to visit the program to talk about his or her job.

- **Group time**—these are times to gather the children together to sing songs, listen to stories, or play games.

- **Special activity**—an activity planned for a small group of children or the whole group. You might plan to get together for a picnic with another provider and her children or make pizza for afternoon snack.

- **Outdoor activities**—including the outdoors as a separate planning category will encourage you to plan for children's outdoor time as thoughtfully as you do for their indoor time.

349

- **Changes to the environment**—the addition of new props or materials, or changes in the arrangement of indoor or outdoor space. For example, you might put some new books on the shelf, place a dishpan full of transportation props next to the blocks, add a collection of keys to sort and classify on the table toy shelf, or plan to move the easels outdoors if the weather stays warm.

What guides the planning process?

Providers have many tools and strategies they can use to help them plan. First, they know what children can and should be doing at a given age and stage of development. Second, providers have specific knowledge about each child. Information gathered through observations and recordings and from talking with parents is invaluable in the planning process. Knowing, for example, that one child is going on a trip may lead providers to provide suitcases and books about trips for the children's play.

Providers use yet another strategy that guides the planning process: they carefully observe how children are using the environment each day. Daily observations provide important clues as to what changes are needed in the environment. For example, if the same toys have been on a low shelf in the room for several weeks, providers may note that there is little interest in them. Putting some toys away, adding new ones, or even changing the location of some toys can gain children's interest. Daily observations can also tell you when something planned is not working. For example, if children are unable to complete the puzzles and often leave them unfinished, the puzzles may be too difficult for them. This tells you to try puzzles with fewer pieces and less complex shapes.

Finally, providers consider what special activities they want to offer in a given week. Special activities are usually planned on the basis of the children's interests. For example, if a child particularly likes bead making, you might look for some craft recipes for making beads. Special activities may coincide with the time of year—in the fall, a walk to collect seeds or dried grasses—or they may simply be activities that providers think the children will enjoy—making applesauce or planting a garden. The special interests or talents of the provider (and the children's parents) are valuable here. An adult's enthusiasm for music or weaving is quickly communicated to the children and can extend the children's interests.

How is planning done?

Weekly planning does not need to be a lengthy process. Finding time for planning, however, can be difficult. Many FCC providers find time to plan before children arrive, after they leave, or during rest time. Parents can also be invited to participate in both the planning and the doing of activities.

A planning form can be very helpful. You can use the form provided in this module or one of your own.

What About Evaluation?

Evaluating the experiences you provide for children is an integral part of the planning process. After you have prepared for and conducted activities, it's helpful to think about the following:

- **What happened during the day?** What types of activities did the children engage in? What did I do to respond to children's actions? What activities did I initiate?

- **How was each child's learning and development facilitated?** What worked well? What did not work well? Did each child have many opportunities to explore, experiment, and learn by doing?

- **In light of the day's experiences, what changes should be made in the environment?** Should I rearrange the furniture and equipment? Should I add new toys or props? Should I try a different style of interaction with certain children? What activities should we repeat?

Taking time to step back and evaluate your program can give you valuable insights into what is working and what changes need to be made.

In this learning activity you will review a sample weekly planning form that includes all the categories discussed. Begin by reviewing the sample form for a group of children including an infant (10 months), a toddler (28 months), two preschool children (3 years and 4 years), and a school-age child (6 years). Then develop a weekly plan using the blank form provided after the example. Finally, implement the plan and evaluate how it worked.

Family Child Care Weekly Plan
(Example)

Week of: _April 4-8_

Theme: _Celebrating Our Diversity_

Skills/concepts to emphasize: _Defining what makes us special, accepting and appreciating people's differences, measuring, exploring how our bodies move._

	Monday	Tuesday	Wednesday	Thursday	Friday
Group time	Read "More, More, More Said the Baby"	Dance the hokey pokey	Sing "If you're happy and you know it..."	Make up a story about being 10 feet tall	Listen to ragtime music and dance with scarves
Special activities	Cut up and taste fruits we never tried: kiwis, mangos, tangelos	Use seed catalogs to plan our garden	Make tracings—hands, feet, or whole bodies	Hang up body tracings from tallest to smallest	Look for people pictures in magazines, make puzzles (older children)
Outdoor activities	Play body tag and crawl through hula hoops	"Measure" things with hands, feet, and tools	Blow bubbles	Use colored chalk	Walk to park

Changes to the Environment

Dramatic Play
Small suitcases; assorted pairs of shoes, hats, and gloves

Blocks
Wooden people and community helpers

Outdoors
Colored chalk
Large boxes to crawl through

Art
"People" colors crayons, paint, and playdough; butcher paper for tracings

Table Toys and Games
Mr. and Mrs. Potato Head
Small blocks and community people

Music/Movement
Hokey pokey tape; scarves; kalimba

Sand and Water
Rubber dolls and clothes to wash
Bubble blowing props

Books
"More, More, More Said the Baby," by Williams
"Anansi the Spider" by McDermott
"I Like Me" by Carlson
National Geographic issues

Miscellaneous
Tools for measuring: chicken bones, shoes, measuring tape, yard stick, scales; unbreakable mirrors

Family Child Care Weekly Plan

Week of: _____

Theme: _____

Skills/concepts to emphasize: _____

	Monday	Tuesday	Wednesday	Thursday	Friday
Group time					
Special activities					
Outdoor activities					

Changes to the Environment

Dramatic Play	Art	Sand and Water
Blocks	Table Toys and Games	Books
Outdoors	Music/Movement	Miscellaneous

For one week, use the plan you developed as a guide. Then answer the following questions:

How did children react to changes in the environment?

_____

_____

_____

How did children react to special activities?

_____

_____

_____

What changes did you make in the plan?

_____

_____

_____

What would you do differently next time?

_____

_____

_____

Discuss your plan and your experiences in using it with your trainer.

IV. Running a Family Child Care Business

In this activity you will learn:

- to comply with laws and regulations governing FCC; and

- to establish sound business practices.

Family child care is both a profession and a business. Because you are self-employed you are learning how to manage a business as well as how to nurture and offer a developmentally appropriate program for children. Running a business involves:

- complying with all laws and regulations applicable to your work;

- developing and implementing policies and procedures for your business;

- maintaining accurate financial records;

- filing and paying taxes;

- obtaining insurance coverage; and

- keeping individual records on children in your care.

Complying with laws and regulations

Your FCC home will run more smoothly if you understand and follow the federal, state, and local laws, rules and regulations governing child care. Some laws or regulations may seem unreasonable. It may be helpful to keep in mind that they were developed to ensure the safety and well-being of children and to protect the provider. If you feel the laws or regulations should be changed, work through appropriate channels to advocate change. In the meantime, stay in compliance with existing laws.

Tax laws impact family child care.

As a self-employed person you are responsible for knowing about and filing all applicable taxes including federal self-employment and federal and state estimated quarterly income taxes. Your quarterly estimates should include your liability for self-employment tax. You are also responsible for withholding FICA and medicare taxes on any person you hire as an assistant in your FCC home. Knowing what kind of expenses you may claim and organizing your records on a regular schedule will make filing your tax return easier. (Refer to the Bibliography and Resource List in the Introduction in Volume I for resources to help you learn more about record keeping and filing taxes.) You can obtain information about allowable deductions for FCC by contacting the Internal Revenue Service at 1-800-829-1040.

It may be wise to consult with a tax expert. Be sure to select someone who understands the family child care business and the applicable tax laws. The cost of an accountant or tax expert is a deductible business expense.

The Americans with Disabilities Act applies to family child care.

The federal Americans with Disabilities Act (ADA) requires child care programs, including family child care, to make reasonable modifications in their policies, practices and procedures in order to accommodate individuals with disabilities. For example, if you care for a child who uses a wheelchair you will need to make your bathroom wheelchair accessible or help the child to use the bathroom. The ADA states that unless providers can clearly prove that caring for a child with a disability would cause "undue hardship," they must accept any child with a disability. One exception is that providers can refuse to care for a child who poses a physical threat to other children. For more information on this Act, contact the Department of Justice Hotline at (202) 514-0301 (voice) or (202) 514-0381 (TDD) in Washington, DC or the Child Care Law Center at (415) 495-5498 in San Francisco, California.

State laws, rules, and regulations protect providers and children.

Most states require either licensing, registration or certification of individuals who provide child care in their homes. Your state licensing authorities can help you find out what regulations or laws apply to FCC providers and how to apply for a license or certificate.

Agencies typically responsible for regulating family child care include:

- Departments of Social Services;
- Offices of Children and/or Families; and
- Departments of Health, Education and Welfare.

Phone numbers for these agencies are listed in local phone directories, normally in the blue pages of government listings. If you are unable to locate an agency, check the phone listings for a child care resource and referral (R&R) agency or contact the Office of the Governor in your state.

Depending on the regulations governing child care in your state and community, you may be in contact with a number of other people including licensing staff, FCC association representatives, parents, other FCC providers, trainers, R & R agency staff, or other agencies involved in registering or licensing homes such as fire, safety and health inspectors.

Regulations for family child care usually address the following topics:

- Number and ages of children in care

- Hours of operation

- Safety, health, sanitation, and nutrition

- Supervision and discipline of children

- Fire prevention and evacuation procedures

- Contingency plans for use in emergencies

- Child abuse and neglect reporting requirements

- Procedures for reporting accidents

- Restrictions on areas of the home to be used for child care

- Medical clearance of the FCC provider, his/her family, and the children in care

- FCC provider training requirements

- Criminal background checks

- Home inspection

Ask the state agency for a copy of the guidelines which affect the operation of your FCC business. Typically these guidelines are under continual revision. Your state may send updates on a regular basis. If so, read them carefully and implement any needed changes. If not, take the initiative to check with the agency at least once a year, then bring your program into compliance with any changes. It's also a good idea to stay in touch with what is happening in your city and county.

Local ordinances and covenants may restrict your family child care business. There may also be local zoning ordinances, homeowner association covenants, or rules set by rental property managers that apply to your FCC business. Perhaps you learned about these ordinances and covenants before you opened your family child care home. Contact your local zoning regulator if you need more information.

Establishing Sound Business Practices

Establishing sound business practices which are simple and take a minimum of time and effort, gives you more energy for working with the children. Most providers want to have flexible policies and procedures because they feel they are offering a service to families. However, you are also operating a business and there are times when you cannot make accommodations for individual families. Think about areas where you are comfortable being flexible and where you will want to remain firm. For instance, your policy may be that parents pay fees on Monday for that week's care. If a parent forgets the payment on Monday you may choose to wait until the next day rather than insisting they go home to get their check. However, if a parent forgets the next day you may decide not to allow them to leave the children until they bring their payment.

Obtaining insurance coverage for your FCC business provides you with peace of mind and financial assistance in the event of an accident.

You may wish to attend a training seminar or contact your local R & R agency to learn about common business practices. Find out what laws or regulations impact your business practices. Specific forms and procedures may be required for medical statements, and reporting accidents or suspected child abuse. Using policies, procedures, and forms to document will help protect you in the event of a lawsuit. An example follows.

While playing outside on the swing set three-year-old Marissa falls off the swing and hurts her arm. Her provider, Ms. Eaton, administers first aid, then calls the parents to let them know Marissa has been hurt and what she did for first aid. Marissa is still crying and she is worried that the child's arm may be hurt worse than it appears. She suggests the parents come to take her to the doctor. As soon as they pick her up, Ms. Eaton fills out an accident report form with details of how the accident happened, the area where it happened, and what she was doing when the accident occurred. Marissa's parents calls Ms. Eaton after visiting the doctor to tell her the child's arm is broken. They are upset and feel she must have been negligent for such an accident to happen. They don't bring Marissa back to the FCC home. Two weeks later Ms. Eaton receives notice she is being sued. The accident report she completed that day provides all the details her attorney needs to prepare her defense.

Developing policies helps avoid misunderstandings.

Policies are the specific guidelines and rules you establish for your FCC business. Including your policies and procedures in a contract with parents will help avoid misunderstandings and may provide legal protection. You probably already have some policies in place.

Typically FCC policies include:

- Hours and days of operation

- Fees

- Payment schedules

- Areas of your home used for child care

- Holidays and vacations (for parents and the provider)

- Meals

- Acceptable behavior

358

- What will happen if a family member comes to pick up a child and appears to be under the influence of alcohol or drugs

- Requirements for signing children in and out

- Toys, clothing and food to be supplied by the parents

- What will happen if a child is ill

- Nap time

- How much notice will be given if care of a child is terminated by the parent or provider

- How you will comply with regulations such as reporting suspected child abuse, prohibitions against spanking and other physical punishment, and administering medications.

Establishing procedures can make a business run more smoothly.

Procedures are the steps you will take to enforce your policies. They typically describe a variety of business practices and tasks. Determining how you will handle everything from interviewing families to handling accidents, and writing it down for yourself in a procedures book will make your business run smoother.

To implement your procedures you may need to develop some forms. Sample forms are included at the end of this learning activity. You can modify or add to these forms to reflect information which may be required by your state or local community. If certain forms are required, you will have to use those instead of developing your own. Even if there are no requirements for documenting and reporting accidents or suspected child abuse, it is wise to develop and use forms and procedures.

Listed below are some of the systems and procedures that many providers have established for running an FCC program. You may find some ideas you want to include in your program.

- **Enrollment procedures.** Before accepting a child into care, have an initial meeting just with the parent(s) followed by a second meeting where the child is introduced to the FCC home while the parent stays on the premises. During the first meeting you can review the policies of the FCC home and explain the contract and enrollment forms which are required before admitting the child. During the second meeting, try to get to know the child and help him or her feel comfortable in your home. If you and the parent agree that the child will be enrolled, you might suggest a third visit where the child stays for two to three hours while the parent is away to ease the transition.

- **Contract and enrollment forms.** Many providers prepare a packet of the contract and enrollment forms to present to parents at the first interview. Enrollment forms would include: a medical statement from the child's doctor stating the condition of the child's health, medications to be administered regularly, immunizations received, and restrictions to activities; a Permission to Transport form to allow the provider to take the child away from the FCC home whether on foot or in the car; enrollment data including the names and work phone numbers of the parents or guardians or other people to be contacted in an emergency, the child's doctor and hospital, who is allowed to pick up the child, special dietary needs, and habits of the child such as "always sleeps with his special blanket;" a notarized Emergency Treatment Form; and forms to participate in the USDA Child Care Food Program if applicable. Provide two copies of the contract so the parents can sign one copy and keep one. Insist that the signed contract is returned with other enrollment forms before accepting a child into care. Update the forms and the contract annually.

- **Participation in subsidized programs.** Programs that offer financial subsidies to parents or providers may help you lower fees or help parents pay for child care. Examples of subsidy programs are the USDA Child Care Food Program which reimburses providers for part of the cost of serving nutritious meals and JOBS subsidies which assist parents with child care costs while training for a new job. These programs require additional paperwork but most providers find it worthwhile to participate because of the benefits they receive. If you offer these benefits to families you will want to include a section in your procedures book about them.

- **Accident reports.** Accident reports are usually required by local laws and regulations. It is important to have the proper forms completed and filed in a timely manner with the appropriate agency. Also, give a copy of the accident report to the parents for their information and document that it was given to them. Include in your procedures book a supply of blank forms and information about who the report must be sent to and when.

- **Child abuse reports.** You will need a system for documenting any injuries or bruises you notice on a child and behaviors that may lead you to suspect child abuse or neglect. A card file will help you keep track of each time a child arrived with an injury, when it happened, and the explanation given (by the child and/or parent) for the injury. All states require FCC providers to file reports of suspected child abuse to designated authorities, usually Child Protective Services. See Learning Activities IV and V in

Module 2: Healthy for a detailed discussion of recognizing and reporting child abuse and neglect.

- **Problem situations.** Develop procedures for those times when parents fail to meet the requirements of your contract. For instance, a non-custodial parent may come to pick up the child from your home. You note that the enrollment form clearly states that this parent is not to pick up the child. Your procedure might be to greet the parent at the door but not allow him or her into your home. Explain to the parent that you are unable to release the child into his or her care. If the parent becomes belligerent, close and lock the door and contact police immediately.

Maintaining Accurate Records

You may have already designed a record keeping system that works well for you. If not, you can try some of the suggestions that follow. Taking time to develop a good filing system and setting aside time every week for updating records will make the task more manageable.

Record keeping can be manageable.

- Keep your business and family records separate and keep your business records separate from records on the children. Set up a separate file for each child. Establish another set of files for saving ideas for activities, sources of supplies and materials, professional articles, and so on.

- When you purchase items for your FCC business, try to pay by check or by charge card, and file your receipts immediately. Your cancelled check or monthly charge card bill will give you an additional record of your purchases. Original sales receipts are required as proof of the purchase.

- Invest in the "tools" you will need to keep good records. This includes sturdy files, labels, and a place to store the files. Inexpensive file cabinets are available at many discount stores or you might want to use a plastic file box, an accordion file, or open crates designed to hold hanging files.

- Establish a regular time for your recordkeeping activities. You may find it most efficient to have a "to be filed" box that you empty once a week, for example, every Friday while the children are napping. If you consider your filing tasks a priority you are more likely to keep your files up-to-date.

- Use a large wall calendar to keep track of important information. The blocks for each day should be large enough so you can easily write in them. Hang the calendar in a convenient place and tie a pen or pencil to a string attached to the calendar.

You might use different pen colors to record different kinds of information. For example, you can record information about your own family activities in red and information about your FCC business in blue.

- Keep your systems simple. As a "self-owned" business, you don't need complicated systems for filing and cross-filing. Design a system that makes sense to you and will be easy to use.

It is important to keep good financial records.

Maintaining accurate financial records is important in running a business. Listed here are the kinds of records providers keep.

- **Attendance records.** You can keep attendance on a calendar or, preferably, a sign-in/sign-out sheet with dates and times indicated that parents initial each day. This is an important record for proving the number of hours your home is used for business daily. It is also required for participation in the USDA Child Care Food Program.

- **Automobile log.** Keep a log of all expenses (repairs, new tires, oil changes) you incur on the vehicle you use for your FCC business. Also keep track of actual miles you drive the car in relation to your business (including the date, destination, how it relates to FCC, and odometer readings) and the total number of miles the car is driven during the year (including non-FCC mileage). Keep a log and a pen or pencil in the car.

- **Direct expenses.** The costs of items used exclusively for the FCC business are considered direct expenses. The full price of these items may be deducted on your tax returns. Such items include: insurance, food, paper products, business supplies, licensing costs including required medical examinations, substitute care costs, and education and books relating to FCC. Additional items such as home improvements required to meet licensing regulations and toys and equipment used only for FCC may be deducted subject to certain limitations. Check with your tax advisor to determine their proper tax treatment. In order to claim deductions you will need receipts. Take time weekly or monthly to total and file expenses by category.

- **Indirect expenses.** Expenses for items which are used for the benefit of your family as well as your business are considered indirect expenses. The allowable deduction for these items is calculated by using a formula which takes into consideration the percentage of time during the year you care for children and how many square feet of your home are actually used for child care. Such expenses include: your home mortgage or rent, utilities, phone, repair of furniture and appliances, maintenance or improvements to areas used for FCC but not required for licensing.

- **Income.** All income, whether from fees charged to parents or subsidies received from a food program or other source, must be reported to the IRS.

- **General information.** When preparing your tax returns you will also need: records showing the purchase price of your home; a property tax bill for the year you started your business; records showing costs of furniture, appliances, carpeting, etc. and the value of each item when you started your business; your FCC license or registration; total square footage of your home and the square footage used for FCC; your previous year's tax return.

Keep records on children in your care.

You will find it helpful to have a folder on each child in care which includes the enrollment forms as well as copies of any reports you have filed, memos to the families, or observations. Forms such as Emergency Treatment and Permission to Transport, as well as the contract and medical statements should be renewed annually. Never share confidential information in children's files with anyone but their own family.

In this learning activity you will think about difficult situations which have occurred in your FCC home. Then you will describe how you handled the situation, noting whether you felt your method was effective. If necessary, you will develop a policy and procedure or revise your existing policy to make it more effective.

Evaluating the Effectiveness of Policies and Procedures

(Example)

Describe a difficult situation:

While I was at the grocery store I saw some diapers on sale and thought I would buy some for the infant I had just enrolled. When I asked the parents to reimburse me for them, they said they thought diapers were included in the weekly fee.

How did you handle it?

I explained that diapers are not included in the fee but offered to absorb the cost of the two month supply I had just bought since there was confusion about my policy.

What are your policies and procedures?

I have a written policy but it didn't cover diapers since I haven't had an infant before. I thought I had told the parents at the interview that they needed to provide the diapers.

What changes are needed to your policies and procedures?

I put in my contract that parents supply diapers as well as other items such as clothing, formula, and baby food. I also wrote down in my procedures book that since parents are responsible for supplying the diapers, I will call and let them know if I see a sale, but will leave it up to them to purchase and bring the diapers.

Evaluating Effectiveness of Policies and Procedures

Describe a difficult situation:

_____

_____

_____

_____

_____

How did you handle it?

_____

_____

_____

_____

What are your policies and procedures?

_____

_____

_____

_____

_____

What changes are needed to your policies and procedures?

_____

_____

_____

_____

_____

Points to Cover During Initial Parent Interview

1. Names and ages of all children to be enrolled:

_____

_____

_____

2. Hours and days care is needed:

_____

_____

_____

3. Special needs of the children/family such as transportation to/from school, restricted diets, or equipment such as cribs or wheelchairs.

_____

_____

_____

4. Health considerations such as allergies (to pets, food, or the environment) or medications taken on a regular basis:

_____

_____

_____

5. Policies, procedures, enrollment forms and contract reviewed with parents:

_____

_____

_____

6. Comments:

_____

_____

_____

Enrollment Form

Complete a form for each child enrolled. If more than one child from a family is enrolled, use a separate form for each child.

Date of Enrollment: _____

Child's Name: _____ Birthdate: _____

Parent(s)/Guardian(s) Name(s): _____

Address: _____ City/State: _____ Zip: _____

Home Phone: _____ Work Phone: _____ (father/guardian)

Home Phone: _____ Work Phone: _____ (mother/guardian)

Names and phone numbers of people authorized to pick up the child: _____

_____

(Note: child will not be released to anyone other than the parent/guardian without prior notice.)

In case of an emergency where a parent/guardian cannot be reached, please contact:

Name: _____ Phone: _____

Days and hours child will be in care: _____

Parents will supply: _____

Provider will supply: _____

Please list any allergies your child has: _____

Doctor's Name: _____ Phone Number: _____

List medications your child takes regularly: _____

Snacks/meals to be provided: _____

What are your child's favorite foods? _____

Are there any food restrictions for your child? _____

What are the child's regular meal times? _____

How long and approximately what time does your child nap? _____

Does your child need a special toy or blanket to sleep? _____

How might your child express negative emotions? Does your child verbalize or act out frustration through physical behavior (biting, pushing, etc.)? Please describe how you typically handle inappropriate behavior.

_____

_____

_____

_____

List your child's favorite toys and activities:

_____

_____

_____

_____

If your child attends school, please list the name and address of the school, teacher's name, and hours child is in school:

_____

_____

_____

Additional information you would like me to know about your child:

I/We certify that the information provided is accurate and complete:

Signature: _____ Date: _____

Signature: _____ Date: _____

Permission to Transport

I/we give permission for _____, or, in an emergency, her designated substitute, to take my/our child, _____, on local trips away from the family child care home whether on foot, by automobile, or public transportation. In automobiles, children will be secured in car seats with a safety belt as appropriate for their age.

Signature: _____ Relationship to child: _____ Date:_____

Signature: _____ Relationship to child: _____ Date:_____

(**NOTE**: This form should be signed by person(s) having legal custody of the child and should be notarized.)

State of _____

County of _____

Sworn to before me this _____ day of _____, 19_____ by _____

_____

Signature of Notary: _____

My commission expires: _____

Permission for Emergency Treatment

In case of an emergency requiring medical treatment, I/we give permission for our child

(Child's name)_____ to receive such treatment services as are deemed in the best interest of the child at the time of the emergency. I/we accept financial responsibility for those services. If possible, I/we will be contacted prior to initiating treatment.

The child's date of birth: _____

The child has known allergies to: _____

The child's doctor is: _____ Phone: _____

Preferred Hospital: _____

Address: _____ Phone: _____

Medical insurance information:

Insurance Co. Name:_____ Policy Number: _____

Policy holder's name:_____ ID Number: _____

Father/Guardian's Name: _____

Employer: _____ Phone: _____

Mother/Guardian's Name: _____

Employer: _____ Phone: _____

The undersigned state they have legal custody of the aformentioned child and request emergency services as indicated.

Signature: _____ Relationship to Child: _____ Date: _____

Signature: _____ Relationship to Child: _____ Date: _____

State of: _____

County of: _____

Sworn to before me this _____ day of _____, 19____ by _____.

My commission expires: _____ Signature of Notary _____

(**Note**: You will want the parents to complete two copies of this form - one to be kept at the child care home and one to be taken along on trips. This form should be signed by the person(s) having legal custody of the child and should be notarized. Attach a picture of the child to the form in case no one is available to identify the child.)

371

SUMMARIZING YOUR PROGRESS

You have now completed all of the learning activities for this module. Whether you are a new or experienced provider, this module has probably helped you develop new managerial skills. Before you go on, take a few minutes to summarize what you've learned.

• Turn back to Learning Activity II, Individualizing Your Program. Review the observations completed for the children in your care. Why are they examples of objective and accurate recordings? How did you use this information to individualize your program for these children?

_____

_____

_____

_____

_____

• Next, review your responses to the pre-training assessment for this module. Write a summary of what you learned, and list the skills you developed or improved.

_____

_____

_____

_____

_____

_____

_____

_____

_____

If there are more topics you would like to know more about, you will find recommended readings in the Introduction in Volume I.

Your final step in this module is to complete the knowledge and competency assessment. Let your trainer know when you are ready to schedule the assessments. After you have successfully completed these assessments, you will be ready to start a new module. Congratulations on your progress so far, and good luck with your next module.

ANSWER SHEETS

Managing a Family Child Care Program

Observing and Recording Information About Each Child's Growth and Development

1. **How did Ms. Gross use a regular activity to gather objective and accurate information about Matt?**

   She recorded what Matt did and said while he made a sandwich.

2. **What are three things Ms. Gross learned about Matt?**

   a. Matt can make a choice.

   b. He can hold a knife and use it for spreading, with assistance.

   c. He can form a simple phrase.

   d. He can complete a task.

   e. He can eat finger foods.

   f. He likes tunafish.

   g. He is open to suggestions.

Planning an Individualized Program to Meet Children's Needs

1. **How did Ms. Sponsel include parents in the planning process?**

   She asked parents to observe their children playing outdoors and let her know what they saw the children doing.

2. **How did Ms. Sponsel use observation information for planning?**

   a. Over the weekend she reviewed her notes and developed plans for introducing new materials and activities during outdoor play in the coming week.

   b. She made a list of things to collect for future activities.

Running a Family Child Care Business

1. **What does Ms. Velardi do to ensure she is in compliance with FCC regulations?**

   She lists questions she has and then looks them up in the regulations and calls her licensing worker to verify.

2. **How does Ms. Velardi minimize the disruption in care for the children and their families?**

   She finds a substitute to care for the children while she is away, lets the parents know well in advance when she will be gone and provides the parents and children an opportunity to meet the substitute.

GLOSSARY

Individualized program   A program in which the environment and the provider's interactions with children are suited to each child's interests, strengths, and needs.

Objective recordings   Written information that includes only the facts about behaviors that are seen and heard.

Planning   The establishment of specific steps to accomplish program objectives.

Systematic observation   Consistent watching, listening to, and recording of what children say and do, according to a particular method.

Module 13:
PROFESSIONALISM

OVERVIEW

Maintaining a commitment to professionalism means:

- continually assessing one's own performance;

- continuing to learn about caring for children; and

- applying professional ethics at all times.

FCC providers offer professional child care services.

A professional is a person who uses specialized knowledge and skills to do a job or provide a service. Being seen as a professional means being viewed with respect. It is sometimes a struggle for child care professionals—especially family child care providers—to have their expertise acknowledged and appreciated. However, when parents and community members see that family child care providers operate professionally, everyone benefits—the entire network of parents, providers, community, and children.

As a family child care provider, you are a member of an important profession. You work with young children at a time when they are developing more quickly than they will at any other period in their lives. You help shape children's views about learning and the world around them. The care you provide influences how children feel about themselves. If you build children's self-esteem during these early years, they will be more likely to succeed in life.

Professionals continue to learn and develop new skills.

Professionalism means providing care based on your knowledge of what children do and how they need to grow and develop. Care based on child development and individual attention is thus one of the bases of professionalism in your field of work. But professionalism also means taking advantage of opportunities to learn more about children and yourself and to develop new skills that will make you more competent. The finest FCC providers continually assess their work and stay open to fresh ideas and new perspectives.

Your professional skills also support families. By being aware of the roles you play in a child's life and building a partnership with his or her parents, you help parents feel competent and good about themselves. When parents have confidence in the reliable, high-quality care you provide, their own performance is improved because they know their children are well cared for in your home.

When you need a service (such as medical or legal advice or electrical repair), you look for a professional business or individual who can meet your needs. You choose professionals because you want:

- the needed service;
- specialized knowledge;
- a commitment to quality;
- dependability; and
- effectiveness.

In all these areas, family child care providers make unique professional contributions. They provide:

- the needed service—a high-quality child development program;

- specialized knowledge—how children grow and develop and how to meet their needs appropriately;

- a commitment to quality—a developmentally appropriate program in a safe and healthy environment;

- dependability—service on a regular basis; and

- effectiveness—a program that helps children begin to build cognitive and creative skills and develop self-discipline and self-esteem.

Stages of Professional Development

Lilian Katz, an early childhood educator, has studied how teachers grow professionally. She suggests that they pass through four different stages of professional development: survival, consolidation, renewal, and maturity. These stages also apply to family child care providers.

Stage One: Survival

Providers new to the field tend to devote most of their attention to learning routines and performing daily tasks. At times they may feel insecure as they face the challenges of establishing a business in their homes and balancing their professional roles with their personal lives. This stage is called survival in part because of the concentrated focus on immediate needs rather than long-term planning. It is important to seek out other providers and training opportunities. Also establish a support network for yourself. Join a professional association. Once you have established your program, you move to stage two, consolidation.

Stage Two: Consolidation

At this stage, providers become more confident and begin to look beyond simply completing the daily routines. Most likely they have developed some systems that work for them, and now have time to find new ways to accomplish routine tasks, handle problems, and consider long-term goals. You may want to continue your learning in order to seek assessment as a Child Development Associate (CDA) from the Council of Early Childhood Professional Recognition, or accreditation from the National Association of Family Child Care. Active involvement in provider associations or professional organizations will be rewarding.

**Stage Three:
Renewal**

Once providers have set up their programs and have experience on the job, they may at times become bored with the day's routines. The isolation of working alone often plays a role in a provider's decline in interest and enthusiasm. Providers in this stage need a renewal—new challenges to rekindle their excitement and commitment to caring for young children. If you are at this stage, you might try attending conferences and workshops, holding an office in a professional organization or a provider association, or pursuing a special interest. For example, you might want to obtain a special endorsement for hourly care; age specific homes; special purpose homes; extended hours; or respite care. These professional activities are important and will provide needed stimulation. Additionally, pursuing nonchild-care related activities can give a boost of energy that will carry over into your family child care business and help you move to stage four, maturity.

**Stage Four:
Maturity**

Providers at this stage are committed professionals. They understand the need to seek new ideas and skills. They continue to grow professionally. If you are a mature provider, you can be a model for people new to the field. In some communities there are systems of mentors or "master providers" that allow you to assist providers entering the field of family child care. You could consider expanding your license or specializing with a specific age group or special-needs children. You might also develop different skills in order to seek new challenges as a trainer or group leader.

**Maintaining a
Commitment to
Professionalism**

Child care is a profession that requires many different kinds of skills. In your work you fulfill the roles of educator, child development specialist, advisor, and nutritionist. Your work is important to the children you care for, their families, and the community.

Maintaining a commitment to professionalism has several positive results. First, it builds self-esteem. Pride comes from learning new skills, acquiring knowledge, and becoming more competent. The sense of success you experience as you become a competent provider is very rewarding.

Second, when you provide professional care, you are helping children grow, learn, and develop to their full potential. Third, your professional behavior helps the field of early childhood education. Family child care is an important component of this field and offers valuable services to families. As you and others provide high-quality programs for children, you build respect for the profession, which can result in more recognition for the important service you provide. And finally, the work you do supports families and helps prepare children for successful living.

Being a family child care provider is not just a job—it's a profession. While you help children grow and develop, you can enjoy your work and continue to enrich your life as a provider and as a person.

Listed below are examples of how FCC providers demonstrate their competence in maintaining a commitment to professionalism.

Continually Assessing One's Own Performance

- Identify areas where performance could be improved. "I can't figure out how to help Johnnie learn to use his words instead of hitting other children. I think I'll look through that book on positive guidance for some ideas."

- Know how to judge their own competence in a certain area. "I'm not providing enough sensory experiences for Drew (6 months). I'll talk with one of the other providers to get some ideas."

- Use parents as resources to address children's needs. "Mr. O'Hare, Carl often wants me to help him with his school work. I'd like to be consistent with your practices at home and what his teachers require. What do you suggest?"

- Compare their own performance against professional standards and guidelines. "I know I should never leave the children unsupervised. I'll wait until after child-care hours to return this plate to my neighbor."

- Participate in professional organizations and/or professional activities. "I think I'll attend this conference to learn more about advocacy."

Continuing to Learn About Caring for Children

- Keep current about procedures and guidelines concerning child development. "During naptime I'll be sure to take a few minutes to review this new policy on reporting suspected incidents of child abuse."

- Keep informed about the latest family child care practices. "I'd like to attend that workshop on curriculum next weekend. I can share the information at my next provider association meeting."

- Apply knowledge and skills on the job. "Helping Sara learn to use the potty was much easier after I read the book, *Toilet Learning* by Alison Mack. The ideas in the book really worked."

- Talk with colleagues about child development and child care. "I think I'll call my resource and referral agency when all the children are napping. Maybe they have some suggestions on how I can plan some projects for the older children during their vacation."

Applying Professional Ethics at All Times

- Maintain respect and confidentiality for each child. "The files that I keep on each child are confidential, Mrs. Robinson. The files include emergency information and health records and things I've noticed about your child—her likes and dislikes. You and Arnisha's father are always welcome to look at her file, but I don't share the files with anyone else."

- Be dependable and reliable in performing their duties and responsibilities. "I'm really tired this morning, but I'll find some energy because I know these children need me. I'll be sure to get some extra sleep tonight."

- Show no personal bias against children because of culture, background, or gender. "I will encourage both boys and girls to express all their feelings."

- Speak out against practices that are not developmentally appropriate. When talking with a parent, you might say, "It's best to wait until Tanya shows signs that she is ready to learn to use the toilet, Mrs. Grisson. Very few children are ready at 17 months."

- Stand up for parts of your program that you believe are appropriate for the children. "Dramatic play helps toddlers make sense of the world. They will still learn the difference between make-believe and fibbing."

- Support your network of family child care providers and protect your field's professionalism by avoiding gossip. "I know you're upset, Janet, but if you don't agree with the association's stand, you really should discuss it with the president. Why don't you set up a time to talk with her next week?"

- Show support for other providers when they need assistance. "I'd be happy to help you rearrange your child care space. How's this Saturday?"

Maintaining a Commitment to Professionalism

In the following situations, FCC providers are maintaining a commitment to professionalism. As you read each one, think about what the providers are doing and why. Then answer the questions that follow.

Continually Assessing One's Own Performance

Ms. Hubbard sinks down into her chair to think at the end of a long day. The morning started out smoothly, but by late afternoon everything was crazy. Clean and dirty clothes were mixed together. Parents had complained earlier in the week that their children had on someone else's clothes. Today she spent 10 minutes finding Joseph's hat and gloves. The gloves were found with Matthew's coat. The hat was near the bathroom where it was left when they came in from outdoors. "This cannot go on," she said to herself. "I have to get more organized. Becky Jackson always seems so organized. Maybe she can give me some pointers."

1. **How did Ms. Hubbard assess her own performance?**

_____

_____

_____

2. **What did she decide to do with the results of her self-assessment?**

_____

_____

_____

Continuing to Learn About Caring for Young Children

Ms. Yoo evaluated her family child care environment to identify three areas where she could improve her skills. Ms. Yoo decided that she would review a module on learning environments (one of the three areas) during the following month and attend an in-service training session on the same topic. Ms. Yoo also asked her trainer to come to her home to observe and then offer suggestions on how her environment could be improved. They planned to meet again in a month to discuss how Ms. Yoo's plan was working and what she was learning.

1. How did Ms. Yoo decide what knowledge and skills she should work to improve?

_____

_____

_____

2. How did Ms. Yoo plan to expand her existing knowledge and skills?

_____

_____

_____

Applying Professional Ethics at All Times

Mrs. Johnson, a parent, arrives to pick up her child, Dora. When she walks in, she notices that another child, Joshua, is climbing to the top of a bookshelf. Ms. Costa (the FCC provider) says, "Hello, Mrs. Johnson. Excuse me a moment." and turns immediately to Joshua. "Joshua," she says, "I know you like to climb and jump, but it is not safe for you to be on this shelf. Let me help you down. You can jump near the pillows where it is safe." When she comes back, Mrs. Johnson says, "Boy, he's wild, isn't he?" Ms. Costa responds, "Joshua really enjoys climbing, he's busy learning about his body and space. Now let me tell you about Dora's day."

1. How did Ms. Costa maintain professional ethics in talking to Mrs. Johnson?

_____

_____

_____

2. How did Ms. Costa interact with Joshua in a professional manner?

_____

_____

_____

Compare your answers with those on the answer sheet at the end of this module. If your answers are different, discuss them with your trainer. There can be more than one answer.

Your Commitment to Professionalism

Many of us believe that being a family child care provider is a great job. We think a provider's work is important to the children and families she works with each day.

As professionals, we are continually reflecting on our feelings about working with children, expanding our knowledge base, and developing positive relations with parents and each other. Yet despite the importance of their work, FCC providers don't always receive the status and recognition they deserve.

These factors may contribute to how you feel about your career as an FCC provider. Consider the following questions:

1. How do you feel about being a family child care provider?

_____

_____

_____

_____

2. Why did you choose this profession?

_____

_____

_____

_____

3. What do you like best about your profession?

_____

_____

_____

4. What would you like to change?

_____

_____

_____

_____

5. What can you begin to do to bring about these changes?

_____

_____

_____

_____

> As you complete the other modules in this training program, you will become more competent in caring for children. Your enhanced knowledge and skills will increase your level of professionalism. This module addresses other ways that can help you stay committed to being a professional provider.

When you have finished this overview section, you should complete the pre-training assessment. Refer to the glossary at the end of this module if you need definitions of the terms that are used.

PRE-TRAINING ASSESSMENT

Listed below are the skills that FCC providers use to maintain their commitment to professionalism. Think about whether you do these things regularly, sometimes, or not enough. Place a check in one of the columns on the right for each skill listed. Then discuss your answers with your trainer.

Skill	I Do This Regularly	I Do This Sometimes	I Don't Do This Enough
Continually Assessing One's Own Performance			
1. Judging my level of competence in caring for children.			
2. Comparing my performance against written procedures and guidelines.			
3. Comparing my performance against the recognized standards of the early childhood profession.			
4. Applying my unique skills and experiences to my work as a provider.			
Continuing to Learn About Caring for Children			
5. Participating in professional early childhood education organizations.			
6. Reading books or articles about child development and early childhood education practices.			
7. Talking with or observing other providers to learn more about managing a group of children.			
8. Participating in training offered by colleges and professional organizations.			

Skill	I Do This Regularly	I Do This Sometimes	I Don't Do This Enough
Applying Professional Ethics at All times			
9. Keeping information about children and their families confidential.			
10. Carrying out my duties in a dependable and reliable way.			
11. Speaking out when child care practices are not appropriate.			
12. Supporting early childhood education practices that are developmentally appropriate.			
13. Showing no personal bias against any child in my care.			

Review your responses, then list three to five skills you would like to improve or topics you would like to learn more about to help you maintain a commitment to professionalism. When you finish this module, you will list examples of your new or improved knowledge and skills.

_____

_____

_____

_____

Discuss the overview and pre-training assessment with your trainer. Then begin the learning activities for Module 13.

LEARNING ACTIVITIES

I. Assessing Yourself

In this activity you will learn:

- to recognize your unique skills and abilities; and

- to use the early childhood profession's standards to assess your own competence.

Each person has special interests and strengths.

Each provider, just like each child, is a unique person with special interests and strengths. You bring your own interests and skills to your profession, and you share them with the children in your care. One provider may share a love for music with children; another may share a love for the outdoors. The children pick up on a provider's enthusiasm and learn to appreciate something new. In turn, providers are able to use their special interests in their work, which makes working more satisfying and fun.

What are you really good at? What do you most enjoy? What do you like best about your work? What would you like to change? These are all questions that providers can ask themselves. The questions will help you focus on what special qualities you bring to your profession.

Because you work independently, you are responsible for offering a balanced program to your children. Within your program, which includes many different learning opportunities, you can provide something special that reflects your own interests and talents.

Begin this learning activity by reading "Being Curious About Yourself" and "Carol Hillman: Gardener, Naturalist, Teacher" on the following pages. The first reading will help you think about yourself; the second tells how one early childhood professional brought her special interests and abilities to the classroom. Although Ms. Hillman works in a school setting, the ideas apply to family child care settings, too. Use the form that follows the readings to answer several questions about how you feel about being a provider. Take time to think about what you really want to say.

Being Curious About Yourself[1]

Who are you? What do you care about? Why are you here? What interests you about children? What gives you pleasure in being with them? Which of your interests do you enjoy sharing with them? What are your goals for them?

Does all this seem obvious—of course you know about yourself? In fact, most of us keep growing in self-understanding, and we learn in the same way we learn about other people—by observing and reflecting on our observations. Why did I get so mad when Marta dropped a cup yesterday? It was an accident. Did it trigger something from my own past that had very little to do with the present situation? Why do I find it so hard to like Jorge? I catch myself being almost mean to him—sarcastic, in a way that just isn't appropriate with little kids. Why do I do that?

Sometimes a friend or colleague can help us think through our self-observations if we're willing to share them. It can be uncomfortable, learning more about ourselves, especially about the parts of ourselves we really don't like. Some people go to therapists to get help with this process, to have someone who can listen thoughtfully to their questions about themselves.

What do you like to do with children? Sing, cook, go on walks, pet animals, have conversations, watch them playing, snuggle, comb hair, and wash faces? Do you get to do what you like to do on your job? If not, could you? If you're a caregiver spending every day with children, it's important that you have many opportunities to be a decision maker, to say, "This is what I want to do next." Not at the children's expense, but in response to both your needs and theirs. If caregivers are contented and growing, children are more likely to be contented and growing too.

Which describes you better: You like parenting children; you like teaching children; you like playing with children? Competence in child care may be based on any of these enjoyments. Parenting is being responsible, taking good care of children, appreciating their growth; if you're experienced as a parent, that may be the role you fall into naturally in child care. Teaching implies particular interest in children's thinking and problem solving, in what they know and understand—and in helping them learn. Playing with children implies being in touch with the child in yourself.

What kind of learner are you? How do you learn best? Different people learn by reading, by taking classes, by observing children's behavior, by discussing their experiences with colleagues and friends, by going to conferences and workshops, by trying things for themselves and seeing what happens. Which of these things work for you? Does your center encourage you to keep learning and give you credit for what you do? A child care center is a *living place* for children and adults. It should be a good place to live together and learn together about the world. What are you learning at your work? What risks are you taking?

---

[1] Reprinted with permission from Elizabeth Jones, "The Elephant's Child as Caregiver," *Beginnings* (Redmond, WA: Exchange Press, PO Box 2890, Redmond, WA 98073, 206-883-9394, 1986), p. 10.

Carol Hillman: Gardener, Naturalist, Teacher[2]

I believe deeply that what you are outside of school affects what you are in school. I have a farm in Massachusetts that has for many years been a resource to me and to the children in my classroom.

There I grow things, looking after the whole process myself. I like having the knowledge that I can grow vegetables or flowers without relying on chemicals. The flowers are just as important as the edible things. I pick and dry many of them, making everlasting bouquets from them. The whole process gives me a feeling of self-sufficiency and a kind of calmness.

Those feelings translate to the classroom in ways that you might not suspect. I come to the classroom with a keen sense of the pleasure it can be to do with what you have, without having to go out and buy things. I try to show the children those same pleasures. We make bird feeders from cups and chenille-wrapped wire. They take the feeders home and have a season's worth of birds coming and going. For me, that is much better than robots, superheroes, or transformers.

Growing things takes attention—you are constantly watching what needs water, what needs thinning, what can be picked. I want to communicate that awareness to children. Every morning we have a meeting, and I ask them what they notice that is different. Almost every day we go outdoors, not just to a playground, but to the woods that surround us on practically all sides. I want the children to become investigators in the natural world: I want them to be curious about the stream, the trees, and the leaves on the ground.

Something else is fed by growing things—my aesthetic sense, a love for beautiful arrangements, shapes, and colors. Many years ago, on my first job after college, I worked at an art gallery in New York City and learned, among other things, how to hang an exhibition. Since then, I have carried with me the importance of placement, whether I am placing blocks on a shelf or plants in a garden.

That, too, carries over to the classroom. The blocks, the baskets of parquetry blocks, the puzzles and pegboards must each stand apart to command their own space and importance. What I am after is a sense of order, not a strict cleanliness—children need messiness, too.

But beyond that sense of order, my experiences in gardens and the wider outdoors have given me a taste for naturally beautiful things. Rather than stickers or pre-drawn forms, the children in my classes make collages from shells and sand, sweetgum pods, the bright orange berries of bittersweet vines, acorns, and pine cones.

Outside my garden, the most important part of my life as a part-time naturalist is raising monarch butterflies. For a number of years, I've worked with Dr. Fred Urquart of Toronto, who was trying to locate the hidden spot where monarchs migrate during the winter months. I've been a part of that search by raising, tagging, and releasing butterflies. Only a few years ago, after a lifetime of tracking the butterflies marked by many people such as myself, Urquart was able to locate the monarch's wintering spot high in the mountains near Mexico City.

_____

[2] Reprinted with permission from Carol Hillman, "Teachers and Then Some: Profiles of Three Teachers," Beginnings (Redmond, WA: Exchange Press, PO Box 2890, Redmond, WA 98073, 206-883-9394, 1986), pp. 21-22.

I have a whole portion of my garden devoted to milkweed, which is the sole food source for monarchs. I find the small caterpillars on the plants and take them into school. During the first few weeks of school each year, the children and I watch the whole metamorphosis—from caterpillar, through chrysalis, to full butterfly. We keep the monarchs in a huge butterfly case for a few days after they emerge. Then, on warm, blue sky days, children take turns holding and releasing the monarchs into the air. It is probably a moment they won't forget.

Taking a Look at Yourself

I think I'm really good at:

_____

_____

_____

_____

I really enjoy:

_____

_____

_____

_____

I can share my interests and skills with children in the following ways:

_____

_____

_____

_____

I would like to be better at:

_____

_____

_____

_____

I would like to know more about:

_____

_____

_____

_____

Discuss your responses with two colleagues. Have they learned anything new about you? Do they see things that you did not see? Use the space below to write what you learned from doing this exercise.

_____

_____

_____

Standards of the Child Care Profession

Every profession sets standards for performance. You should have developed your own set of policies and procedures. Part of being a professional is having written statements of your philosophy, policies, and procedures. These statements can help you implement your plan for high-quality care for children and can support you as a professional FCC provider. If you need to update these statements, there are resources that can help you formulate your ideas.

The child care profession has several statements of standards. You should become familiar with all of them. These standards are not intended to restrict you; effective providers are always prepared to adjust daily routines to meet individual children's needs and interests. These standards act as guides. In using them, you, other early childhood professionals, and parents can confirm that you are providing high-quality care.

Several documents are accepted by the early childhood profession as indicators of professional work. Reviewing these documents can help you evaluate your performance.

- The statement on *Developmentally Appropriate Practice in Programs Serving Children Birth Through Age 8*, developed by National Association for the Education of Young Children (NAEYC), gives guidelines for the kinds of practices that are suitable for children at particular ages and stages of development. Appropriate activities and teaching practices are outlined for children from infancy through age 8.

- The *Child Development Associate (CDA) Competency Standards for Family Day Care Providers* are the core of the CDA program. They are statements of the skills needed to be a competent provider and are used to assess FCC providers seeking the CDA credential. These standards, also called Competency Goals, are further defined into 13 Functional Areas. The modules in this training program can help you to begin acquiring the skills and knowledge in each of the 13 Functional Areas. After completing this training program you may be interested in continuing to develop the competencies needed to seek a CDA credential.

- The *Accreditation Criteria* of the National Association for Family Child Care (NAFCC) in Washington, DC, 1987 are another source of guidance. NAFCC accredits family child care homes that offer high quality child care services. The process includes a provider self-assessment validated by two outside individuals.

Reviewing these documents and completing the self-assessments for each of the modules in this training program should give you a comprehensive picture of your capabilities. This review will also identify areas you need to know more about and skills you need to develop or improve.

For this learning activity you will need a copy of NAEYC's *Developmentally Appropriate Practice in Early Childhood Programs Serving Children from Birth Through Age 8* so you can review the section on programs for the age categories for which you provide care. You can order one through NAEYC's toll-free number: 1-800-424-2460. Write a paragraph about one aspect of developmentally appropriate practice that is particularly meaningful to you, and discuss how NAEYC's statement relates to what you do as a provider.

_____

_____

_____

_____

_____

_____

_____

_____

_____

_____

_____

_____

_____

_____

_____

_____

_____

_____

Discuss your statement with your trainer.

LEARNING ACTIVITIES

II. Continuing to Learn About Caring for Children

In this activity you will learn:

- to continue to expand your knowledge and skills; and
- to make short- and long-range professional development plans.

Continued learning has many benefits.

No matter how many years you have been working with young children or how much you already know, it is important to continue to learn more about your profession.

- **There is always new information to be learned**. Professionals need to keep up with the latest developments in the field. New research often leads to new, more effective strategies for working with children. Learning and growth are ongoing for the child care professional.

- **Continual learning makes you an active, thinking person**. Providers who are always learning new things are more interesting people and are more likely to inspire the children in their care. If you enjoy learning, you are more likely to help others enjoy it, too. Providers who keep learning always have new ideas to bring to their family child care setting.

- **You care about children**. Each article or book you read and every discussion or conference you participate in may give you new insights or help you resolve nagging problems. Suppose, for example, that a child with special needs joins your group. You may have to learn new ways to meet this child's needs. Because you care about all young children, you are always alert for new and helpful information relating to their development.

- **You want to grow professionally**. A commitment to continue learning can lead to improved performance. Learning also leads to an increased feeling of confidence that could allow you to take on new challenges or give you the confidence you need to discuss a problem with a parent.

- **Continual learning is affirming.** You may rediscover ideas you'd tucked away. The process of learning tends to affirm the good work you've been doing and the knowledge you already have.

There are many ways to continue learning.

How can providers keep growing and learning? In addition to participating in this training program, there are many other ways. You might:

- join professional organizations;
- read books and articles;
- network with other professionals in the field;
- observe other providers; and
- take advantage of training opportunities.

Professional organizations help keep you up-to-date.

Professional organizations help you keep up-to-date on the latest information and current issues in the profession. These organizations offer newsletters, books, brochures, and other publications with useful information and helpful tips. Their conferences provide a way to meet others with similar interests and concerns. Many organizations have local affiliates that meet regularly.

The following are descriptions of the major professional organizations in the child care profession.

Association for Childhood Education International (ACEI)
11141 Georgia Avenue, Suite 200
Wheaton, MD 20902
(301) 942-2443

Established in 1892, ACEI is represented in all 50 states and many nations abroad. The Association addresses the care and education of children from birth through adolescence.

The Children's Foundation
725 15th Street, NW
Washington, DC 20005-2109
(202) 347-3300

The Children's Foundation strives to improve the lives of children and those who care for them by providing a voice for children and their families on issues of critical concern—welfare reform; federal food assistance programs for children; health care and housing; affordable, high-quality child care; and enforcement of court-ordered child support—at the national and local levels. It offers practical publications and a Project Information Clearinghouse.

The Council for Early Childhood Professional Recognition
1341 G Street, NW, Suite 400
Washington, DC 20005
(202) 265-9090 or (800) 424-4310

The Council is the national credentialing program for early childhood educators. Its goal is to improve the quality of early childhood programs by assessing, improving, and recognizing the skills of education staff in child care settings. The Council awards the Child Development Associate (CDA) credential, the nationally recognized credential for child care workers.

National Association for the Education of Young Children (NAEYC)
1509 16th Street, NW
Washington, DC 20036
(202) 232-8777 or (800) 424-2460

With more than 60,000 members, NAEYC is the largest early childhood professional organization in this country. This group publishes *Young Children*, an early childhood journal of ideas, findings, and issues in child care. NAEYC also publishes books, posters, and other media materials on child care issues. NAEYC's annual national conference (and area and state chapter conferences) offers professional training on a range of important topics. The conferences are also wonderful opportunities to meet other providers as well as writers and researchers in the field. Ask your trainer for information on joining your local NAEYC affiliate.

National Association for Family Child Care (NAFCC)
1331-A Pennsylvania Avenue, Suite 348
Washington, DC 20004
(800) 359-3817

NAFCC is the national voice for family child care providers. This membership organization is a national support network for family child care providers and advocates of the profession. On the national level, it participates in legislative advocacy. For individuals, NAFCC provides training information. Its publications include a quarterly newsletter and *How to Start a Family Day Care Business*.

Zero to Three
National Center for Clinical Infant Programs (NCCIP)
2000 14th Street, North
Suite 380
Arlington, Virginia 22201-2500
(703) 528-4300

NCCIP is a group of professionals from a wide variety of disciplines concerned with supporting infants and toddlers and their families. This group publishes a newsletter, "Zero to Three," as well as other publications of interest to professionals working with children under 3. NCCIP's annual conference provides a good opportunity to meet people in other fields who are also working with young children.

National Black Child Development Institute (NBCDI)
1023 15th Street, NW, Suite 600
Washington, DC 20005
(202) 387-1281

NBCDI is a group that advocates on behalf of the growth and development of black children. It organizes and trains networks of members to voice concerns regarding policies that affect black children and their families. NBCDI sponsors an annual conference that focuses on critical issues in child care development, education, foster care and adoption, and health. NBCDI also publishes the *Black Child Advocate*, a quarterly newsletter.

National Institute for Hispanic Children and Families
2000 Rosemont Avenue, NW
Washington, DC 20010
(202) 265-9885

This group considers the child care needs of Latino children and analyzes how those needs compare with the needs of other children. The group also reviews and assesses legislation affecting Latino children and their families.

Save the Children, Child Care Support Center
1340 Spring Street, Suite 200
Atlanta, GA 30309
(404) 885-1578

A major focus of Save the Children has been to enrich the community by increasing the availability of family child care and to connect providers to resources within the country. The organization sponsors an annual conference to advance the knowledge and skills of family child care providers as providers and leaders in the child care field.

Southern Early Childhood Association (SECA)
P.O. Box 56130
Little Rock, AR 72215-6130
(501) 663-0353

SECA (formerly known as SACUS) comprises early childhood educators, teachers, providers, administrators, researchers, teacher trainers, and parents in the United States and abroad. The group provides a voice on local, state, and federal issues affecting young children. An annual conference is held to exchange information and ideas. SECA also publishes materials on the latest issues in child development and early education. Publications include *Dimensions* (a quarterly journal), *Tires Are Tools for Learning*, and *Issues of the 80s*. SECA has 13 state groups.

You can read books and articles.

Books and articles help you expand your knowledge and skills. You can review articles or chapters in a book during naptime or after hours. A list of recommended resources is included in the Introduction to this training program. You can check with your trainer, local association or R&R agency about resources you can borrow.

Networking is a way to share ideas and get support.

Networking is spending time with people who perform similar tasks to share ideas, information, and experiences. It is a good way to find solutions to problems, gain new knowledge, or help fellow providers cope with difficult situations. You can network with one other person or with a group. Group networks can include other child care professionals in the local community or in the state. Meetings can be very informal, perhaps in the evening or on a Saturday. They can also be formal, with speakers and a detailed agenda. What is important is that providers meet, share ideas, and get support in coping with the demands of their work.

Observe other professionals to gain a new perspective.

You can learn a lot by visiting the home of another provider and even visiting a child care center. Because each provider is unique, you can observe others and learn new approaches to solving discipline problems, managing a transition time, or coping with feeding three hungry children at one time.

When observing another provider's home, plan to spend some orientation time. Give the children a chance to get used to your being there, and in a relatively short time they will be acting their normal selves. Before you arrive, talk with the other provider about your goals and reasons for observing. This may help pinpoint the time of day that you should arrive, and it may help the other provider feel more relaxed about being observed.

Participate in training on topics related to your job.

Training is another way to keep up-to-date in the child care field and develop new skills. You can attend courses offered by community groups. County extension agencies offer nutrition courses, and public school adult-education programs offer courses on a wide range of topics. College or university courses or a local training agency may also be options. Your participation in this self-instructional training program will enhance your knowledge of child development and your child care skills.

Begin this learning activity by reviewing your answers to "Taking a Look at Yourself," in Learning Activity I. Pick one item from your responses to "I would like to be better at" or "I would like to know more about." Consider the sources of assistance available to you: the public library, workshops, professional organizations, your trainer, and other providers. Identify what specific resources can help you with the task or topic you have selected. Use the form on the next page to list what you find.

Continuing to Learn About Caring for Children

I want to improve or learn more about:

_____

_____

_____

_____

_____

_____

_____

Resources I can use:

Source	Contact Person
Public library	
Workshops	
Professional organizations	
Trainer	
Providers	

Developing plans for continued learning helps you reach your goals.

Now that you have identified resources to help you in an area you want to work on, you need to plan how and when to use those resources. When you develop a plan, you clarify what you want to achieve—your goal—and how you will go about achieving it. With a written plan in front of you, you feel like you're already making progress. And you are! Knowing where you're going and how you're going to get there makes it easier to take each step and to recognize your goal when you reach it. As you take each step and check it off on your plan, you can visualize your movement toward your goal.

You can improve your skills in the following ways:

- Take advantage of opportunities that come your way. Attend workshops and training offered by community groups, local colleges, resource and referral agencies, or other groups.

- Use other providers as resources, and offer yourself to them as a resource. Visit and talk with each other often to share ideas and to discuss concerns.

- Review how you manage your time. If you look closely at how you spend each day, you may find some time-wasting activities. Finding ways to do things faster or better may leave extra time for reading, listening to tapes, watching videos, studying, and reassessing how you are doing in your work.

- Set specific goals for yourself. Try to do something on a regular basis to fulfill them.

In Learning Activity I, Assessing Yourself, you identified skills you would like to improve. You also identified skills that you're good at. The chart you just completed helped you think about resources that are readily available to you. Use the results of these two activities to make plans for your professional development. For the short term you may want to focus on skills you think most need improving. For the long term you may want to build on an area you are strong in and become even more skilled—so that you can share your competence with others while you increase your self-confidence.

In this learning activity you will make some short- and long-range plans. Think about your own professional goals. Then identify possible barriers and decide how to overcome them. Read the example on the following page, and fill out the chart that follows.

Plan for Professional Development
(Example)

Short-Range Plan

What would I like to do right away to improve my skills?

- *Take a course on how to guide mobile infants' behavior.*

- *Learn more activities for infants to do outside.*

- *Review Module 8, Self.*

What barriers might hinder me from completing these plans?

- *It's hard to find time to complete the learning activities and still care for children.*

- *I don't have any resources on helping infants learn self-discipline.*

What can I do to overcome these barriers?

- *I can arrange child care for my own children for an evening or Saturday morning on a regular basis so that I can have more time to work on the modules.*

- *I'll send away to NAEYC for two brochures: "Helping Children Learn Self-Control" and "Love and Learn: Discipline for Young Children."*

Long-Range Plan

What would I like to be doing a year from now?

- *Be an active member in one professional association.*

- *Complete the Caring for Children in Family Child Care Program.*

- *Seek a CDA credential.*

- *Begin college courses in early childhood education.*

What barriers might hinder me from completing these plans?

- *It takes time to be an active member of any group.*

- *The time and energy I need to do the modules compete with the time I need to be part of a professional organization and to pursue my personal interests.*

- *Courses at technical institutes and colleges cost money.*

What can I do to overcome these barriers?

- *I can arrange for time on a regular basis to pursue my long-range plan by trading responsibilities with others or hiring assistants.*

- *I can join the professional organization and restrict my involvement to attending meetings and conferences until I have more time.*

- *I can set up a schedule for completing the modules, which will help me stay on track.*

- *I can set up regular times to pursue my personal interests and spend time with family and friends.*

- *I can find out about student loans and scholarships, and I can check with local training agencies about other ways to take for-credit courses.*

- *I can make sure all credits can be transferred.*

Plan for Professional Development

Short-Range Plan

What would I like to do right away to improve my skills?

_____

_____

_____

_____

What barriers might hinder me from completing these plans?

_____

_____

_____

_____

What can I do to overcome these barriers?

_____

_____

_____

_____

Long-Range Plan

What would I like to be doing a year from now?

_____

_____

_____

_____

What barriers might hinder me from completing these plans?

_____

_____

_____

_____

What can I do to overcome these barriers?

_____

_____

_____

_____

Discuss your plans with your trainer. What barriers can you overcome? Agree on an overall plan to achieve your goals, both short and long term.

III. Applying Professional Ethics at All Times

In this activity you will learn:

- what it means to act in a professional manner; and
- to identify professional behavior.

Professionals do what is right rather than what is easy.

As discussed in Learning Activities I and II, being a professional involves assessing one's knowledge and skills and continually building on them. But professionalism is more than having expertise. It has to do with how you apply your knowledge and skills daily as you work with parents, children, and others. It means doing your work to the best of your ability. And it involves your actions in the child care setting and in the community. Professionals need to do what is right rather than what is easy. Practicing professionals are committed to doing what is best for all children in their care, on every occasion. Here are some examples.

Ethics of Family Child Care	Unprofessional Behavior	Professional Behavior
Maintaining confidentiality about children and their families. Refusing to discuss children with parents other than their own. Restricting conversations to times when children are not present.	Talking about a child in front of the child or with a parent other than the child's. *"Did you notice how dressed up Tommy always is? It's as if his parents are trying to impress me. I'm glad your child comes in play clothes."*	When trying to identify ways to help a child, discussing the problem confidentially with another provider without specifying the individual. *"Sometimes parents bring their children to my home in inappropriate clothing. What do you do in this situation?"*
Being honest, dependable, and reliable in providing care. Being consistent in availability and performance. Having written policies that specify availability, philosophy, and procedures.	Paying more attention to adults and personal tasks than to children. Not being dressed when children start arriving. Doing housework and personal tasks while providing care. *"You kids can watch TV while I make a few phone calls."*	Being ready to work every day on time and prepared to provide high-quality child care. *"I plan my schedule so that I have a half-hour to prepare for the children's arrival that is free from other duties. I also take regular vacations to energize myself."*

407

Ethics of Family Child Care	Unprofessional Behavior	Professional Behavior
Treating parents with respect even during difficult situations.	Getting angry at a parent who is late and demanding that he or she do better. Talking to other parents or acquaintances about parents. *"This is the third time you've been late this week. Don't you know I need to get on with my personal life?"*	Talking to a parent who always comes late about the problem this causes and discussing possible solutions. *"Mrs. Cranson, my child care day ends at 6:30. If you can't get here by then, is someone else authorized to pick up Jennifer?"*
Treating each child with respect regardless of gender, culture, or background. Treating each child as an individual; avoiding comparisons.	Teasing children if they cry. Asking one child to behave just like another child. *"Why can't you go potty like Timothy does?"*	Comforting a child who is hurt or upset. Including activities and materials that reflect the cultures and backgrounds of all children. *"It's OK to cry. Do you want to tell me about it?"*
Making sure activities, practices, and routines are developmentally appropriate.	Making all children do the same activities or trying to meet all children's needs on a strict schedule. *"Wake up, Damian, it's time for everyone to eat. You've been sleeping long enough."*	Talking with parents about appropriate activities for their children's stages of development. *"Children Pam's age love to carry things around the house in buckets."*
Providing a good model for learning and for language and communication skills. Modeling the standard language form of grammar and sentence structure. Never using profanities in front of children.	Using non-standard grammar, slang, or profanities with children. *"Free play is over now. I don't want to see no more of your junk on the floor."*	Using standard grammar. Using complete sentences when talking with children. *"Free play is over now. It's time for everyone to pick up the toys."*

Ethics of Family Child Care	Unprofessional Behavior	Professional Behavior
Dressing to do the job. Being conscious of dress, grooming, and hygiene.	Wearing clothes that hinder movement and that you have to worry about. *"We can't paint today because I don't want to risk getting my new sweater dirty."*	Wearing comfortable clean clothes so that you can play with and care for children: clothes you can sit on the floor in, bend and lift in, and move quickly in when necessary. *"I'm most comfortable in wide skirts or slacks that let me sit on the floor easily with the children."*
Recording information appropriately.	Not taking the time to record needed information because it's too much trouble. *"No one ever reads accident reports. I'm just wasting my time filling one out."*	Keeping good records to aid in making accurate reports to parents. *"Lori's mother said she really likes my message board. She can look on the chart and see what Lori's day was like."*
Advocating on behalf of children, families, yourself, and others. Letting people know the importance of child care work.	Belittling family child care work as "only babysitting" or denying that it is a profession. *"As soon as I can, I'm going to get out of babysitting and get a real job."*	Joining a professional organization. *"I'm really glad I joined NAEYC. Their materials really help me be a better provider."*

In this activity you will list examples of how your behavior conforms to the ethics of the child care profession. Then you will read several case studies and identify examples of your own professional behavior.

Ethics of Family Child Care	Examples of Your Own Professional Behavior
Maintaining confidentiality about children and their families. Refusing to discuss children with parents other than their own. Restricting conversations to times when children are not present.	
Being honest, dependable, and reliable in providing care. Being consistent in availability and performance. Having written policies that specify availability, philosophy, and procedures.	
Treating parents with respect even during difficult situations.	
Treating each child with respect regardless of gender, culture, or background. Treating each child as an individual; avoiding comparisons.	
Making sure activities, practices, and routines are developmentally appropriate.	
Providing a good model for learning and for language and communication skills. Modeling the standard language form of grammar and sentence structure. Never using profanities in front of children.	

Ethics of Family Child Care	Examples of Your Own Professional Behavior
Dressing to do the job. Being conscious of dress, grooming, and hygiene.	
Recording information appropriately.	
Advocating on behalf of children, families, yourself, and others. Letting people know the importance of child care work.	

Ethical Case Studies[3]

The following situations are adapted from an article in *Young Children*, the professional journal of the National Association for the Education of Young Children. After reading each one, write down what you think a professional would do. Then plan a time to discuss your responses with your trainer and a group of colleagues.

1. Case Study: The Working Mother

Timothy's mother has asked you not to allow her almost 4-year-old son to nap past 1:30 in the afternoon. She says, "Whenever he naps he stays up until 10:00 at night. I have to get up at 5:00 in the morning to go to work. I am not getting enough sleep." Along with the rest of the children, Timothy takes a one-hour nap almost every day. He seems to need it in order to stay in good spirits in the afternoon.

What should a professional do?

_____

_____

_____

_____

_____

_____

2. Case Study: The Aggressive Child

Eric is a large and extremely active first-grade child who often frightens and hurts the younger children. The parents listen to what you say but feel that the behavior is typical for boys his age. A mental health specialist has observed the child, but her recommendations haven't helped either. Meanwhile, Eric terrorizes other children, and parents are starting to complain. You are becoming stressed and tired, and your patience is wearing thin. You are spending so much time dealing with Eric that you are worried that the other children are not getting the attention they need.

What should a professional do?

_____

_____

_____

_____

_____

---

[3] Adapted with permission from Stephanie Feeney, "Ethical Case Studies for NAEYC Reader Response," *Young Children* (Washington, DC: NAEYC, May 1987), pp. 24-25.

3. Case Study: The Divorced Parents

Mr. Martin is the recently divorced father and custodial parent of 2-year-old Tracy. Carla, the girl's mother (and the noncustodial parent), comes to your home several times a week to visit Tracy. Tracy's father has changed since the divorce. He always has a stressed expression on his face and avoids contact with you. Tracy is now absent 2 or 3 days per week and usually arrives late when she comes. Tracy's father became very angry at you when Tracy's bag was misplaced. Efforts to talk with him have been unsuccessful. Despite the absences, Tracy has seemed healthy and well-adjusted, though in recent weeks she has had difficulty playing with others.

Carla has heard rumors that her former husband is behaving strangely. She tells you she is unable to reach her ex-husband by telephone or pick Tracy up at the times specified in the court agreement. She asks what is happening and if you have concerns about her daughter's father.

What should a professional do?

_____

_____

_____

_____

_____

_____

When you have completed these case studies, plan a time to discuss your responses with your trainer and other providers. These are difficult situations to handle, and it will help you to discuss your ideas.

L E A R N I N G   A C T I V I T I E S

IV. Becoming an Advocate for Children and Families

In this activity you will learn:

- to recognize the importance of being involved in advocacy for children and families; and

- to become involved in advocacy efforts.

How You Can Become an Advocate[4]

Advocacy is working for change. This often means speaking out on issues that may affect children and families or on issues that affect your own working conditions.

A first step in becoming an advocate is to understand the importance of advocacy. This means recognizing how public and private policies affect children's lives and accepting that children need a strong voice to ensure that the programs they attend support their development. Advocates must ask themselves: "What can I do to ensure adequate attention to children's needs by policymakers, elected officials, administrators, schools, businesses, and other groups?" Answering this question requires making a commitment to act.

Advocacy efforts try to improve the circumstances of children's lives so they get what they need to grow to their full potential. FCC providers are especially well informed on this issue in terms of both theory and practice. Advocates commit themselves to sharing their knowledge with others. They move beyond good intentions and take action, overcoming the fear of becoming involved. Because they realize that the problems faced by children and families are a collective responsibility, they take the crucial, transforming step from concern to action.

Professionals can expand their commitment to children, families, and their profession when they act on their beliefs and share their knowledge with others. FCC providers can contribute to advocacy in at least six ways.

---

[4] Adapted with permission from Stacie G. Goffin and Joan Lombardi, *Speaking Out: Early Childhood Advocacy* (Washington, DC: National Association for the Education of Young Children, 1988), pp. 2-5.

Contribution 1: Sharing Your Knowledge

Your professional beliefs and knowledge are based on an understanding of child development, experience caring for children, and relationships with parents. Therefore, you can make important contributions to policy debates about the developmental needs of children and the characteristics of safe and nurturing environments. FCC providers need to assume responsibility for sharing their knowledge with parents, policymakers, and other decisionmakers. You can help decisionmakers focus on the role of policy in enhancing children's development. As an advocate you can become a catalyst for change.

Contribution 2: Sharing Your Professional Experiences

You work with children and their families daily. You experience firsthand the impact of changing circumstances—such as unemployment, layoffs, furloughs, family illnesses, and the conflicts between work and family responsibilities—before decisionmakers are informed that these issues are "new trends." When children and families receive services from agencies, you are firsthand observers and monitors of whether children's needs are being met. As a result, you have the opportunity—and a professional responsibility—to share the personal stories that give meaning to group statistics. Personal experiences help professionals become more persuasive. Without sharing confidential information, FCC providers can describe how policies affect children and families.

Contribution 3: Redefining the "Bottom Line" for Children

The debate about programs for young children is often tied to other policy issues such as welfare, job training, and teenage pregnancy. Funding for children's programs is often seen as an investment in children's future productivity.

Joining children's issues with broader political issues and social concerns is an effective political technique. It can expand the base of support and help frame children's issues in ways consistent with accepted social values.

The profession's unique perspectives on children, however, also enable FCC providers to speak out for children's inherent "worth." You know that childhood is a meaningful time for development in its own right.

If policies for children and families are developed solely on the basis of "return on investment," children will suffer when investors seek a higher return or decide to pull out of the "market." FCC providers must remember that these strategies are simply means to achieve a desired end. They must not undermine the "bottom line" of advocacy—encouraging policies that promote children's healthy development.

415

Contribution 4: Standing Up for Your Profession

Family child care is a growing profession that provides a valuable service to children and their families. Therefore, providers need to speak out on behalf of family child care as a profession—and for the special expertise needed to be a professional.

Many people don't know that providing child care requires a distinctive, professional knowledge base or that the quality of care children receive depends on the training and compensation of child care professionals. FCC providers know firsthand about how they feel when others view them as merely "babysitters" rather than child care professionals. They need to share these stories, too. For example, at a national training conference, an FCC provider shared how she felt when a parent repeatedly wrote on the weekly check for child care fees, "For babysitting." After several weeks of accepting checks with this notation she mustered her courage to tell the parent that she was a professional, providing quality care for his child.

Advocacy efforts on behalf of family child care are most effective when providers emphasize the benefits of their work for children and families. Providers must begin to exercise their own power to speak out on issues that affect their profession.

Contribution 5: Involving Parents

Your daily interactions with parents provide many opportunities to share common concerns and goals for children's well-being. You are in a unique position to help parents recognize their power as children's primary advocates—for both their own and other people's children.

Parents can be especially effective advocates on behalf of their children. Parents represent a critical consumer voice. By involving parents, providers can dramatically expand the constituency speaking out for children.

Contribution 6: Expanding the Constituency for Children

FCC providers may have ongoing relationships with other individuals and agencies who provide services for children and families—public school administrators and teachers, health care providers, religious organizations, and professional and volunteer groups. These interactions provide natural opportunities to inform others about the developmental needs of children, appropriate caregiving practices, and the supports that families need.

You can choose from many courses of action once you make a commitment to become an advocate for children, their families, and your profession. Here are a few of the choices:[5]

• Share ideas for appropriate practice with other providers and parents (instead of just observing disapprovingly).

---

[5] Adapted with permission from Stacie G. Goffin and Joan Lombardi, *Speaking Out: Early Childhood Advocacy* (Washington, DC: National Association for the Education of Young Children, 1988), pp. 14-15.

- Explain to parents why children learn best through play (instead of bemoaning that parents are pushing their children or giving in and teaching with inappropriate methods and materials).

- Establishing and/or participating in FCC Providers Associations (instead of feeling frustrated by your isolation and wishing that you had other providers to call or meet with).

- Write a letter to the editor of a newspaper or magazine to respond to an article or letter (instead of just complaining about how other people don't understand the needs of children, their families, or their providers).

- Establish or join and participate in an association of providers (instead of wishing such a group existed).

- Write to your state or federal legislators about a pending issue and share your experiences as a way to point out needs (rather than just assuming someone else will write).

- Meet someone new who is interested in working with children and ask her or him to join a professional group such as the National Association for the Education of Young Children (NAEYC), the National Black Child Development Institute (NBCDI), the National Association for Family Child Care (NAFCC), or others listed in Learning Activity II (instead of just wondering why the person isn't involved).

- Ask a friend to go with you to community meetings where issues of concern to children and families will be discussed (instead of staying home because you don't want to go alone).

- Volunteer to represent your professional group in a coalition to speak out on the educational needs of young children (instead of waiting to be asked or declining because you've never done it before).

- Work and learn with others—for example, your local provider association—to develop a position statement on a critical issue (instead of saying "I don't really know much about this topic.").

- Volunteer to speak at a school board meeting about NAEYC's position statement, *Developmentally Appropriate Practice in Early Childhood Programs Serving Children from Birth Through Age 8* (1987) (instead of resigning yourself to the fact that your school system doesn't understand much about early childhood education).

In this activity you will consider your own feelings about advocacy and develop a plan for becoming an advocate. Review the suggestions included in this learning activity, then answer the following questions.

Becoming an Advocate

1. **What contributions would you like to make as an advocate for children, families, and your profession?**

    _____

    _____

    _____

    _____

    _____

2. **What obstacles might prevent you from being an advocate and how can you overcome them?**

    _____

    _____

    _____

    _____

    _____

3. **Describe below an advocacy step you can take this month:**

    _____

    _____

    _____

4. **Describe below an advocacy step you can take within six months:**

    _____

    _____

    _____

5. **Describe below an advocacy step you can take within one year:**

    _____

    _____

    _____

    _____

Discuss your responses with your trainer.

V. Taking Care of Yourself

In this activity you will learn:

- to recognize the importance of taking care of yourself; and

- to take care of yourself physically, emotionally, socially, and intellectually.

Providers need to take care of their own needs.

As a provider, you have the important responsibility of taking care of the needs of children. You also have a responsibility to take care of yourself. The most important resource you have to give children is yourself—your caring, your energy, and your commitment. You cannot do this when you aren't at your best. To provide good care for children, you need to be in good physical and emotional health. You also need to feel that you are appreciated, meaningfully connected to others, intellectually stimulated, and performing a job worth doing.

Taking care of yourself means considering your needs and well-being in four areas: physical, emotional, social, and intellectual.

Health is very important to a person who cares for children. Without physical stamina and good health, a provider is not adequately prepared to work with children for long hours every day. Taking care of your physical well-being means being sure you eat foods that are good for you, get enough rest, and exercise several times a week.

The way you feel about yourself, your work, and the world affects how you interact with the children and adults around you. The more positive you feel about yourself, the better you will be able to care for children. When you start to feel worried or depressed, it's good to talk with family or friends about your concerns and to take some time to think about yourself.

Having people to talk to is essential for survival. A trusted person with whom to share your joys, frustrations, and ideas can be very important in determining how you feel about yourself as a person and as a provider. The person may be another provider, spouse, relative, or friend. What is important is that you have someone (at least one, but preferably several people) with whom you can exchange ideas, feelings, resources, and moral support.

Most adults enjoy learning something new and being challenged. Like children, adults need to continue to explore, experiment, and learn. Your learning can be about work-related issues such as child development and about many other topics as well.

In this learning activity you will assess how well you are taking care of yourself. Record your activities for two days. For Day 1 record your activities for today. Review your answers, note areas where you could take better care of yourself, and try to improve your schedule tomorrow. Record that schedule under Day 2. You might want to repeat this activity several times over a longer period of time.

Taking Care of Myself

	Day 1	Day 2
Physical Well-Being		
Did I eat three balanced meals?		
How much sleep did I get? (Is that average?)		
Did I get any exercise?		
Emotional Well-Being		
Did I have a generally positive outlook?		
Did I take a few moments to relax after a stressful situation?		
Social Well-Being		
Did I spend time with someone I care about?		
Did I talk through a day's problem with a friend or colleague?		
Intellectual Well-Being?		
Did I read anything for information or interest—a book, an article, the newspaper?		
Did I learn something new?		

Discuss this activity with your trainer and make a commitment to take good care of yourself. Use the space below to note what actions you will take.

I will do the following things to take care of myself:

S U M M A R I Z I N G   Y O U R   P R O G R E S S

You have now completed all of the learning activities for this module. Whether you are an experienced provider or a new one, this module has probably helped you maintain or begin a commitment to professionalism. Before you go on, review your responses to the pre-training assessment for this module. Write a summary of what you learned, and list the skills you developed or improved.

If there are topics you would like to learn more about, you will find recommended readings listed in the Introduction which can be found in Volume I.

Discuss with your trainer your responses to this section. Let your trainer know when you are ready to schedule the assessments. If you have not completed all 13 modules, when you have successfully completed these assessments you will be ready to start a new module. Congratulations on your progress so far, and good luck with your next module.

If you have completed all 13 modules, this will be your final assessment. Congratulations on accomplishing your goals!

Maintaining a Commitment to Professionalism

Continually Assessing One's Own Performance

1. **How did Ms. Hubbard assess her own performance?**

   a. She thought about how the day had progressed.

   b. She considered feedback from parents.

   c. She thought about how she felt about the day's events.

2. **What did she decide to do with the results of her self-assessment?**

   a. She decided to become more organized.

   b. She decided to talk to Becky Jackson, another provider, to get some pointers.

Continuing to Learn About Caring for Children

1. **How did Ms. Yoo decide what knowledge and skills she should work to improve?**

   a. She completed a self-assessment.

   b. She talked with her trainer to identify areas for improvement.

   c. She set specific goals.

2. **How did Ms. Yoo plan to expand her existing knowledge and skills?**

   a. She selected a module to review.

   b. She planned to attend training.

   c. She planned an observation and feedback visit from her trainer.

   d. She scheduled a follow-up meeting with her trainer.

Applying Professional Ethics at All Times

1. **How did Ms. Costa maintain professional ethics in talking to Mrs. Johnson?**

   a. She greeted the parent politely when she arrived.

   b. She responded to Mrs. Johnson's comments in a positive way.

   c. She maintained confidentiality by not discussing Joshua's behavior with an adult who was not Joshua's parent.

2. **How did Ms. Costa interact with Joshua in a professional manner?**

   a. She acted quickly to ensure Joshua's safety.

   b. She used positive guidance techniques to direct Joshua to a safe place for jumping.

GLOSSARY

Competence	The ability to do something well.
Ethics	A set of principles, standards, or guidelines that direct acceptable behavior—what is right or good rather than quickest or easiest.
Job description	The official written statement describing a provider's responsibilities.
Maintaining confidentiality	Sharing information only with people who have a right to know.
Networking	Spending time with people who perform similar tasks to share ideas, information, and experiences.
Professional behavior	The consistent, thorough application of knowledge, skills, and ethics.
Professionalism	A commitment to gaining and maintaining knowledge and skills in a particular field, and to using that knowledge and those skills to provide the highest-quality services possible.